Social Marketing Casebook

Jeff French,
Rowena Merritt
and Lucy Reynolds

§SAGE

Los Angeles | London | New Delhi
Singapore | Washington DC

nsmc

leading behaviour change

First published 2011

SAGE Publications Ltd
1 Oliver's Yard
55 City Road
London EC1Y 1SP

SAGE Publications Inc.
2455 Teller Road
Thousand Oaks, California 91320

SAGE Publications India Pvt Ltd
B 1/I 1 Mohan Cooperative Industrial Area
Mathura Road
New Delhi 110 044

SAGE Publications Asia-Pacific Pte Ltd
33 Pekin Street #02-01
Far East Square
Singapore 048763

Library of Congress Control Number: 2011921125

British Library Cataloguing in Publication data

A catalogue record for this book is available from the British Library

ISBN 978-0-85702-543-2
ISBN 978-0-85702-544-9 (pbk)

Typeset by C&M Digitals (P) Ltd, Chennai, India
Printed in India at Replika Press Pvt Ltd
Printed on paper from sustainable resources

Social Marketing Casebook

SAGE has been part of the global academic community since 1965, supporting high quality research and learning that transforms society and our understanding of individuals, groups, and cultures. SAGE is the independent, innovative, natural home for authors, editors and societies who share our commitment and passion for the social sciences.

Find out more at: **www.sagepublications.com**

CONTENTS

ABOUT THE AUTHORS

Professor Jeff French has over 30 years' experience of evaluating and developing leading behaviour change projects, social marketing programmes and communication strategies at international and local levels. Jeff and has published over 80 chapters, articles and books in the fields of behaviour change, social marketing, community development, health promotion and communications. He is Visiting Professor at Brunel University and Brighton University, a Fellow at King's College London and teaches at four other UK Universities. Until 2009 Jeff managed the National Social Marketing Centre and is currently Chief Executive of Strategic Social Marketing Ltd.

Dr Rowena Merritt has more than 10 years' experience working in the communication and marketing fields in the private and public sectors. She currently works as the Research Manager at the National Social Marketing Centre and previously led on Local Practitioner Development where she set up the award-winning National Demonstration Site scheme, funded by the Department of Health. Rowena has published widely and regularly guest lectures at a number of universities in Britain, Hong Kong and the USA.

Dr Lucy Reynolds founded the National Social Marketing Centre's widely acclaimed evidence resource, ShowCase, and is an expert in UK and international social marketing evidence. Lucy has published widely on social marketing theory and practice, in academic, health and environmental journals, as well as appearing on Radio 4. Lucy is a senior consultant at Finnamore, the UK's largest independent health consultancy, where she specialises in health inequalities, performance transformation and assets management.

ACKNOWLEDGEMENTS

We would like to thank all the people who helped us in preparing the vignette and case studies for this book; without their input this book would not have been possible. We would also like to thank the National Social Marketing Centre in England for their help and support in developing this book.

INTRODUCTION

In this Introduction we will explore why governments, public institutions, non-governmental organisations (NGOs) and private companies are increasingly applying social marketing principles to help develop more effective social change programmes. We will also introduce the five key features that are reflected again and again in successful programmes:

- Citizen Orientation
- Clarity of Purpose
- Coalition Building
- Combination of Approaches
- Continuation, Learning and Evaluation.

These five key features recur in most of the case studies throughout the book. If you are interested in one of these features in particular you can scan the book for examples of how it can be enacted by looking out for the relevant symbol.

Citizen Orientation

Clarity of Purpose

Coalition Building

Combination of Approaches

Continuation, Learning and Evaluation

WHY WE NEED SOCIAL MARKETING

This book focuses on the process of developing effective social change programmes, which help people change their behaviours to bring about social progress. This is a process we call social marketing. Social marketing is not a new approach, but rather a field of applied study – just like commercial sector marketing. Social marketing has been developing since the 1970s, and over the last ten years has been increasingly taken up by governments and NGOs around the world as a practical and systematic way to develop social change interventions. Social marketing is also increasingly being applied because it has been shown to make a useful contribution to tackling many of the big social challenges faced by communities and their governments.

All societies face a number of key challenges over the coming years. These include, but are not limited to:

- The need to ensure that spending on public services makes things better, as perceived by citizens, but also represents good value for money and ideally saves money.
- The balance of current evidence suggest that tackling chronic disease will require a programme of both clinical intervention and primary prevention focused on behaviour change.
- Environmental challenges such as global warming and CO_2 emissions require big changes in both the lifestyles that people aspire to and the behaviours they undertake.
- Inequality and social exclusion are increasing within countries and between regions.
- People who most need services are often the least likely to have access to them.
- Most states are experiencing increases in growth in social, welfare and healthcare budgets as a percentage of GDP. This trend is probably not sustainable into the medium to long term.

In addition to these big social challenges, many social change programmes suffer from a number of substantial weaknesses (French and Mayo, 2006):

- Many social programmes that aim to change behaviour are constructed by policy makers and driven down into the system and communities. This 'top down' or 'expert led' approach which is often politically driven by ministers or by 'experts' is often not informed by insight[1] into the behaviours and beliefs of the target group, with the result that interventions are frequently misunderstood or viewed as irrelevant by the people who they are intended for.
- Many projects are throwaway interventions ('short shelf life'). Behaviour change programmes are often developed by politicians or experts, as a means of demonstrating activity or concern around an issue high on the political/media agenda. Timescales are often short term, with little baseline evidence for action and evaluation of impact. Short term awareness raising campaigns are usually driven by a need for organisations or governments to demonstrate activity or manage political agendas rather than promoting real change.
- Many programmes are not adequately performance managed. Activity is focused around developing intervention products – often social advertising, tool kits, training programmes or web services – with the result that vital planning, insight and evaluation stages are neglected. This focus on activity results in programmes that are often not guided by what target groups say will help and also often do not have widespread stakeholder engagement to ensure programme sustainability.

---

[1] See Chapter 1 for a fuller explanation of 'insight'.

○ There is often a lack of coordination and integration between the blizzard of policy directives and programmes from across government. This results in public programmes that provide contradictory advice, competing incentives or disincentives.

○ Many public programmes either have vague, unquantifiable aims or at the other extreme have unrealistic goals.

○ Few programmes utilise a full intervention mix of education, design, support services and control measures with strong coordination between these key modes of intervention.

○ Often programmes are insufficiently funded or sustained over an adequate length of time to achieve agreed outcomes.

These challenges can seem both complex and intractable. However, whilst the issues that behaviour change programmes seek to address are complex in their causes, the solutions are not always complicated. There is a growing body of evidence and many examples of good practice[2], which demonstrate how well-planned and executed behavioural change programmes, based on social marketing planning principles, can be highly effective in reducing the impact of current and future social challenges. In this book we explore some of this strong practice to learn how this has been done.

LEARNING FROM THE PRIVATE SECTOR

Change management in the public sector is often driven by a focus on business planning, service delivery and better systems management. Recently, there has been a concerted effort in many countries to import such disciplines from the private sector, as a way of increasing efficiency and effectiveness. The adoption of systematic business processes is, however, a second-order activity in most private-sector organisations.

The principle function of businesses is winning customers, delighting them and developing products and services, not the other way round. Many of the basic business processes for developing products and services are now well established and the delivery of excellence in service or product is seen as no more than a baseline requirement for success in the business world. Over the last thirty years in the business sector, there has been more and more emphasis on delivering excellence by ensuring a consistent customer-centric approach, which not only focuses on creating value for customers, but also on building an ongoing relationship with them.

This shift from a product and service orientation towards a customer-focused orientation has been profound in the private sector, but much less marked in the public sector. However, as an approach to developing social change programmes, social marketing is driven by these same two essential 'customer'- (or 'citizen'-) focused drivers:

1 Create value for the citizen.
2 Develop an ongoing relationship with them, which ensures they become part of the solution to the social challenges facing society.

---

[2] See National Social Marketing Centre ShowCase good practice case study database at www. thensmc.com and Tools of Change at http://www.toolsofchange.com/en/topic-resources/

THE NEED FOR CITIZEN-CENTRIC PUBLIC AND NGO SERVICES

Staff who work in the public or NGO sector do so for many reasons, but one underpinning motivation is the sense of satisfaction that such a career can offer. In practice, however, employees can find themselves dealing with the vagaries of working within a service that is often perceived to be bureaucratic, self-serving and inefficient.

Developing the means for sustained organisational change and service improvement through a process of satisfying citizen needs is about developing a new culture that actually builds on the core public-sector and NGO ethos of social welfare, citizen support and community solidarity. This cultural bedrock can be used to develop a new ethos focused not on service provision but on meeting citizens' needs. Such a shift should result in a culture that is motivated, progressive, ambitious and constantly striving to improve services, not for the sake of efficacy or to satisfy 'managers', but for the benefit of services users. A 'citizen needs' driven approach to service improvement should also create a new respect from the public for public and NGO services.

Social marketing, with its associated concepts and operational principles, offers organisations the opportunity to achieve such a change.

THE STRUCTURE OF THIS BOOK

In Chapter 1 of this book, we set out the key social marketing concepts and principles that can be used to develop and implement successful social programmes aimed at helping people to change their behaviours. In this chapter we explore why social marketing should not be confused with social advertising[3] or social media[4].

In Chapter 2, we describe a five-stage approach to planning and implementing these concepts and principles.

The remaining chapters of this book then give real-life examples of how the social marketing approach has created real value for citizens by generating change around issues such as infant fatalities or environmental pollution.

THE FIVE KEY FEATURES OF THIS BOOK

When discussing social marketing with colleagues from around the world, we often talk about the importance of applying the 'social marketing mindset'. But what is this mindset?

---

[3] Social marketing focuses on understanding people and behaviour and seeks to make a positive impact on them. Social advertising can contribute to this, but only if it can be shown to have a positive impact on the behaviours being addressed.

[4] New and social media can be valuable in communicating to and proactively engaging audiences, but social marketing is much wider than this and goes beyond the use of new media.

In Chapter 1 we explore the eight principles, or 'Benchmark Criteria', that can help you to identify whether an intervention is a social marketing programme. We also discuss the 4Ps of the Marketing Mix and the 'deCIDES' intervention mix.

These conceptual tools are all helpful for understanding and identifying social marketing. However, the nature and practice of social marketing is not without its debate. As with any field of practice that draws on a wide range of theory, science and experience, practitioners rigorously debate issues such as the value of the 4Ps, the ethics of the 'Exchange' concept and the place of competitive analysis in social marketing.

With this inevitable ongoing debate in mind during the process of writing this book, we have sought to identify a small number of crucial features that reflect the social marketing mindset. To ease the task of remembering them, we have named them the '5Cs', and believe they lie at the heart of effective social marketing interventions. The 5Cs are set out below:

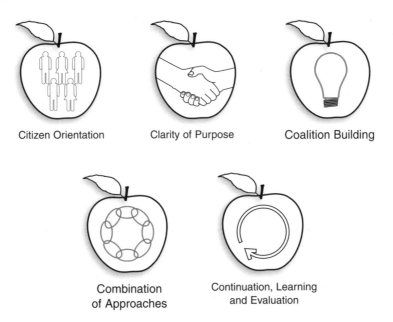

Citizen Orientation   Clarity of Purpose   Coalition Building

Combination
of Approaches

Continuation, Learning
and Evaluation

Customer orientation is the most important of the 5Cs. This is because this is the key principle that drives every aspect of social marketing. The five key features of the social marketing mindset can be understood as follows.

CITIZEN ORIENTATION

Many behavioural change interventions are based on evidence derived from published studies, as well as analysis of other forms of needs data such as service utilisation, epidemiological data or demographic statistics. This information is vital, but is not sufficient in its own right to develop effective behavioural interventions. By contrast, the commercial sector invests heavily in market research to understand people's motivations, needs, wants, fears and aspirations, as well as understanding why they would, or would not, buy a specific product or use a specific service. Public behaviour-change interventions need to follow this example, enhancing their understanding of the challenge by understanding potential target audiences:

> We must be relentlessly customer focused. Many people want a single point of contact for a range of services. The public are not interested in whether their needs are met by Department X or Agency Y, they just want a good, joined up service where X and Y talk to each other and share the information the public have provided. We should strive to meet this demand. (Gus O'Donnell, Cabinet Secretary, quoted in UK Cabinet Office, 2006)

As the UK Cabinet Office has stated, if we don't understand what really matters to the people we are trying to reach, we will waste time and money, and risk compromising public service providers' reputations, by offering services which customers don't recognise as being for them and have difficulty accessing:

> We will base our management of those services on an illusion, recording as a triumph each duplicative and unnecessary phone call because it has been dealt with within the target time allowed. The complex social problems of exclusion, many of which can be alleviated by early intervention, will remain intractable. (UK Cabinet Office, 2006)

COALITION BUILDING

Another vital key to success is the development of coalitions, both internally and externally. Working with external stakeholders can provide:

- Useful insight into consumer behaviours. For example, the development of the obesity Social Marketing Strategy in the UK (see Chapter 19) involved many manufacturing and retail organisations, who contributed valuable insight into behaviours of key target groups/consumers.
- Strategic advice and support within the wider political environment. Political stakeholders can circumnavigate the hierarchical processes of government by providing direct access to ministers. At a local level, stakeholders can be used to provide additional resources or access to target audiences.
- Organisations close to target groups can act as 'main message givers', or advocates and exemplars of change. For example, see the case study about the adoption of child car-safety sets in Chapter 3.

It is vital that behaviour-change programmes are planned and implemented across institutional, departmental and, if possible, sector borders. A multi-faceted approach, where diverse stakeholder partners combine with a joint vision of what they want to achieve, has a much higher chance of success than single initiatives developed in silos.

There is also empirical evidence that investing in partner and stakeholder engagement increases the impact and sustainability of programmes. It is 'vital that any behaviour change programme should be developed in partnership with stakeholder organisations' (NICE, 2007).

CLARITY OF PURPOSE

Behaviour-change programmes require a set of clear, measurable and realistic behavioural objectives that can be achieved within the timescales of the specific programme. Often many governmental and NGO programmes have poorly articulated, unrealistic, or, in the opposite extreme, no clear discernible objectives. Programme objectives need to be based on thorough research into what has been achieved elsewhere; what the system is capable of achieving; and what the target audience think and believe. Programme objectives also need to be achievable and realistic. According to Bill Novelli, picking the wrong goal is one of the mistakes that government organisations and NGOs commonly repeat:

> Too often, people create an elegant plan around the wrong premise or the wrong goal. A successful programme, no matter how we define it, has got to begin with very clear, realistic, measurable goals. (Quoted in Fenton Communications, 2001)

COMBINATION OF APPROACHES

It is always critical to ensure policy coherence, despite numerous examples of programmes across government which have contradictory aims and objectives:

> It follows from the evidence presented here that there is no single intervention, and no simple remedy, that can reduce the burden of chronic diseases. As we have learned from our experience with tobacco, it requires a prolonged commitment of skills and resources in a multi-setting, multi-factor, multi-strategy approach. (Ministry of Health Planning, 2003)

All successful behavioural programmes employ a combination of strategies to achieve change. However, a key error often made in the public sector is for behavioural change programmes that have achieved success in one particular environment to be transported directly to another without any of the key processes that have been outlined in the previous section. What combination of interventions that worked with one specific target group on a specific issue and at a point in time may not work in other situations. For example, if we are considering increasing or developing a tax to help reduce the consumption of fatty foods we may look to the evidence about what has worked in other areas such as tobacco consumption. However, as the following quote makes clear, what works in one area may not work in another:

> Studies of tax, price and behavioural change policies applied to tobacco and alcohol products in many countries provide persuasive evidence of their impact on decreasing consumption of those products. These policy interventions may serve as models for similar approaches for lowering consumption of highly saturated fats or other energy-dense foods. However, critical differences among these types of interventions may limit their generalizability to food consumption. (Goodman and Anise, 2006)

Generally the most successful social change programmes consist of a number of interventions that are mutually reinforcing. In the next chapter we will explore the five main domains of intervention that can be applied in social programmes: Design, Education, Information, Support and Control. Each of these domains of intervention should be informed by the social marketing principles set out in Chapter 1.

CONTINUATION, LEARNING AND EVALUATION

Effective evaluation is crucial to ensuring that the effect of a programme, and its value for money, are assessed. Part of getting value from an investment involves capturing any learning from it, so it can be fed back into future work. While researchers and academics can provide help in this area, it is also important to gain input from key partners, stakeholders and the target audience, and to assess impact both on the selected target audience and the wider delivery system. The focus should be on being able to assess impacts on people's behaviour: what they are actually doing as a consequence of the work.

Assessing the extent to which a programme's aims and objectives have been achieved will require a focus on short-, medium- and long-term indicators. As well as assessing behaviour change, it is also vital to consider other wider impacts, such as:

- Knowledge – the extent to which information was understood and retained.
- Attitudes/beliefs – the extent to which information was valued and incorporated into people's inherent attitudes.
- The wider system – e.g. partner and stakeholder relationships, community and media responses, services and systems.

It is also important when thinking like a social marketer to review and assess: efficiency, effectiveness, equity, quality, engagement and the success of the project management processes. It is also important to undertake an assessment of the cost effectiveness and cost–benefit of, as well as the return on, investment (ROI) from your social marketing programme.

Ultimately it is important to assess programme outcomes against intended outcomes, including behavioural and other impacts.

As well as measuring impact, social marketers have a duty to share learning (both around what worked and what did not) with practitioners who come after them. To do this, it is necessary to make sure that there is a formal writing-up of evaluation findings in a report, which is easy to understand and digest.

Other forms of knowledge transfer should also be employed, to promote understanding of what has been learnt. Finally, it is important to give feedback to commissioners and funders of interventions to discuss the findings and reflect on the implications for ongoing strategy development and future commissioning.

HOW TO USE THIS BOOK

This book is not meant to be a collection of 'perfect' examples. Our chosen case studies all faced their own challenges during research, implementation and evaluation, and all responded as best they could within sometimes challenging circumstances. However, we have brought together a selection of stories from the field, to show you what social marketing can look like in practice, and to enable you to learn from practitioners' experiences – both good and bad.

Many of the case studies and vignettes featured in this book are also available in full on the National Social Marketing Centre's ShowCase resource. ShowCase is an online case study database, which features successful UK and international projects and programmes that have used social marketing techniques and principles to achieve tangible changes in behaviour. With case studies written against the planning process and some featuring engaging video clips, users can follow the journey teams took and find detailed information on the 'how' of delivering a social marketing intervention, as well as outcomes achieved. The case studies provide honest reflections and practical tips so that users may capitalise on others' achievements and avoid similar mistakes and barriers.

ShowCase
Social Marketing Case Studies

You can visit ShowCase via the NSMC website at www.thensmc.com.

You can read this book from front to back, or you can dip in where your interest takes you. Each chapter stands alone, but we hope that together they make a stronger sum, and provide lots of examples of how and why social marketing can be applied. As you work your way through this book, or if you go straight to case studies that interest you, try to reflect on the five elements of the social marketing mindset we have outlined above.

In the following chapters we will return to each of the 5Cs, and each one is featured in most of the case studies that are included in this book. In each case study you will be able to see how the social marketing mindset has been applied to develop interventions that are driven by an aspiration to provide value to citizens, though a process of developing interventions that are based on a deep understanding of their needs and views.

INTRODUCTION RECAP

This Introduction has set out the rationale and some of the drivers for the application of social marketing principles to help design and deliver more effective social change programmes. It has also introduced the five key features that we feel represent the crucial elements of a 'social marketing mindset'. These features are: Citizen Orientation, Coalition Building, Clarity of Purpose, Combination of Approach, and Continuation, Learning and Evaluation.

SELF-REVIEW QUESTIONS

1 Write a sentence that sets out the essence of each of the five mindset features.
2 Assume you are writing a recommendation for your manager about why a social marketing approach should be taken to tackle a specific issue. Set out an argument for applying a social marketing approach and explain how adopting a social marketing mindset will help deliver a better and more effective programme.

REFERENCES

Fenton Communications. (2001). *Now Hear This: The 9 Laws of Successful Advocacy Communication*. Washington, DC: Fenton Communications. Available to download at: www.fenton.com/FENTON_IndustryGuide_NowHearThis.pdf.

French, J. and Mayo, E. (2006). *It's Our Health: National Review of Social Marketing*. London: Consumer Focus (formerly the National Consumer Council).

Goodman, C. and Anise, A. (2006). What is known about the effectiveness of economic instruments to reduce consumption of foods high in saturated fats and other energy-dense foods for preventing and treating obesity? Copenhagen: WHO Regional Office for Europe. Available online at: www.euro.who.int/document/e88909.pdf.

Ministry of Health and Planning, Victoria, BC. (2003, Nov.). Prevention that works: A review of the evidence regarding the causation and prevention of chronic disease. Chronic Disease Prevention Initiative, Paper No. 2. Victoria, BC: Ministry of Health Planning.

NICE (UK National Institute for Health and Clinical Excellence). (2007). *Guidance on Behaviour Change*. London: NICE.

UK Cabinet Office. (2006, Oct.). Customer insight in public services: A 'primer'. London: Cabinet Office. Available online at: www.cse.cabinetoffice.gov.uk/UserFiles/File/Customer_Insight_Primer.pdf.

1 THE KEY PRINCIPLES AND CONCEPTS OF SOCIAL MARKETING

ABOUT THIS CHAPTER

In this chapter we will consider what social marketing is, and how it is increasingly being used around the world by organisations in the public, private and NGO sectors to enhance the effectiveness of programmes designed to improve people's lives (French and Mayo, 2006).

Nearly every big policy challenge facing governments requires action to change behaviour (Australian Public Service Commission, 2007; Darnton, 2008). For example, obesity, alcohol misuse, infection control, recycling, saving for retirement and crime reduction are all essentially about helping people change to deliver better lives for individuals and at the same time helping society as a whole. At a population level, little progress is being made in many of these fields. Additionally, questions relating to the legitimacy of state intervention, in what can be considered private matters, are often raised (Reeves, 2010). More recently, the need to ensure value for money when investing government spending has also become a live debate (UK COI, 2009a).

As discussed in this chapter, governments and NGOs are becoming increasingly alert to emerging evidence from fields such as social psychology, behavioural economics and neural sciences, all of which are developing new evidence and theories around approaches to social behavioural change. In parallel with these developments, social marketing has, over the last 25 years, been developing a growing body of theory, evidence (Gordon et al., 2006) and experience that is starting to have a profound influence on the delivery of both national and local efforts to promote social good. Social marketing is, Nancy Lee suggested at the world social marketing conference in Brighton in 2008, a 'best of breed' approach to developing effective social change programmes that are based on sound evidence, user insight and systematic planning.

WHAT IS SOCIAL MARKETING?

The two words 'social' and 'marketing' can appear to be antagonistic. 'Social' programmes, politics and movements are about making the world a better place; whilst commercial-sector 'marketing' is the process of developing value and wealth for people who already possess resources and capital. The potential clash of basic philosophy is clear and raises the fundamental question: 'is it possible to apply any form of 'marketing' thinking when attempting to tackle 'social' issues? We believe the answer to this question is 'yes'. In this chapter, we will review what social marketing is, and how it can enhance attempts to bring about social good. By working through the case studies in this book, we aim to clarify and demystify social marketing, so that the reader can develop a clear understanding of what social marketing is and is not. The reader should also be able to assess whether an intervention, regardless of what it is called, is or is not applying a social marketing approach. This is important not for any dogmatic or ideological reasons but rather because the key social marketing concepts and principles set out in this chapter and explored in this book are based on sound evidence and experience about what works and what does not.

In summary, this chapter provides an overview of key social marketing concepts and principles. These concepts and principles are reflected in the vignettes and case studies within this book. Chapter 2 goes on to describe a social marketing planning framework that embodies these key principles.

DEFINING SOCIAL MARKETING

In 1971 Kotler and Zaltman published social marketing: An approach to planned social change. This paper marked the first time the phrase 'social marketing' was used in an academic journal, but in reality social marketing approaches were being applied from the 1960s onwards, in both developing and developed countries.

There have been, and continue to be, a developing range of formal definitions of social marketing. For example:

> Social marketing is a programme planning process that promotes the voluntary behaviour of target audiences by offering benefits they want, reducing barriers they are concerned about and using persuasion to motivate their participation in program activity. (Kotler and Roberto, 1989)

> Social marketing is the application of commercial marketing technologies to the analysis, planning, execution, and evaluation of programs designed to influence the voluntary behaviours of target audiences in order to improve their personal welfare and that of their society. (Andreasen, 1995)

> Social marketing is the use of marketing principles and techniques to influence a target audience to voluntarily accept, reject, modify or abandon behaviour for the benefit of individuals, groups, or society as a whole. (Kotler et al., 2002)

Formal definitions vary across the literature, but three key elements commonly appear in the vast majority of these definitions:

- Social marketing's primary purpose is to achieve a particular social good (rather than commercial gain) and its primary focus is on achieving specific behavioural objectives.
- It consists of a finite and coherent set of concepts and principles that can be used in policy formulation, strategy development and implementation of social change programmes.
- It is a systematic process that is defined by learning and evaluation.

Social marketing, like any form of social endeavour, is accompanied by a lively and ongoing debate about its theoretical and practical base, and what should or should not be included under the title. However, authors increasingly agree that it has a number of defining principles and concepts and that it is a coherent approach that can be used to shape policy development and delivery in a broad range of public sector arenas.

Social marketing is also widely accepted to be a systematic planning and delivery methodology, drawing on techniques developed in the commercial sector, but also drawing on experience from the public and non-profit sectors about how to achieve and sustain positive behaviours and how to construct, deliver and evaluate effective programmes of action.

By the very nature of its focus – helping to influence behaviour for social good – social marketing needs to be a multi-disciplinary, trans-theoretical field of study and practical endeavour. Social marketing draws on many theories, models, research approaches, feeder disciplines and forms of analysis to build a rich understanding of why people act as they do and how we can help them to either maintain positive behaviours or change their behaviour for their own and society's benefit. Like commercial-sector marketing, social marketing applies a rigorous and systemic approach to developing, testing, refining and measuring return on investment.

Social marketing is a set of evidence and experience based concepts and principles together with a systematic approach to understanding behaviour and modifying it for social good. It is not a science but rather a form of 'technik' (from the German): a fusion of science, practical 'know-how' and reflective practice aimed at continuously improving the performance of social programmes. To reflect this assessment of the current state of social marketing theory and practice in this book, we use the functional definition of social marketing developed by French et al. (2010):

> Social marketing is the systematic application of marketing alongside other concepts and techniques, to achieve specific behavioural goals for social good.

THE WORDS MATTER LESS THAN THE APPLICATION OF THE PRINCIPLES

If you do an internet search for the term 'social marketing' you will quickly discover that it is used to describe a wide range of interventions, but especially social media, social advertising, or media advocacy. There is nothing wrong with any of these forms of intervention but they are not social marketing as we understand the term. In addition there are many forms of social programme, including civic-education programmes, mass-media information campaigns and community-engagement programmes, many of which apply elements of social marketing practice but not the full suite of principles. Again there is nothing wrong with such approaches but it is important to be clear about when a social marketing approach is being applied and when just specific elements of the social marketing approach are being applied to another form of intervention.

It is therefore important to look beyond the terms people use to describe their work, and to get to the substance of what they do and how they do it. The 'benchmark criteria' set out in this book act as a checklist to help review whether what you are doing, reading about or hearing about is consistent with social marketing principles or not.

Finally, it needs to be recognised that fully implementing the principles and planning processes of social marketing can represent a big challenge for any individual or organisation. There are few 'perfect' social marketing interventions that apply every single principle and systematically work their way through every step of a full planning process. Real issues such as deadlines, the need to spend money and pressures from policy makers, managers and communities often mean that compromises need to be made. This is the reality of developing and implementing social marketing interventions. The vignettes and case studies in this book demonstrate how it is possible to apply many of the principles of social marketing, whilst at the same time managing the real world pressures that every practitioner faces. The point is not to apply social marketing principles set out in this chapter in a mechanical way, but rather to apply them as a reflective practitioner, making judgements about what needs to be done in the particular circumstances that you find yourself in. Being clear about when and how you might need to make a few short cuts or compromises and what you can do to minimise the impact of these on the integrity of the programme is part of what you will gain from reading this book.

SOCIAL MARKETING BENCHMARK CRITERIA

The 'Customer Triangle' is a diagrammatic representation of the eight benchmark criteria that are described below (Figure 1.1).

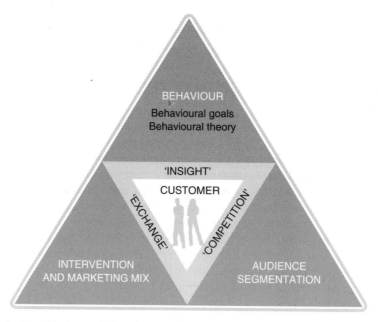

Figure 1.1   The Customer Triangle

Source: French and Blair-Stevens (2005).

These eight 'benchmarks' describe the key concepts and principles of social marketing, and include: Customer Orientation, Exchange, Competition Analysis, Insight, Theory, Behavioural Focus, Segmentation and Method Mix.

1 CUSTOMER ORIENTATION

This is about more than just understanding people. It involves 'seeing things through their eyes'. This means understanding people's social context, the challenges they face and their coping mechanisms. Adopting a customer orientation perspective requires finding out, through different types of audience research, about the lives, needs, fears, aspirations and concerns of your target audience. This should include direct research with the target audience, observation, collating intelligence from existing data and seeking the views of key people who understand or influence the audience. A key risk to avoid is assuming that we know what people want. The aim is to develop interventions that are informed by what we know will motivate people rather than starting from the premise that people need to understand and then change in line with what experts recommend.

2 BEHAVIOURAL FOCUS

The bottom line for social marketing is about measuring changes in behaviour. However, the focus is not just on 'changing' behaviour, but on being able to influence and sustain positive behaviours over time. This means that, in some instances, such as recycling, what we are aiming to do is to encourage people to keep doing a positive behaviour. Social marketing interventions recognise the dynamic and changing nature of behaviour and do not treat it as a simple on/off switch. They recognise that achieving sustainable behavioural change or maintenance requires sustained action. The establishment of clear measurable behavioural goals is one of the most important principles of social marketing. These goals need to be realistic and achievable. As Bill Novelli states:

> Picking the wrong goal is one of the mistakes non-profits repeat the most too often, people create an elegant plan around the wrong premise or the wrong goal. (Quoted in Fenton Communications, 2001)

A successful social marketing programme starts with very clear, realistic and measurable behavioural goals.

3 THEORY INFORMED

Theory is used in social marketing to inform both problem understanding and programme design. Selecting and using behavioural theory involves looking at the underlying ideas about what may influence behaviour in a given situation. A good example of using theory can be seen in the 'Liverpool's Challenge' case study in Chapter 6. The key principle of using theory in social marketing is to use it to understand significant influences on behaviour, and select a theory, or set of theories, that will help explain and pre-empt interventions that will influence target audience behaviour. Later in this chapter, we summarise 24 factors drawn from behavioural change theory and research that can be used as a checklist when analysing behavioural challenges and developing potential interventions.

4 DEVELOPING INSIGHT

'Insight' (IDEA and UK Local Government Association, 2008) is about moving from an initial focus on developing a broad understanding of the lives and behaviours of people towards a more focused, deeper understanding of what is or is not likely to engage a target audience or motivate them in relation to a particular behaviour. The key task is to identify 'actionable insights' which are meaningful to the audience and which the social marketer can do something about. Developing insight moves beyond selecting interventions based on evidence reviews, demographic data, and problem identification and mapping to incorporate understanding about why people act as they do and what they believe would help them to change. Insight is developed through a process of discovering why people behave in the way that they do, what they value and what they say about what will help them. Understanding beliefs, attitudes, barriers to change and potential enabling factors is key. It is also often very helpful to understand why some people carry out the positive behaviour you want to promote as these people can often provide vital clues about the benefits and costs involved.

5 UNDERSTANDING THE EXCHANGE

Rewards and barriers for both problem and desired behaviours need to be considered when planning a social marketing intervention in order to develop a valued exchange proposition. An exchange proposition is an offer that is made to a target audience, which they will value sufficiently to willingly bear the cost either of maintaining, or of changing, specific behaviours.

Benefits that result from an exchange in social marketing can either be tangible or intangible. Bagozzi (1975) suggests that social marketing is a form of 'complex exchange', where value or benefits tend to be intangible in nature. The emphasis on creating value through marketing activity is reflected in Vargo and Lusch's 'Service-dominant Logic Theory' (Vargo and Lusch, 2004; Lusch and Vargo, 2006). The focus of social marketing is on creating value for the 'customer' through every aspect of service delivery, rather than just providing a product. The value of a product is not in the physical product itself, but in the service, benefit or value it provides to the customer. This means that in social marketing the core product is the benefit people will get from undertaking the behavioural goal of the programme.

A key factor in developing a powerful exchange proposition is therefore to ensure that what is offered is something that is valued by the target audience, and not just those proposing the change. Sometimes exchanges are positive (i.e. people get a physical, social or psychological reward or benefit); sometimes exchanges can be negative (i.e. people will face a penalty, social disapproval or some other form of negative consequence if they continue to adopt a particular behaviour). In addition, some exchanges are 'passive' (i.e. they require little cognitive engagement), whilst others involve 'active' decision-making (i.e. a rational assessment of the exchange, and a conscious decision to act in a particular way).

Both positive/negative behavioural reinforcement and passive/active decision-making are spectrums rather than absolute categories. However, if we combine the notion of rewarding or penalising a behaviour with the notion of active or passive decision-making, it is possible to construct a 'value/cost exchange matrix' to represent these various forms of exchange (Figure 1.2).

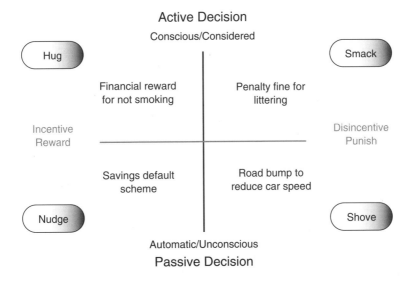

Figure 1.2 Value/cost exchange matrix

Source: French (2010a).

Exchange requires a full appreciation of the real 'costs' and 'value' to the audience. This can include things such as time, effort, money and social consequences. The key aim with a positive exchange is to maximise the potential offer and its value to the audience, whilst minimising the costs of adopting, changing or maintaining a particular behaviour.

With negative exchanges the important issue is to make sure that the cost is one that has meaning to the target audience. For example, imposing a penalty fine that is set at a rate that the audience does not consider high enough, or where they believe there is little chance of being caught, will probably not bring about the desired change.

6 THE COMPETITION

When seeking to influence behaviour there will always be a range of competing factors that will work to undermine the desired change. A key social marketing principle is to understand what may be competing with what you are promoting. In social marketing, there are two main types of competition: external and internal competition. External competition comes from the influence of those people, environments, systems, social norms or organisations that directly or indirectly promote a counter-behaviour, or influence people to maintain an unhealthy or social undesirable behaviour. Competitive forces, such as anti-health advertising and promotions, negative social norms and stress-inducing environments make it harder to motivate people to adopt a desired behaviour. Internal competition includes such things as people's feelings and attitudes about something; the pleasure involved in the thrill of risk taking; the difficulty of giving up an ingrained habit; or addiction. Competition analysis in social marketing leads to the identification of countervailing forces and the systematic development of strategies to reduce the impact of these external and internal competitive forces.

7 SEGMENTATION

Segmentation is a social marketing process that involves assigning people to groups that exhibit similar characteristics, beliefs values and behaviours in order to develop specifically targeted interventions deigned to help them change behaviour. Traditionally, targeting of approaches has tended to concentrate on characteristics such as age, gender, ethnicity, income. Segmentation examines alternative ways that people can be grouped and profiled, for example by their beliefs, values and aspirations or by their actual behaviours. This process of grouping people with similar characteristics helps social marketers to understand both the differences between people, and the types of intervention that might help different groups to change. There is no single 'right way' to segment, but in social marketing programmes segmentations that focus on both behaviour and motivations are the most helpful when it comes to developing potential interventions.

8 METHODS MIX

The last key principle of social marketing is to develop a tailored, evidence- and insight-led mix of interventions, to bring about the desired behavioural goal. In most cases a single intervention is less likely to be effective than multi-component interventions. For example, just 'informing' someone of something may have some limited effect, but if this is combined with practical support and a chance to actively consider it with guidance (education) it is more likely to be effective. A key task in social marketing is then to establish the right mix of interventions given the available resources and time.

   The intervention mix described by the de-CIDES intervention framework (French et al., 2010) can help guide the selection, coordination and combination of different intervention types that will be used in a programme. (See Figure 1.3 and Table 1.1.)

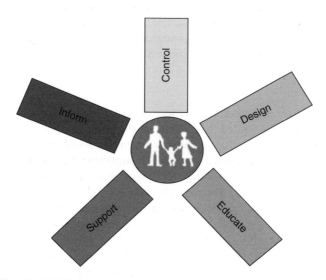

Figure 1.3   The de-CIDES five intervention domains

Source: French et al. (2010).

Table 1.1   The de-CIDES five intervention domains

INFORM/COMMUNICATE:

- inform/communicate/prompt/trigger/remind/reinforce/awareness/explain

EDUCATE:

- enable/engage/train/skill development/inspire/encourage/motivate

SUPPORT:

- service provision/practically assist/promote access/social networks, social mobilisation

DESIGN:

- alter: physical, product, social, organisational, systems, technology

CONTROL/REGULATE:

- control/rules/require/constrain/restrict/police/enforce/regulate/legislate/incentivise

If we combine these five domains of intervention with the four types of exchange, we are able to draw up an intervention matrix (see Figure 1.4) that can be populated with different types of intervention. The selected intervention mix should be informed by all available evidence, data and insight.

All of the case studies in this book use a combination of intervention types and different forms of exchange. You can use the matrix in Figure 1.4 to plot which combination each uses as you read the case studies. You can also use this intervention matrix to help describe and record the intervention mix for social marketing programmes that you develop.

As well as de-CIDES, another common way of thinking about the marketing mix is by referring to the 4Ps of marketing: Product, Price, Place and Promotion (Borden, 1964). Despite their age, the 4Ps are still used by both commercial and social marketers, to ensure that marketers focus on all four of the key marketing domains when developing interventions (Table 1.2).

	Hug	Nudge	Shove	Smack
Control				
Inform				
Design				
Educate				
Support				

Figure 1.4   The social marketing intervention mix matrix

Source: French (2010b).

Table 1.2   The 4Ps marketing mix

Product	The thing being provided, i.e. the product or service.
	In social marketing terms, the programme, campaign, project, service, etc.
Price	A similar concept to 'Exchange'.
	What it costs the person to get the product or service – not just money – but also time, effort, social consequences, etc.
Place	Where the product or service can be delivered
	Where the customer can be reached/engaged
	Where the customer takes up the service or product
Promotion	The package of things that will highlight and promote the product or service – incentivise and encourage its adoption/purchase, the media promotion

The 4Ps have been criticised by some (e.g. Nelson, 2010) for focusing too heavily on the planner (rather than the target audience), and for putting 'product' first on the list of tasks. However the 4Ps are often used when planning social marketing interventions, providing a useful intervention checklist, and we have made reference to them in several chapters of this book to illustrate how they have been applied.

USING SOCIAL MARKETING STRATEGICALLY

The eight social marketing benchmarks outlined above form the core of what this book is about. The principles are reflected in our chosen case studies, and can be used as a guide to good practice as well as a useful checklist when developing social marketing interventions.

It is common for people initially to think of social marketing as something that is used to develop a particular programme or campaign. While this can be the case, it can also be used strategically to inform policy development, analysis and strategy selection.

Figure 1.5 illustrates how social marketing can be used strategically to assist policy analysis, support strategy development and then guide implementation and delivery, as well as operationally to plan programmes, campaigns or other interventions.

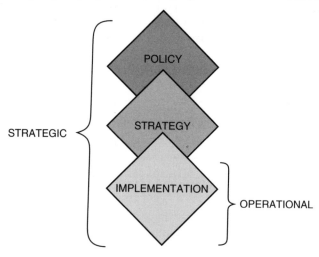

Figure 1.5   The social marketing process

In Chapter 2 we explore why and how social market principles can be applied to assisting with the development of policy and strategy in more depth.

INFLUENCING BEHAVIOUR

In addition to applying the social marketing principles set out above, social marketers also need to be aware of the growing evidence base about how to effectively change behaviour, and to have a working understanding of some of the underlying science of behavioural change. The issue of behaviour change, even for the social good, is not without its political, ethical and ideological dilemmas. Commentators, academics and politicians from all points along the political spectrum often feel uncomfortable with the idea that people's behaviour can be modelled, predicted or changed (Buchan, 1988). Many citizens also share this disquiet, principally unsettled by the fear that behaviour-change interventions imply that we can circumvent people's free will.

However as Ormerod (1988) contends, much of this perceived fear can be reduced by the knowledge that complex systems such as human behaviour, even if driven by what appear to be simple rules, result in behaviours that cannot be controlled or predicted in a very precise way. The best that we can currently say with assurance is that we have a certain amount of knowledge about why people act as they do; what can influence this; and how to develop and deliver programmes that have a greater chance of success. It must always be remembered, however, that it is unlikely that there will ever be a simple approach to behaviour change that will work in every circumstance.

There is strong evidence to demonstrate that what most of us know from experience: that simply telling someone to do something is no guarantee of success (Mulgan et al., 2004). We know, instead, that if we want to help people to change behaviours, we need to consider other factors such as looking at the timing, context and situation involved, all of which will influence whether someone is likely to follow what we propose. The tone and feel of the approach, along with the social context, can be hugely important. If others are supporting what you are proposing, this social effect on the person can be hugely important, particularly if the person values or appreciates the other people supporting a particular course of action.

PUTTING THEORY INTO PRACTICE

Recent findings from a variety of fields of study have all helped to expand and enhance our understanding of how and why people behave as they do.

This learning gives us a powerful set of principles, which can be used to help design more effective social change interventions. In particular, there is a much wider appreciation now that while behaviour can be 'rationale' and the result of conscious consideration, in practice many decisions flow from emotional engagement, social influence and environmental prompts.

What we now know is that many of the decisions we make that influence our behaviour are not the result of active decision-making. Rather, as discussed above, they are unconscious and automatic. These 'decisions' are influenced by our social and emotional contexts and by factors such as timing, and our physiological state. The following set of 24 principles summarises much of what we currently know about influencing behaviour, drawn from fields of study that include management, psychology, policy development, economics, design, sociology, biology and communication studies:

1   Change in behaviour is usually a process not an event, and often entails several attempts before success. When delivering intervention programmes there is a need to be persistent, sustain interventions over time and offer multiple paths to success.

2   A desire or acceptance of the need for change must be present in the target audience. Some people will already want to change their behaviour; others will need to be persuaded to consider a change.

3   People need to feel involved and engaged. Participatory involvement often creates bigger behavioural change effects. Wherever possible, involve, consult and engage people in both designing and delivering interventions.

4   Active consideration often leads to more permanent change. If people have a chance to explore and consider issues, this often helps them reconsider attitudes and beliefs that help them change their behaviour or maintain a positive behaviour.

5   People can be taught critical thinking skills that can help them take more control over their lives and resist media, social and environmental influences on their behaviour.

6   People are often motivated to do the 'right thing' for the community as well as themselves and their families. Interventions that appeal to people's sense of community togetherness tend to be more successful.

7   Social relationships and social support have a strong and persistent influence on behaviour. Working with and through key influencers improves the impact of behaviour-change programmes. Use the power of group norms and behaviour to inform and engage people in change, let them know that others are changing and use the power of group action.

8   People can be 'locked into' patterns of behaviour and need practical help to break or unfreeze these. Programmes that provide practical support to change, are easy to access and require small steps tend to be more effective.

9   Beliefs and values influence how people behave. Programmes should start by understanding target audience beliefs and attitudes and use these to inform the development of behaviour change services and products.

10   Behavioural experience can influence beliefs and values. Programmes that move people to behaviour as quickly as possible, i.e. give them a chance to try the thing that is being promoted work best. It is not always necessary to rely on shifting attitude first. Often behaving differently often leads to a shift in attitude.

11   Change is more likely if an undesired behaviour is not part of an individual's coping strategy. Avoid 'telling people off' for 'bad' behaviour if they are using it to cope with life. Demonstrate an understanding of the reasons for their behaviour and offer realistic and attractive alternatives that give practical support to change.

12   People's perception of their own ability to change can either enhance or detract from attempts to change. So, it is best to develop services and support that will build people's confidence, knowledge and skills.

13   People's perception of their vulnerability to a risk and its severity is key to understanding behaviour and developing effective interventions. Focus on understanding people's perceptions and how they view the risks associated with the behaviour. Also focus interventions on people's views and frame risks in ways that they can understand and are meaningful to them.

14   People's perceptions of the effectiveness of the recommended behavioural change are key factors affecting decisions to act. This factor means that we need to set out – in terms that people value – the benefits and potential impact of the change that is being promoted.

15 People influence and are influenced by their physical, social and economic environments. There is a limit to a person's capacity to change if the environment militates against the desired change. Deliver programmes that tackle the underlying environmental, social and economic barriers to change as well as personal factors.

16 People are loss averse. They will put more effort into retaining what they have than acquiring new assets or benefits. Stress potential losses associated with the behaviour as well as the positive gains that can be accrued from change.

17 People often use mental short cuts and trial-and-error approaches to make decisions, rather than 'rational' decision-making. An understanding of these short cuts or heuristics should be used to develop interventions and develop new 'scripts' associated with the behaviour you are trying to influence.

18 The more beneficial or rewarding an experience, the more likely it is to be repeated. Maintaining positive behaviour can be assisted by reinforcement. Behavioural interventions should seek to reward desired behaviours and when appropriate penalise inappropriate behaviour. Interventions should also seek to support positive behaviour by maintaining a relationship with people which affirms their new behaviour and encourages them to build on it.

19 Many people are often more concerned with short-term gains and costs, and tend to place less value on rewards or costs that might happen in the future. Programmes should emphasise short-term as well as long-term benefits and seek to reduce short-term costs.

20 People are more likely to change behaviour if they value what is being offered or in the case of a negative penalty that the penalty has meaning and real consequences for them. Offers and penalties need to be presented in a way that people find meaningful and understandable.

21 Change is more likely if the actions that have to be taken are easy and specific. Making the first step to change very easy also helps engage people in the start of a change process. Keep interventions specific and promote them in a way that the target audience views as relevant and appealing.

22 People can be helped to change by designing services and environments in a way that encourages people to act and does not involve complex choice decisions. Design services and environments that encourage 'mindless choosing', i.e. by removing the need for complex choices, for example making only low or non-alcoholic drinks available at social functions will encourage fewer people to get drunk.

23 Many people are bad at computation and risk assessment. Many of us do not understand numbers, risk ratios or odds. Test the users' understanding of numerical and risk-based messages before using them. Convey risks and factual numeric information in ways that the target audience can understand and find compelling, for example the number of Olympic-sized swimming pools full of water that can be saved by fitting a low-volume flush toilet.

24 Communications and media can have a powerful effect on people's attitudes, beliefs and consequently behaviour. However, this effect is not mainly concerned with information transmission. Media can however help to build up impressions of relationships between issues, set the agenda for public debate and create emotional responses as well as transmit information.

This list is drawn from hundreds of papers and books, but the reader is directed to the following texts which provide useful summaries of state-of-the-art thinking: Hornick (2002), Ariely (2007), Brafman and Brafman (2009), Ciladidi (1994), Kahneman (2003), Dawney and Shah (2005), Thaler and Sunstein (2008), Mulgan et al. (2010), French et al.

(2010), Du Plessis (2005), UK COI (2009b, 2009c), Cottam and Leadbeater (2004), Design Council (2010), Challenger et al. (2009), Earls (2007), Grist (2010), Goldstein et al. (2007), Dolan et al. (2010).

This 24-point summary of common human traits and tendencies can be considered when planning and implementing social marketing interventions.

CHAPTER RECAP

The main features of social marketing can be understood by reference to the eight benchmark criteria set out in this chapter. Social marketing draws on many fields of study to develop client- or citizen-focused strategies for promoting behaviour change. There are very few perfect social marketing programmes that exhibit every feature set out in this chapter, but it is possible for programme designers and practitioners to apply as many of these evidence-based principles as possible.

In this chapter we have introduced the terminology and key social marketing concepts that we use throughout the following chapters. We have also agreed our definition of social marketing as:

> The systematic application of marketing alongside other concepts and techniques to achieve specific behavioural goals for social good.

In the next chapter we will learn how to plan a social marketing programme, using the 'Total Process Planning Model'.

SELF-REVIEW QUESTIONS

1   List the eight benchmark criteria for social marketing, and summarise the key characteristics of each.
2   Set out your own definition of social marketing in not more than 30 words.
3   List some of the key social marketing models that have been introduced in this chapter and some of the key features of each one.

REFERENCES

Andreasen, A. (1995). *Marketing Social Change: Changing Behaviour to Promote Health, Social Development, and the Environment.* San Francisco: Jossey-Bass.

Ariely, D. (2007). *Predictably Irrational: The Hidden Forces that Shape Our Decisions.* London: HarperCollins.

Australian Public Service Commission. (2007). *Changing Behaviour: A Public Policy Perspective.* Available online at: www.apsc.gov.au/publications07/changingbehaviour.htm.

Bagozzi, R. (1975). Marketing as exchange. *Journal of Marketing*, 39: 32–9.

Borden, N. (1964). The concept of the marketing mix. *Journal of Advertising Research*, 4 (June): 2–7.

Brafman, O. and ,Brafman, R. (2009). *Sway: The Irresistible Pull of Irrational Behaviour*. London: Virgin.

Buchan, J. (1998). *Frozen Desire: An Inquiry into the Meaning of Money*. London: Picador.

Challenger, R., Clegg, C. and Robinson, M. (2009). *Understanding Crowd Behaviours*. Leeds: Leeds University Press.

Ciladidi, R. (1994). *Influence: The Psychology of Persuasion*. London: Collins.

Cottam, H. and Leadbeater, C. (2004). Health: Co-creating services. Red Paper No. 1. London: The Design Council.

Dann, S. (1977). Anomie, ego-enhancement and tourism. *Annals of Tourism Research*, 4(4): 184–94.

Dann, S., Harris, P., Sullivan-Mort, G., Fry, M. and Binney, W. (2007). Reigniting the fire: A contemporary research agenda for social, political and nonprofit marketing. *Journal of Public Affairs*, 7(3): 291–304.

Darnton, A. (2008). *Reference Report: An Overview of Behaviour Change Models and Their Uses*. London: Government Social Research Unit. Available online at: www.civilservice.gov.uk/Assets/Behaviour_change_reference_report_tcm6-9697.pdf.

Dawney, E. and Shah, H. (2005). *Behavioural Economics: Seven Principles for Policy Makers*. London: New Economics Foundation.

Design and Technology Alliance Against Crime. (2010). Design out crime using design to reduce injuries from alcohol related violence in pubs and clubs. London: The Design Council.

Dolan, P., Hallsworth, M., Halpern, D., Kind, D. and Vlaev, I. (2010). *Mindspace: Influencing Behaviour Through Public Policy*. London: Institute for Government; UK Cabinet Office.

Du Plessis, E. (2005). *The Advertised Mind: Ground-breaking Insights into How Our Brains Respond to Advertising*. London: Millward Brown & Kogan Page.

Earls, M. (2007). *Herd: How to Change Mass Behaviour by Harnessing Our True Nature*. London: John Wiley.

Fenton Communications. (2001). *Now Hear This: The 9 Laws of Successful Advocacy Communication*. Washington, DC: Fenton Communications. Available to download at: www.fenton.com/FENTON_IndustryGuide_NowHearThis.pdf.

French, J. (2005). *The Big Pocket Guide to Social Marketing*, 1st edn. London: The National Consumer Council.

French, J. (2010a). The value/cost exchange matrix. Presentation given at the 20th University of South Florida Social Marketing Conference, June 2010. Download at: www.strategic-social-marketing.org.

French, J. (2010b). The social marketing intervention mix matrix. Presentation given at the Open University, Nov. 2010. Download at: www.strategic-social-marketing.org.

French, J. and Blair-Stevens, C. (2010). *Improving Lives Together: The de-CIDES Framework*. London: Westminster City Council..

French, J., Blair-Stevens, C., Merritt, R. and McVey, D. (2010). *Social Marketing and Public Health: Theory and Practice*. Oxford: Oxford University Press.

French, J. and Mayo, E. (2006). *It's Our Health!* London: National Consumer Council.

Goldstein, N., Martin, S. and Cialdini, R. (2007). *Yes! 50 Secrets From the Science of Persuasion*. London: Profile Books.

Gordon, R., McDermott, L., Stead, M. and Angus K. (2006). The effectiveness of social marketing for health improvement: What's the evidence? *Public Health*, 120: 1133–1139.

Grist, M. Steer. (2010). *Mastering Our Behaviour Through Instinct, Environment and Reason*. London: Royal Society of Arts.

Hornick, R. C., ed. (2002). *Public Health Communication Evidence for Behaviour Change*. New Jersey: LEA.

IDEA and the UK Local Government Association. (2008). Insight: Understanding your citizens, customers and communities. London: RSE Consulting.

Kahneman, D. (2003). A psychological perspective on economics. *American Economic Review*, 93(2): 162–8.

Kotler, P. and Roberto, W. (1989). *Social Marketing: Strategies for Changing Public Behaviour*. New York: Free Press.

Kotler, P., Roberto, W. and Lee, N. (2002). *Social Marketing: Improving the Quality of Life*. Thousand Oaks, CA: SAGE.

Kotler, P. and Zaltman, G. (1971). Social marketing: An approach to planned social change. *Journal of Marketing*, 35: 3–12.

Lusch, R. F. and Vargo, S. L. (2006). Service-dominant logic: What it is, what it is not, what it might be. In Lusch and Vargo (eds), *The Service-Dominant Logic of Marketing: Dialog, Debate, and Directions*. New York: M. E. Sharpe.

Ministry of Health Planning, Victoria, BC. (2003, Nov.). Prevention that works: A review of the evidence regarding the causation and prevention of chronic disease. Chronic Disease Prevention Initiative, Paper No. 2. Victoria, BC: Ministry of Health Planning.

Mulgan, G. (2010). Influencing public behaviour to improve health and wellbeing: An independent report. London: Department of Health.

Mulgan, G., Aldridge, S., Beales, G., Heathfield, A., Halpen, D. and Bates, C. (2004, Feb.). Personal responsibility and changing behaviour: The state of knowledge and its implications for public policy. London: Prime Minister's Strategy Unit.

Nelson, S. (2010). *Naked Marketing: How the 4Ps Have Destroyed Business and What To Do Instead*. London: Management Books 2000Ormerod, P. (1998). *Butterfly Economics: A New General Theory of Social and Economic Behavior*. London: Faber & Faber.

Reeves, R. (2010). *A Liberal Dose? Health and Wellbeing: The Role of the State, An Independent Report*. London: Department of Health.

Thaler, R. and Sunstein, C. (2008). *Nudge: Improving Decisions about Health, Wealth and Happiness*. New Haven and London: Yale University Press.

Thomas, M. and Brain, D. (2008). *Crowd Surfing: Surviving and Thriving in the Age of Empowerment*. London: A & C Black.

Turning Point. (2004). *The Manager's Guide to Social Marketing: Using Marketing to Improve Health Outcomes*. Seattle: Turning Point. Available to download at: www.turningpointprogram.org/Pages/pdfs/social_market/smc_managers_online.pdf.

UK Cabinet Office. The Cabinet Office Emergency Planning College, York, UK. Website: http://epcollege.com/.UK COI (Central Office of Information). (2009a). *Payback and Return on Marketing Investment (ROMI) in the Public Sector*. London: Central Office of Information. Available online at: http://coi.gov.uk/blogs/bigthinkers/wp-content/uploads/2009/11/coi-payback-and-romi-paper.pdf.

UK COI (Central Office of Information). (2009b). *Communications and Behaviour Change*. London: Central Office of Information.

UK COI (Central Office of Information). (2009c). *How Public Service Advertising Works*, ed. J. Lannon. London: Central Office of Information and the Institute of Practitioners in Advertising.

US National Cancer Institute. (2005). *Theory at a Glance: A Guide for Health Promotion Practice*. Washington, DC: US Department of Health and Human Services. Available to download at: www.cancer.gov/PDF/481f5d53-63df-41bc-bfaf-5aa48ee1da4d/TAAG3.pdf.

Vargo, S. L. and Lusch, R. F. (2004). Evolving to a new dominant logic for marketing. *Journal of Marketing*, 68: 1–17

2 PLANNING SOCIAL MARKETING

ABOUT THIS CHAPTER

All of the case studies in this book undertook some form of planning to develop the interventions that they put in place. Systematic and transparent planning is a key defining feature of social marketing.

This chapter will set out a basic guide to planning social marketing interventions. Whilst a growing number of social marketing planning guides and models are available, most focus on 'operational' planning (i.e. for on-the-ground delivery). However, social marketing principles can also be used to guide and inform policy formulation and strategy development as well as operational programme planning. There is a need, then, to distinguish between strategic and operational social marketing planning.

THE NEED TO ACT STRATEGICALLY AS WELL AS OPERATIONALLY

'Strategic Social Marketing' is a process that applies social marketing principles to inform the development of an organisation's overall strategy, to ensure delivery against its organisational goals in relation to behaviour change. Strategic Social Marketing can be defined as:

> The application of social marketing principals and concepts to inform and guide strategic goal development, intervention selection and evaluation. (French, 2010)

Strategic Social Marketing is concerned with informing and guiding the key strategic processes of goal setting, intervention selection and evaluation planning. Thinking strategically also means that specific social marketing interventions can be linked to overall organisational strategies. For example, in the field of obesity there is a need for governments to look at food production policies, and legislation relating to the promotion of food products. These overarching strategic objectives need to be linked to specific behaviour change programmes, such as those set out in Chapters 6 and 19 of this book.

There are a number of social marketing planning frameworks and models which the social marketer can either use or adapt to their own situation. The case studies in this book have employed a variety of different models, but they all used some form of transparent planning process. One of the best known social marketing planning models is the five-stage 'Total Process Planning' (TPP) model (French and Blair-Stevens, 2005), which is the basis for the UK National Social Marketing Centre's (NSMC) online planning tool.

This tool has now been developed by the NSMC in to a free online tool that can be found at the NSMC website (see the webaddress list at the end of this chapter). This site also hosts a number of helpful planning tools for each step of the five-stage model, as well as a growing number of case studies, available on the ShowCase collection, which illustrate how social marketing has made a positive contribution to many social challenges. This chapter sets out a short form of the NSMC's TPP planning framework, to illustrate the main steps and tasks when planning a social marketing project.

THE TOTAL PROCESS PLANNING MODEL

Very few social marketing programmes work their way through every step of a prescribed planning model. Most people tailor and adapt an approach to a best fit with the context and issues that they are working on. The important thing is not to follow any model to the letter, but to adopt a systematic approach that is transparent and appropriate for your situation, and that applies to as many social marketing principles as possible.

The TPP social marketing planning model consists of the five stages set out in Figure 2.1.

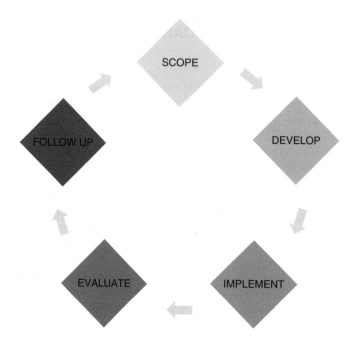

Figure 2.1 The social marketing planning model

SCOPING STAGE

Though all stages of social marketing planning are important, investing time in the scoping stage is particularly critical. This helps to avoid a tendency to start generating and crafting solutions before a deep understanding of the customer is achieved. It also ensures that a clear behavioural focus is identified from the start, and helps to ensure that relevant theory and ethical issues are considered early in the process.

Insights gained during scoping are used to inform the development of a working proposition about what will help bring about change and the selection of appropriate methods that can be taken into the next testing and development stage. The scoping stage ends with the production of a Scoping Report, which summarises findings from the activities set out below.

SCOPING INVOLVES THE FOLLOWING TASKS

Setting out the rationale for the intervention:

- Sets out why action is needed on the identified social issue; who the target audience is; and why they have been selected. Sets out the need for action, the relevant policy and/or organisational context and the overall strategic objectives of the project sponsor(s).

Situation Analysis:

- SWOT[1] and STEEPLE[2] analysis: A review of organisational strengths and weaknesses, opportunities and threats analysis and a review of relevant social, technological environmental, ethical, political and legal issues that may impact on the programme of behaviour are carried out.
- Competition analysis and Force Field analysis: List and assign relevant weighting to factors influencing adoption of the behaviour including positive enabling factors and barriers to change. Analysis of what or who may be influencing the target audience to act in a way that is detrimental or positive and assessing relevant weight of the influence.
- Evidence review, gather information about what is known about how to tackle the issue from published and unpublished sources, i.e. case study reports interviews with others who have undertaken work in the field.
- Asset mapping: recording of all assets including: social networks, community assets, environmental assets, stakeholder assets that could be used to tackle the problem.

TARGET AUDIENCE PROFILE AND SEGMENTATION

- Describe the primary audience, i.e. the people you are seeking to influence. Also, set out the secondary and tertiary audiences, i.e. the people who are influencing or could influence the primary audience these can often be intermediaries such as parents.

---

[1] Setting out: Strengths, Weaknesses of current interventions and services in relation to the issue and Opportunities and Threats in relation to the issue drawn from the STEEPLE analysis.

[2] STEEPLE analysis is the process of identifying and ranking in order of influence issues that may have an impact on the behaviour you are focused on influencing, the factors are: Social, Technological, Environmental, Ethical, Political and Legal issues.

○ Data analysis, including gathering and analysis of: service uptake data, demographics, geographic data, relevant behavioural data including risk taking and protective behaviours.

○ Target audience insight and understanding, developed from existing published material and qualitative and quantitative target audience research such as surveys, focus groups and observational studies.

○ Setting out an initial audience segmentation. Cluster people based on attitudes beliefs, knowledge and behaviours.

INTERVENTION PROPOSITION

○ Describe the exchange and how it will be promoted based on target audience insight and understanding, you will also need to set out how the proposed behaviour will be positioned with the target audience. In the case of a positive behaviour change, e.g. recycling. How the benefits will be maximised and costs reduced. In the case of a problematic behaviour, e.g. driving too fast, how the costs will be maximized and the benefits reduced. In the case of non-rational choice situations, set out how the choice environment will be structured, or what , policy or service transformation will be introduced. Use the value cost matrix in Chapter 1 to describe the exchange.

○ Set out the possible Intervention and marketing mix, refer to the de-CIDES intervention modes and the 4Ps marketing mix to describe the proposed interventions.

INITIAL MARKETING OBJECTIVES, SET OUT:

○ Cognitive objectives: measuring knowledge.

○ Affective objectives: measuring beliefs and attitudes.

○ Psychomotor: measuring behaviour change or sustained behaviour. Note: All objectives should be: SMART[3].

WHY INVEST IN SCOPING?

The advantages of investing in a robust scoping stage include:

1 Ensuring that subsequent resources and time invested in addressing the challenge(s) can be used to greatest potential effect.

2 Providing a valuable way to begin to engage and mobilise key partners and stakeholders, who (whatever interventions are selected) will be crucial to ongoing work.

3 Providing important baseline understanding and insights on which all subsequent work can be based.

4 Helping to grow the evidence base by setting out clear hypotheses and objectives that can subsequently be tested, evaluated and reported on.

DEVELOPMENT STAGE

This is where the interventions selected as a result of scoping are taken forward. By this point you should have a good understanding of your target audience; analysed their behaviours; set goals; engaged with key stakeholders; and produced a scoping report. You are now in a position to develop a specific intervention plan.

---

[3]Specific, Measurable, Achievable, Relevant, Time bound.

Crucial to this is undertaking pre-testing of ideas with the audiences, checking that the evidence and assumptions are relevant and actionable, and adjusting plans accordingly. The development stage involves planning your intervention mix, maintaining stakeholder engagement and, where appropriate, building a working relationship with external partners.

The output should be a social marketing business plan with SMART objectives to be executed in the implementation stage.

MARKETING INTERVENTION MIX STRATEGIES

- Set out which combination of the five intervention modes will be used: 1) Inform, 2) Educate, 3) Support, 4) Control, 5) Design, and how the 4Ps of marketing will be applied.
- Describe product: core, actual and augmented product (see Chapter 1 for an explanation of each element) objects or services offered to assist adoption. Set out the price/costs that will be associated with adopting the behaviour and how they will be reduced and what Incentives and disincentives will be used. Describe the place, e.g. ensuring convenient access, opportunities to engage and attractiveness. Finally, set out your promotion strategy, how the desired behaviour will be promoted.

PRE-TESTING AND PILOTING

- Set out how you will pilot test the proposed interventions and the timetable, and plan for this pilot phase.

REPORT ON THE IMPACT OF THE PILOT PROGRAMME

- Reporting on impact (the immediate effect of the intervention/s on issues such as knowledge gain, attitude and beliefs) , outcome (the medium-term effect on behaviour and return on investment).

SET OUT THE FULL BUSINESS PLAN

- Justify the final intended audience segmentation and set out SMART behavioural objectives for each audience.
- Set out the recommended intervention mix that will be used and project milestones, e.g. when will the launch take place, when will the first review take place? Detail the anticipated impact and outcomes over the designated time frame.
- Set out the resources required from main sponsors, partners and stakeholders and how they will be deployed against the de-CIDES intervention mix and the 4Ps marketing mix you have proposed.
- Include a plan for stakeholder and partner engagement.
- Detail how the programme will be managed and its reporting and governance arrangements.

IMPLEMENTATION STAGE

The tasks you will need to consider include: preparing for the intervention launch; spotting opportunities and dealing with problems during delivery; monitoring and evaluating the process as it unfolds; gathering feedback from staff and stakeholders involved in delivery;

and monitoring the wider environment for any changes or developments that might impact upon the intervention.

Depending on the feedback from key stakeholders, you may be required to adjust the implementation plan. A key concern throughout is successfully delivering the intervention and achieving the desired impact on the target audience's behaviour within the timescales you have identified. Specific tasks will include:

- Staff support and development
- Stakeholder and partner management
- Ongoing review and managing risks associated with the project
- Opportunity spotting, horizon scanning and programme adjustment
- Data gathering and recording for assessing process efficiency
- Regular reviews of progress using agreed tracking data
- Reporting to sponsors and stakeholders.

EVALUATION STAGE

At this stage, the impact of the intervention is formally reviewed and assessed. The aim of evaluation is to identify the strengths and weaknesses of your intervention, determine if it is making a difference and measure its return on investment. You will be required to gather detailed information about how the intervention has worked and what it has achieved. You will need to deliver an evaluation report to report back to all sponsors, stakeholders and partners. This evaluation report should include:

1 Introduction including: project rational and governance
2 Aims and objectives
3 Ethical considerations
4 Ownership: intellectual property, sign-off responsibility
5 Evaluation timetable
6 Methodology including: resources used, study design, e.g. use of pre- and post-assessment, the use of control groups. Tools used to collect and analyse data and references to any theoretical models and how results will be analysed
7 Data reporting , setting out your findings
8 Analysis and conclusions and recommendations.

FOLLOW-UP STAGE

The evaluation stage should not be seen as an end-point but the stage when the results of the evaluation are considered by key players and stakeholders, the implications digested and forward plans made as appropriate. Good follow-up helps to promote learning, enhance the evidence base and recognise and value the contributions of those involved.

This final stage in the process is one which can often be overlooked. But it is important to see it as an opportunity to communicate outcomes and lessons learned to your funders, stakeholders and a wider audience.

Sharing the findings of evaluation means that future developments and interventions can build on learned success and failures. This increases the prospect that successful interventions will enter mainstream thinking and practice.

OTHER TOOLS AND FRAMEWORKS

The TPP is just one of many social marketing planning frameworks and there are numerous other models that can be used. These range from simple one-page written plans, such as that set out by Hastings and Elliot (1993), to models such as the ten-step approach advocated by Kotler and Lee (2008), or the seven-doors approach advocated by Sean Kidney and Rick Sission (see the web address list at the end of this chapter). An alternative, comprehensive framework is the six-stage CDCynergy social marketing edition tool (see web address list at the end of this chapter). This model is a six-step approach and includes many tools that can be used along the way. Another useful eight-step model called the BEHAVE-based marketing plan is set out by Strand and Smith (2008). The four-step STELa planning model is also now available as a downloadable app for smart phones and computers (again see the web address for this programme). There are also numerous other models, such as the WHO COMBI model (2004), that contain elements of social marketing principles, and many specialist social marketing companies and institutions who have developed their own planning models. What all of these models share is the inclusion of the social marketing principles set out in Chapter 1, and a commitment to a systematic and transparent development process.

Each of these planning approaches has advantages and disadvantages from the perspective of the social marketer. Some are very simple to apply; others are more comprehensive and require more effort. The key issue to consider when selecting a social marketing planning model is the scale and complexity of the behaviour you are seeking to influence. Social marketing can be applied to small-scale local projects (for example, see Chapter 4) or large-scale, sustained national programmes (see Chapter 19). Clearly, when a large-scale investment is being made in a social behaviour change programme, a more thorough planning approach and reporting process is required.

QUALITY ASSURING SOCIAL MARKETING PLANNING

It is not possible to develop an exact formula that can be universally applied for delivering population-focused behaviour programmes that will result in success every time. However, there is an emerging set of principles that can aid us in the development and application of interventions (French et al., 2010; Klassen, 2010; Suter, 2009). These features are summarised in the following quality assurance list that can be used to test the utility and strength of social marketing plans.

SOCIAL MARKETING QUALITY ASSURANCE PLANNING CHECKLIST

1   Clear aims and measurable behavioural objectives should be set out in the programme plan together with the target audience(s) and segments that will be the focus of the intervention should be explicit.
2   Programmes should set out how funding and other resources will be applied and over what time period. A clear expected return on investment case should be set out to justify the level of planned investment.
3   The programme should be endorsed by policy makers, commissioners and managers and deliverers of the programme. The programme plan should set out the political, policy, managerial and institutional commitment to the programme.

4   The programme team should capture what evidence about effective practice from reviews and case studies, observational data and target audience psychographic data is being used to formulae insight and interventions.

5   The programme plan should set out a clear rationale for the programme and why particular interventions have been selected. The programme plan should also indicate the theoretical perspectives and models that have been used to inform planning that is congruent with the form, focus and context of the intervention.

6   The programme plan should demonstrate that target group(s), stakeholders and partners have been involved in needs assessment, target setting, delivery and evaluation.

7   The programme plan should set out how prototype interventions or pilots will be tested and used to develop full-scale programmes.

8   The plan should set out how the programme will be funded to the level required to achieve impact and how it will be sustained over the recommended time-scale for delivery. Plans should also set out key milestones, in developing and delivering the programme. These milestones should cover process, impact and outcome milestones.

9   Programme plans should set out how coalitions, stakeholders, partners and interest groups will be engaged over the lifetime of the intervention. The plan should also set out the mechanism for coordinated action between international, national regional and local delivery, and how decision-making, governance and coordination of the programme will operate.

10   Key barriers and enabling factors and other risks should be identified in the programme plan together with what actions will be taken to address these factors.

11   Evaluation, performance management, learning and feedback mechanisms are clear in the programme plan. Evaluation should encompass short-term impact measures for tracking purposes, process measures of efficiency and outcome evaluation related to the specific objectives of the programme.

12   All programme plans should be recorded and published, the plan should be based on a proven planning template such as TPP.

These characteristics can be used as a checklist to test the likely impact of social marketing interventions and programmes, and as a checklist when developing a social marketing plan.

CHAPTER RECAP

In this chapter we have looked at how social marketing principles can be used to inform policy, strategy and operational planning. If social marketing principles are used in the development of social programmes, a better understanding of the issues and possible solutions is likely to be developed. We have introduced a definition of strategic social marketing:

The application of social marketing principles and concepts to inform and guide strategic goal development, intervention, selection and evaluation.

The main focus of this chapter has been on one of the defining features of social marketing: the application of a systematic and transparent approach to intervention development, implementation and evaluation. Whilst there is no one correct way to plan social marketing interventions, and there are now a variety of social marketing planning models for the practitioner to select from, there should always be a written plan that stands up to interrogations by those delivering the intervention and those sponsoring it. We have introduced a simple five-step approach to planning (TPP) and set out a number of recommended sub-steps under each of these five main stages. We have also introduced a checklist of features of effective programme planning. The more of these features that are included in the development and execution of social marketing programmes, the more likely they are to demonstrate impact. The case-study chapters that make up the rest of this book use a variety of planning approaches but each study was developed by applying the main planning principles set out in this chapter.

SELF-REVIEW QUESTIONS

1 List the five key steps in the TPP planning framework, and as many of the sub-tasks as you can remember.
2 List at least three reasons why you think the 'scoping' stage is a key stage in social marketing planning process.
3 Review any of the case-study chapters in this book, using the 12-point 'Planning Quality Assurance' from this chapter, and make an assessment about how many of the characteristics of effective planning are evident in the case study.

REFERENCES

Andreasen, A. (1995). *Marketing Social Change.* San Francisco: Jossey-Bass.
French, J. (2010, Nov.). Why nudges are seldom enough. Key note presentation given at the Open University Sterling University Annual Social Marketing Conference, Milton Keynes.
French, J. and Blair-Stevens, C. (2010) *Big Pocket Guide to Social Marketing,* 1st edn. London: National Consumer Council, National Social Marketing Centre.
French, J., Blair-Stevens, C., Merritt, R. and McVey, D. (2010). *Social Marketing and Public Health: Theory and Practice.* Oxford: Oxford University Press.
Hastings, G. and Elliot, B. (1993). Social marketing practice in traffic safety. In *Marketing of Traffic Safety* (pp. 35–55). Paris: OECD.
Klassen, A. (2010). Performance measurement and improvement framework in health, education and social services: A systematic review. *International Journal for Quality of Health Care,* 22(1): 44–69.
Kotler, P and Lee, N. (2008). *Social Marketing: Influencing Behaviors for Good.* Thousand Oaks, CA: SAGE.
Stand, J. and Smith, W. (2008). Social Marketing: A practical resource for social change professionals. Washington, DC: AED. Available online at: www.aed.org/Publications/upload/Social-Marketing-Behavior-Book.pdf.
Suter, E. (2009). Introduction to integration: Ten key principles for successful health systems integration. *Healthcare Quarterly,* 13: 16–23.
WHO (World Health Organization). (2004). *Mobilizing for Action: Communication-for-Behavioural-Impact (COMBI).* Tunis: WHO Mediterranean Centre for Vulnerability Reduction (WMC).

USEFUL WEBSITES

The UK National Social Marketing Centre social marketing planning tool: www.thensmc.com/document-sharing.html.

CDCynergy social marketing planning tool: http://www.orau.gov/cdcynergy/demo/.

Seven doors model of social marketing planning: www.media.socialchange.net.au/strategy/7_Doors_Model.html.

STELA Social Marketing planning App: www.Strategic-social-marketing.org.

The Community toolbox: http://ctb.ku.edu/en/tablecontents/index.aspx.

The Global Social Marketing network: www.socialmarketers.net/index.php/home.

3 DEVELOPING CULTURALLY SENSITIVE INTERVENTIONS

VIGNETTE: 'HINDUISM AND H$_2$O', LONDON SUSTAINABILITY EXCHANGE

KEY WORD: CULTURAL AWARENESS

Londoners of Hindu faith have enthusiastically taken up water saving, thanks to a community-led initiative that makes the link between Hindu beliefs and water conservation.

Research with Hindu Community members and leaders enabled programme planners to understand how effective faith beliefs can be in encouraging people to adopt sustainable lifestyles, and to plan a programme of practical advice, tools and support that responded to this insight. Interventions included 'Temple Talks', outreach work with Hindu temples and training of Community Champions to deliver free home water audits.

As one participant noted, 'it makes sense to Hindus because respecting nature is our "dharma" or our duty and so we can vibe with their message easily' (Female, 23–35, Greenwich).

This case study is available in full on ShowCase, at: www.thensmc.com

This vignette makes the point that, if we want to develop successful interventions, we need to have a deep understanding of what motivates the target audience we are trying to reach.

ABOUT THIS CHAPTER

As we discussed in Chapter 1, customer understanding is essential when developing successful social marketing interventions. In this chapter you will:

○ Learn how a detailed appreciation of the target audience's cultural and religious beliefs enabled a successful intervention to be developed, to increase use of child car safety seats.

○ Explore how the methods mix can be tailored to be culturally appropriate, once sensitivities or potential triggers have been identified and understood.

CASE STUDY: INCREASING THE USE OF CHILD RESTRAINTS IN MOTOR VEHICLES IN A HISPANIC NEIGHBOURHOOD

Clare Pickett, The National Social Marketing Centre; Gregory R. Istre; Martha Stowe; Mary A. McCoy; Katie N. Womack; Linda Fanning; Laurette Dekat, Injury Prevention Center

This case study appears in full on the National Social Marketing Centre's ShowCase resource (www.thensmc.com).

PROJECT OVERVIEW

Young children restrained in child safety seats have an 80 per cent lower risk of fatal injury than those who are unrestrained, but minority and low-income populations are less likely to use restraints in motor vehicles than the general population (Istre et al., 2002). In 1997, a preliminary survey of Hispanic pre-school aged children in west Dallas, Texas, revealed much lower car restraint use among this group than among pre-school aged children of other origin in the rest of the city (Womack, 2001). There were few reports of successful programmes to increase child restraint use among the Hispanic population so the Injury Prevention Center (IPC) of Greater Dallas undertook to implement and evaluate a programme tailored to this population.

This multi-faceted programme incorporated cultural beliefs and developed community networks to increase the use of child safety restraints in an Hispanic neighbourhood in the west Dallas area of Texas. A series of educational and engagement activities were conducted in the target area by trained bilingual staff, most of whom were residents of the local neighbourhood. Activities were carried out at neighbourhood parties, in a local community health centre, daycare centres, churches, community centres and shops. Child motor vehicle restraint use was evaluated through structured observational surveys and following the intervention revealed a significant increase in child restraint use in the community.

PROJECT RATIONALE

Child-passenger motor-vehicle crashes are the leading cause of death for children ages 1 to 14 (IPC, 2010). However, many of these deaths and injuries associated with motor-vehicle crashes can be prevented by using proper child-passenger safety restraints, such as car seats and booster seats.

Properly securing a child in a correctly installed child safety seat reduces the risk of serious and fatal injuries. All states in the US have child restraint laws that require child safety seats for infants and children fitting specific criteria. Texas law requires all children under the age of eight to be properly restrained in a child safety seat, unless the child is taller than four feet, nine inches (Womack, 2001).

Texas has one of the highest populations of citizens of Hispanic origin, home to 8.6 million in 2008, contributing to 36 per cent of the population (US Census Bureau, 2006–8).

 ## AIMS AND OBJECTIVES

The IPC was established in 1992 by health, government and business leaders in a strategic attempt to tackle the increase in injuries and trauma-related deaths in Dallas. In 1997 one problem area the IPC targeted was the use (or lack) of child safety seats in order to prevent death and injury. Child safety seats not only save lives but they also save money: every $46 spent on a child safety seat saves the government $1,900 in societal costs and every $31 spent on a booster seat saves $2,200 (IPC, 2010).

Initial scoping research indicated that the lack of child safety seats was more prevalent in minority and low-income populations, an estimation which was substantiated following further research among the Hispanic population of Dallas. As such the primary aim of the project was to increase the use of child safety restraints – as defined as child safety seats or booster seats – in motor vehicles in the target area of west Dallas, Texas, among the Hispanic population.

A secondary aim was also set: to reduce the number of child injuries and fatalities occurring due to the lack of use of child safety restraints.

 ## IDENTIFYING THE TARGET AUDIENCES

The team were able to effectively segment their target audience based on their scoping research. A flow-chart showing the information used to determine the primary target audience is presented in Figure 3.1.

Minority and low-income populations: child restraint use less common

Hispanic population: minority and typically low-income population

Dallas: high Hispanic population, particularly in the west of the city

Scoping research: low child restraint use among Hispanic population in Dallas

Targeted: parents of Hispanic pre-school aged children

Segmented: mothers of Hispanic pre-school-aged children in particular

Figure 3.1   The segmentation process: using data to identify the target audience

Source: Injury Prevention Centre of Greater Dallas.

The team first considered minority and low-income populations as child safety restraint use was found to be less common among these groups. The Hispanic community were selected due to their high population density and low income. A preliminary survey also revealed that pre-school-aged children among the Hispanic population were less likely to use child restraints (Womack, 2001). In particular, parents were targeted among this group, especially mothers who were more commonly supervising their children. Three adjacent zip codes in the west sector of Dallas were chosen.

SCOPING RESEARCH

To determine the extent of the problem and identify possible target audiences, a review of the academic literature was initially conducted. After the review was completed, a variety of Texan state data (emergency response data, police data and hospital data) was analysed. This analysis found that a disproportionate percentage of car accidents involved those of Hispanic origin.

To understand the issues further, a preliminary survey amongst the Hispanic community, assessing pre-school-aged children in west Dallas, Texas, to investigate the use of car seats, was then conducted. The survey found that the percentage using child restraints was much lower in this population (19 per cent of those surveyed) than among pre-school children of all races in the rest of the city (62 per cent) (Womack, 2001).

Having chosen and further segmented their target audience to the Hispanic population, most notably parents and mothers in particular, the team conducted six focus groups with their target audience to obtain insight and information in order to develop an intervention to increase the use of the child restraints within the Hispanic community.

The knowledge gained in these focus groups informed the design of the intervention. For example, the researchers had originally planned to implement a very popular incentivised intervention which was designed in North Carolina, whereby those observed using a car seat correctly would be stopped and given a prize/coupon. The focus group in this instance rejected this approach as they advised that the community will simply collect the prize and not actually use the car seat. Secondly, the researchers were prepared to recruit famous people to champion the importance of car seats. Again the focus group said no, mothers are the only ones who are trusted in the Hispanic community and as such are the only people that members of the community will listen to. (See Figure 3.2.)

ACTIONABLE INSIGHTS

Key insights gained during the focus groups with members of the Hispanic community within the target area of west Dallas, Texas, contributed greatly to the design of the intervention. Underpinning most of these key insights was the fact that child safety-seat use was simply not part of the tradition or culture of the Hispanic community and therefore was not the 'norm'. To be effective, the interventions needed to address this and incorporate various aspects of the Hispanic culture into the use of car safety seats.

Figure 3.2   A community priest blesses the car seats
Source: Injury Prevention Centre of Greater Dallas.

The key insights are detailed below:

○ The importance of religion. One of the most fundamental insights was the importance of religion within the Hispanic community and existence of fatalism and destiny, the belief that any potential accidents were 'in God's hands'.

○ Lack of knowledge. There was often a lack of similar regulations in their native countries so those who had recently immigrated to the US were particularly unaware of child restraint laws and their importance.

○ Perceived safety. There was a perception of safety as the parents believed that they were safe drivers and therefore less likely to be in an accident.

○ Lack of information. There was a decided lack of information about child seats and their importance as such parents were not aware of how valuable they are.

○ The use of shock tactics. The focus group stressed the need for drama and gore to get the message across – this was surprising as this is not true for other ethnic groups who are usually put off by it.

○ Media channels. The researchers found that the members of the community did not read as much but were more inclined to watch television or listen to the radio. The focus groups also identified mothers as authority figures to help communicate the message.

 STAKEHOLDER ENGAGEMENT

The intervention was funded by the US National Highway Traffic Safety Administration, the National Center for Injury Prevention and Control and the Centers for

Disease Control and Prevention. Activities were carried out at neighbourhood parties, in a local community health centre, daycare centres, churches, community centres and shops.

The IPC worked with several groups and community organisations to carry out the project, including:

- Physicians, nurses and staff at a local health centre
- Staff of the daycare centres and grocery stores
- Texas Department of Transportation and the Texas Department of Health
- Dallas Police Department
- Staff and members of a local community centres.

BARRIERS

COMPETITION

An analysis of the internal and external competitors and barriers which might affect the programme was conducted. Key factors included:

- Religion and sense of safety. The main internal competitors identified were the target audience's perceived sense of safety and their views on religion and fatalism.
- Resistance. The two main factors were resistance from the children and unsupportive fathers/male family members. The team found that the men were less likely to use seat belts as they perceived it to undermine their masculinity and by proxy they were also less likely to use child safety seats.
- Community politics. A further barrier was involving the Hispanic community in the project. There are community politics, changing dynamics and other variables which can be very unpredictable – maintaining an intervention in this environment is hard work.

In addition to the identified competitors, a number of barriers were identified during the focus groups:

- Disinterest and apathy. Initially the team found it difficult to engage the Hispanic community. It was found that they often had been asked their opinion on various issues but they had since been ignored or there had been no follow-up.
- Uninterested in traffic-safety issues. The team found it especially difficult to engage them regarding this particular issue. They were not interested in traffic-safety issues but were much more concerned about reducing the levels of violence and crime within their community. Therefore it was very hard to get their views and engage this group as this was a low priority issue for them.
- Lack of trust. There was also an inherent lack of trust surrounding outsiders entering their community and asking questions.

To overcome these initial challenges, it helped that one project lead had worked with this community before and so was more readily accepted and trusted than most. The team also provided an exchange for their participation. For example, by providing exercise classes for the women and organising a session with an outside speaker on how to deal with violence.

MARKETING MIX

The programme used a mix of methods to encourage, enable and educate regarding the use of child safety seats among Hispanic parents. The interventions were developed using the Safe Communities model which uses a 'bottom-up' approach and is developed from standardised educational programmes. It has four distinguishing features:

1   Injury data analysis from multiple sources
2   Expanded partnerships
3   Resident involvement
4   An integrated and comprehensive injury control system.

The intervention was then adapted to the Hispanic community and was further modified based on the insights from the six community focus groups.

Details of the interventions, against the four elements of the marketing mix are as follows:

PRODUCT

- The core product, the benefit promised, is the ensured safety of the child when travelling in the car. By extension, the core product is also the reduced risk of child fatality and injury when travelling in the car.
- The actual product, the desired behaviour, is the correct use of child car safety seats.
- The augmented product included to address the issue of fatalism. Local priests were asked to bless the child safety seats in a ceremony before they were distributed.

EDUCATIONAL CLASSES

- Child safety-seat classes were conducted in Spanish and English by bilingual certified child-passenger safety technicians.
- The classes sought to highlight the importance of using child safety seats during all car trips, regardless of length of travel.
- The classes were held bi-weekly at the only county-sponsored community primary-care health centre in the target area and at other locations in the community on request.
- Parents were required to attend an hour-long training class on the proper use and installation of child safety seats before they received a seat.
- During the child safety seat classes videos of graphic car-crash footage were used, highlighting what happens in an accident to a crash dummy with a child in their arms.
- Included seat-belt demonstrations and what to do when a child does not want to sit in the safety seats.

TRAFFIC-SAFETY WORKSHOPS

- These were delivered by the IPC staff and included information about vehicle safety, driver's licence and traffic laws, immigration and social-security laws and proper installation and use of child safety seats.

PRICE

The research showed that the target audience were typically a low-income earning group and indeed poverty was a factor when it came to the poor standard of vehicles they drove. The research also showed that the target audience had many priorities competing for their time. Therefore, the team needed to consider the price of taking part for the target audience, both in monetary and non-monetary terms.

- ○ Monetary. Free traffic safety and child safety-seat training workshops and parents were offered the incentive of a car seat for a low cost of $10 if they attended. These car seats were subsidised by a separate grant obtained from the Texas Department of Transportation; parents were asked to pay for a seat but were not denied a seat if they were unable to pay.
- ○ Non-monetary. Activities also addressed the issues of importance to the community other than child safety restraints. The team gave them information on immunisations, home safety tips, domestic violence, child abuse and community resources. Plus the exercise classes taught by the staff to help develop a bond with the mothers and provide an exchange for their input.

PLACE

The interventions were delivered through the local primary-care health centre, daycare centres and community venues in the target neighbourhood such as neighbourhood block parties, health fairs and local festivals. (See Figure 3.3.)

- ○ Health centre. Educational classes were held at the health centre. Class instructors also participated in health fairs and special events organised by the health centre, distributed pamphlets about child safety seats and seat-belt use and conducted child safety-seat inspections and demonstrations.
- ○ Daycare centres. At the daycare centres a week-long intervention for children, parents and daycare staff included seat-belt demonstrations, child safety-seat training for daycare centre employees and traffic-safety workshops for parents.
- ○ Neighbourhoods. Interventions which were implemented in several neighbourhoods in the target area included neighbourhood block parties, health fairs, child safety-seat inspections, traffic-safety workshops and the delivery of educational messages at local festivals.

PROMOTION

A lack of knowledge and a lack of information were two of the key insights from the focus groups so effective and accurate communication was an essential element to the methods mix. The language barrier was also an issue so all activities and information were in Spanish and English.

KEY MESSAGES

Key messages were developed to be clear, simple and meaningful. It was crucial that these messages be consistent across all locations and channels of distribution and moreover

Figure 3.3   Community events

that this was common practice elsewhere both in the US and internationally. Thus the intervention included emphasising and re-emphasising the importance of child seats and the penalties for not using them. Key messages were:

○ Child safety seats are important and they save lives.
○ Children are not safer in their parents' arms or on their lap when travelling.
○ Car safety seats must be used for all journeys, regardless of the length of the journey.

MESSENGERS

Insight from the focus groups highlighted the importance of mothers who were seen as authority figures within the Hispanic community.

○ The team recruited an active mothers' group. Three local mothers were hired as liaisons to promote child safety-seat use over a nine-week period in five daycare centres. Strategies developed by the liaisons included information booths, raffles and games designed to promote child safety-seat use.
○ At local schools, churches and neighbourhood events, a Hispanic policewoman known as 'La Protectora' (the protector) held classes in Spanish and English for parents and children to explain child safety laws and procedures.
○ Trained bilingual staff, most of whom were also residents of the target area, conducted all the activities.

KEY MEDIA CHANNELS

In order to reach as much of the target audience as possible, the messages were conveyed through various media including printed materials, television and radio. Classes at the health centre were advertised through the local health clinic, at churches, community centres and botanicas (traditional healers) and on local Spanish-language radio and television shows.

PRINT MATERIALS

○ Educational pamphlets about the programme were distributed at the botanicas, churches, community centres and the health centre.

○ Paediatricians at the health centre reinforced the importance of using child safety seats by distributing 'prescriptions' for proper child safety-seat use to patients. These were prescription pads that had been pre-printed with instructions for parents to get a car seat for their child and a phone number they could call to sign up for a class.

MONITORING AND EVALUATION

Child-restraint surveys were performed by trained observers, using survey forms developed by the Texas Transportation Institute (TTI) which had been used for the past 13 years for longitudinal studies of restraint throughout Texas. Beginning in February 1997, surveys were conducted as vehicles entered parking lots at three types of locations in the target area:

1   The community health centre where the intervention was implemented
2   Daycare centres that also received the interventions
3   The parking lots of eight grocery stores which were patronised predominantly by Hispanics.

Observations at the grocery-store parking lots were considered to be most representative of the community as a whole. Children who were restrained in accordance with Texas state law were considered properly restrained. The safety seats were not examined in detail to determine whether they were appropriately tightened and tethered.

A total of 7,413 observations among pre-school-aged Hispanic children (under 5 years old) were conducted from 1997 through to 2000: 2,246 (30 per cent) of these were conducted at the health centre, 2,735 (37 per cent) at daycare centres and 2,432 (33 per cent) at grocery-store parking lots. Additionally, 4,137 comparison observations were done by TTI on pre-school-aged children of all races in other parts of Dallas.

The TTI survey also observed driver seat-belt use both at the target areas and other parts of Dallas as driver seat-belt use was believed to be a necessary factor in child restraint use, although it is not the sole determinant.

Since IPC did not have access to morbidity data and the number of deaths was too small to prove a significant change, observations of child-restraint use was used as the main indicator for the programme's impact.

FINDINGS

Three years after the interventions were launched the use of safety restraints among Hispanic pre-school-aged children increased to 73 per cent (from an initial prevalence of 21 per cent).

By the third year of the programme, vehicle restraint use among Hispanic pre-school-aged children had surpassed restraint use among pre-school-aged children in the rest of Dallas and by the sixth year of the programme, restraint use among clinic attendees had surpassed 85 per cent.

By 2000 (after three years):

○ More than 3,000 child safety seats had been distributed to Hispanic families in the target area during the survey period.
○ Use of restraints among Hispanic pre-school-aged children increased significantly in all three settings.
○ Use of restraints among Hispanic pre-school-aged children attending the health centre (73 per cent) had surpassed use in the rest of Dallas (69 per cent) as measured in the TTI survey.
○ The predominant impact of the programme in the overall community (as measured by the surveys in grocery store parking lots) was seen among children younger than 2 years.
○ Observed driver seat-belt use also increased significantly in each of the three settings, whereas the TTI survey showed little change in driver seat belt use in other parts of Dallas.
○ There was a strong association between child-restraint use and driver seat-belt use at all of the observation sites. The association remained strong after results were stratified by year, setting, age of the child and type of vehicle.

The programme was found to be most successful among parents who attended the community health centre – the main site of intervention activities – and in the pre-school-age group. However, overall, the trend of increasing use was significant in all three settings across all age groups.

 LESSONS LEARNT

The programme owed its success to:

○ Its ongoing, multi-faceted nature
○ Its integration of cultural and religious factors
○ The use of Hispanic teachers in child safety-seat classes
○ The efforts of the community health-centre staff in integrating safety messages into the clinical routine
○ The feedback received from surveillance data about progress in the programme.

For a programme to be successful in increasing child-restraint use, it must also target driver seat-belt use. The team observed little increase in child restraint use in vehicles in which drivers did not wear a seat belt. Furthermore, it was pertinent whether there was a male/female driver as males were less likely to use seat belts and child seats as they perceived it to undermine their masculinity.

Although they found a significant increase in child-restraint use in the community (as measured by the grocery-store and daycare-centre surveys), this remained significantly lower than use at the health centre, indicating that there is much work still to be done.

Some of the increase in restraint use at the health centre may have been due to a 'social desirability' effect – parents going to the health centre may have been more conscious about practising car seat safety. Although the overall trend in restraint use in the rest of Dallas was relatively flat, there were some fluctuations from year to year, which may have reflected other community factors at work that influenced child-restraint use.

In retrospect, to have improved further on their successes, the team had would have liked more active mothers groups as they believe more support from the mothers of the community would have helped to distribute the message further. Ideally they would have conducted more focus groups as insight from the target audience were key to the design and format of intervention. They also would have managed their own staff differently. For the project the team received a hard and intensive grant which meant that the work was to be conducted during a short and ambitious timeframe. This meant that the nature of the work was very labour intensive and the staff were worn out. Considering that the results were not immediate, this type of work is extremely demanding especially when benefits are not seen straight away and it can be challenging to keep the staff motivated. More people and more resources would have eased the pressures on staff somewhat.

Despite this, the programme was a success and was able to equal or exceed the use of child safety seats among the Hispanic population as compared to the general population.

CHAPTER RECAP

This chapter has shown how an understanding of a target audience's deep-rooted beliefs can be used to trigger positive behaviour change. Without a deep level of insight from the programme team, this target audience's fatalism could have been a significant barrier to change.

In the next chapter we will learn how community insight and support in a UK setting enabled programme planners to overcome significant community opposition, in order to co-create a successful approach to increasing smoking cessation.

SELF-REVIEW QUESTIONS

1 For this programme, research and engagement activities were carried out via neighbourhood parties, community health centres, places of worship and shops. When considering a specific target audience, what assets do you have within your community and how might you use these to gain cultural and religious understanding?

2 In this case study, the target audience was 'minority and low-income populations'. This led to the selection of the Hispanic community, due to their high population density and low income. What ethical sensitivities might arise from selecting a specific target audience in this way, and what steps might you need to take to minimise these?

3 One of the key insights for this programme was that the target audience's religious faith led to fatalism around road safety – 'we're in God's hands'. In response, a priest was asked to bless the car seats before they were distributed. For a behaviour-change intervention you are trying to achieve, how might you respond to a similarly fatalistic, faith-based attitude?

REFERENCES

Injury Prevention Centre of Greater Dallas. (2010). Child passenger safety. Accessed August 2010: www.injurypreventioncenter.org.

Istre, G., McCoy, M., Womack, K., Fanning, L., Dekat, L. and Stowe, M. (2002). Increasing the use of child restraints in motor vehicles in a Hispanic neighbourhood. *American Journal of Public Health*, 92: 1096–9.

Safe Kids USA. (2009). Child passenger safety. Available at: www.usa.safekids.org/our-work/programs/buckle-up/child-passenger-safety.html. Accessed August 2010.

US Census Bureau, American Community Survey. (2010). Hispanic or Latino origin by specific origin. 2008 American Community Survey 1-Year Estimates. Available at: http://factfinder.census.gov/. Accessed August 2010.

US Census Bureau, American Community Survey. (2010). Texas – ACS demographic and housing estimates 2006–2008. Available at: http://factfinder.census.gov/. Accessed August 2010.

Womack, K. (2000, Jan.). *Survey of Front Seat Occupant Restraint Use in Eighteen Texas Cities*. College Station, TX: Texas Transportation Institute.

4 COMMUNITY-BASED SOCIAL MARKETING

VIGNETTE: WAY TO GO!

KEY WORD: COMMUNITY-BASED SOCIAL MARKETING

Car emissions have a large impact on children's health. Research indicates that parents are concerned when they learn about the impacts of cars on children, however, they are currently unaware of these impacts. Way To Go! is a programme that has been developed to reduce the impact of cars on the environment through a strategic approach for fostering sustainable behaviour through community-based social marketing. The Way To Go! school programme is designed to encourage children to walk, bike, ride-share and take public transport to school rather than driving. When an individual signs up for this programme they receive a Way To Go! kit. This kit provides environmental facts, statistics and the rationale for a traffic reduction programme. It stresses traffic-safety information and the importance of choosing the best routes to school. This kit suggests ways to generate enthusiastic and sustainable involvement forms and models to use as the programme is implemented. It involves using mapping strategies and the development of safe walking and biking strategies.

More than 450 have requested the Way To Go! kit, with some schools reporting almost a 50 per cent increase in the number of children that are walking to school. One school reduced the number of cars dropping off children from 150 to just four. More information about this case can be found at: www.cbsm.com/.

This vignette reveals the positive impact using a community social marketing approach can have.

ABOUT THIS CHAPTER

As we discussed in Chapter 1, in order to develop sustainable projects, engaging stakeholders and partners from the start is vital for achieving long-term success. In this chapter you will learn:

- The value of taking a community approach to addressing a problem which is the cultural norm.
- Stakeholders are not a homogeneous group, and therefore engagement with them should be tailored to meet their needs and expectations.

○ From the outset, this project focused on building strong links with volunteers and workers, and focused on developing an intervention which would fit into Brinnington alongside existing services, so it would be readily accepted by the target audience and existing service providers.

CASE STUDY: LOSE THE FAGS: REDUCING SMOKING PREVALENCE IN A DEPRIVED COMMUNITY IN NORTH WEST ENGLAND

Fiona Spotswood, Bristol Social Marketing Centre; Sarah Clarke, NHS Stockport

This case study appears in full on the National Social Marketing Centre's ShowCase resource (www.thensmc.com).

PROJECT OVERVIEW

The Lose the Fags project is located in Brinnington, a housing estate in Stockport, Greater Manchester, England. The project is led by NHS Stockport, in partnership with the National Social Marketing Centre (the NSMC).

Although only covering a small locality, it is important for NHS Stockport to focus on Brinnington housing estate as it is ranked the most deprived area in Stockport (Neighbourhood Renewal Strategy, 2009) and in the top 3 per cent most deprived areas for England and Wales. It has relatively high unemployment, low education levels, premature death and poor health (IMD, 2007).

Due to the extremely high smoking prevalence (54 per cent) (Neighbourhood Renewal areas Residents' Survey, 2007), a targeted project was developed for the Brinnington estate residents. The project was community-based and NHS Stockport developed partnerships with established local services such as the Children's Centre and the Stockport Sports Trust's community fitness centre. After 18 months of scoping and development work, the project was launched in July 2009 and is still continuing at time of writing.

PROJECT RATIONALE

Brinnington Neighbourhood Renewal Area has a population of 6,508 and is predominantly white (97.4 per cent) with more people than average under 16 years old (Profiling Stockport, 2010). People in Brinnington consider themselves to have worse health than the Stockport and national averages (ibid.). They are also twice as likely to be unemployed compared to the national average. People in Brinnington are less likely to have formal qualifications than people across Stockport and are more likely to rent their accommodation from the local authority than the national average (ibid).

In 2007, a survey of 600 Brinnington residents found that 54 per cent smoked (Neighbourhood Renewal areas Residents' Survey, 2007), which was significantly higher than the Stockport average of 18 per cent and the national average of 24 per cent (Banister and Burgess Allen, 2007). NHS funded smoking cessation services had initially attracted residents, but only 186 quit attempts were made in 2007/8 and numbers were declining quickly. In 2008/9, only 145 people accessed services (Stop Smoking Service Equity Profile, Stockport NHS).

In 2007, social marketing was identified by the Associate Director of Public Health and the Tobacco Lead at NHS Stockport (then Stockport Primary Care Trust (PCT)) as a tool which might enable the PCT to engage with the target group of routine and manual workers living in Brinnington, who had not been engaged by more traditional communication methods.

 AIMS AND OBJECTIVES

The behavioural problem in Brinnington was that too few people were accessing smoking-cessation services, with numbers accessing services steadily declining, despite evidence that NHS smoking-cessation services make quit attempts more likely to succeed. Therefore, the aim of the project was to design a social marketing intervention, which would create an increase in the number of quitters registering with local NHS smoking-cessation services.

In 2008/9, the year prior to the intervention launch, there were 145 quit attempts by smokers who accessed cessation services. This is equivalent to 5.6 per cent of the smoking population accessing services, compared with a Stockport average of around 10 per cent. Services included a local smoking-cessation advisor based at the main Brinnington GP practice and the 'Quit for Life' drop-in group. Other services accessed in Brinnington included a pharmacy service. The SMART objective set was to double the number of quit attempts through all local services, including the two new services (at the Target Life Lapwing Community Fitness Centre and Children's Centre) within 12 months of project launch.

 IDENTIFYING THE TARGET AUDIENCES

A multi-stage segmentation process was implemented to enable 'Lose the Fags' to be carefully positioned to best meet the needs of the defined target audiences. Three segments were identified, based on demographic and psychographic factors, and based on the Stages of Change model (Prochaska et al., 1994):

- Contemplators: Lose the Fags was designed to target contemplator smokers in Brinnington (i.e. those who are already considering quitting smoking). Research from the baseline survey suggested that there was a large segment (around 70 per cent) of contemplators whose needs were not being met by existing services.
- Women with pre-school-age children: The target audience of contemplators was segmented by gender and age. Women with pre-school-age children formed one target segment. These women were aged 18 to 40 and required childcare facilities to attend any clinic or group. Such facilities, however, were not available. They were also experiencing the pressures of adjusting to motherhood, financial strain and confusion over competing health messages. Smoking was an ingrained part of their lives, and yet they desired to give up with the right kind of support; in a friendly, familiar environment with people 'like them' and with child care so they could focus on themselves.
- Adult male contemplators: Research indicated that it was culturally unacceptable for men to admit wanting help, or to be seen to be asking for it. Existing support groups were seen as women-oriented. Support for men's quit attempts would have to be disguised in some way, to alleviate the psychological costs of asking for support.

SCOPING RESEARCH

Qualitative primary research formed a core part of the scoping stage. The research aimed to identify key insights which could help the Solutions Team[1] develop interventions. The research was completed in five distinct phases.

PHASE 1: EXPLORATORY RESEARCH

In order to gain an initial understanding of the barriers and motivations towards smoking cessation in Brinnington, five mixed-gender focus groups were held during spring/summer 2007. The groups included:

1 Hardened smokers with no intention of quitting
2 Smokers who had tried but failed to quit
3 Smokers who were contemplating quitting
4 Successful quitters
5 Those currently in the process of quitting.

Research objectives were to explore the experiences of successful quitters and those who had dropped out of services, to understand why existing cessation services had achieved limited success. A series of interviews were also held with key health professionals in Brinnington to explore possible improvements to smoking cessation services to make them more consumer-oriented.

ACTIONABLE INSIGHTS

There were a number of key insights which emerged from the scoping research, and which were used to develop the intervention.

○ Lack of trust: Trust in 'authority' and health 'messages' was very low. Brinnington residents are bombarded by 'outsiders' offering help and this is perceived as them being bossed around and patronised. The intervention and the process of developing the intervention had to be co-created with key community members, or it would be rejected as mere interference. Co-creation and community involvement became the guiding principle of the project.
○ Utilising established local services: Co-creation informed the selection of 'Lose the Fags' partners. Local service-delivery partners were selected, who were already trusted by local people. Selected partners were the Target Life Lapwing Centre (a community sports facility run by Stockport Sports Trust) and the Brinnington Children's Centre. Additional team members, known already in Brinnington, were selected from the existing smoking-cessation service.
○ Loss of social life: For people in Brinnington, quitting smoking also meant giving up key aspects of their social life, like the morning social cigarette at the school gate. Even though people might be considering quitting, the jump between contemplation and action was large. The baseline survey for 'Lose the Fags' indicated that 40 per cent of smokers in Brinnington were thinking of quitting, but only 3.3 per cent were definitely planning to quit.

---

[1] The Solutions Team comprised local community members, community-based stakeholders and Stockport NHS workers. The team was convened to guide core parts of the intervention development process.

The job of the 'Lose the Fags' team was to enable these contemplators to take a step towards quitting, without becoming overwhelmed. A texting service was set up for this purpose. Texting was perceived as less daunting than telephoning to make an appointment. The texter would receive a phone call from a local team member to then make further arrangements for treatment.

○ Fear of asking for help: Men in Brinnington struggled to actively ask for help. The Lapwing Centre is a community leisure centre offering classes and individual fitness programmes. There is a gym, various community rooms and a thriving boxing club. The fitness Instructors at the Lapwing were suggested as ideal new service providers. Men could feel they were simply going to the gym, and ask for support in an ad hoc way, reducing their psychological costs. The gym is also open until 9 p.m., so able to fit around shift patterns.

○ The need for 'me' time: For women with young children, childcare is an essential accompaniment to any daytime service. Also, research identified that self-esteem, perceived self-efficacy and confidence were all very low amongst Brinnington's young mums. Offering a smoking cessation service in a familiar environment was therefore essential. The Children's Centre is central in Brinnington and familiar to many young mothers. Crèche facilities were available, and support workers in all roles were able to signpost female attendees of the centre to the new smoking-cessation sessions.

PHASE 2: FOLLOW-UP PRIMARY RESEARCH

Once target segments had been identified, two further focus groups were conducted with these groups in Summer 2007. The purpose of this research was to gain additional insight into their lifestyles, what moves and motivates, and what their interests, fears and pleasures were.

PHASES 1 AND 2: KEY FINDINGS

○ Key barriers and motivations for quitting were largely in line with national research into smoking amongst routine and manual workers.

○ Brinnington smokers were tired of being 'nagged' into quitting and were unlikely to succeed or make an attempt because their support networks consisted of smokers, providing a real fear of being ostracised.

○ Life in Brinnington often has smoking at its centre – socialising at the school gate, drinking in the pub, waiting in queues for local services, chatting to neighbours or family.

○ There was a drive to quit, primarily because of financial worry but also because of the fear of ill-health and desire to be a positive role model for children.

○ For women with pre-school-aged children, childcare facilities provide time to focus on themselves and are therefore essential to any intervention.

○ Low confidence was a considerable barrier to community participation, and services in a trusted, safe and well-known environment with familiar faces were essential.

○ Given the complexity of their lives, ease of access to Nicotine Replacement Therapy (NRT)[2] would also be vital.

---

[2] NRT is nicotine replacement therapy; pharmaceutical products which can help quit attempts by alleviating withdrawal symptoms and cravings. NRT can take the form of the nicotine patch, nicotine inhaler, nasal spray, gum, sublingual tablet and lozenge.

○ Men were more likely to work, often in shift patterns, so out-of-hours access to support would be essential. However, men struggled to admit they needed support and most men refused to do so. Therefore, a service with a concrete distraction away from the smoking-cessation element was needed.

 PHASE 3: COMMUNITY CONSULTATION

As stated at the beginning of this case study, developing community support and the support of key stakeholder organisations and potential partners is often key to the success of social marketing programmes. After the focus groups and interviews were completed, two phases of consultation were held with members of Brinnington's community, including: health-service providers and managers; ex-smokers; current smoking-cessation service users; community-group leaders and organisers; and smoking-cessation service providers.

In the first consultation workshop, held in March 2008, key findings from the primary research phase were presented to the group. Participants were then split into smaller working parties to discuss developing appropriate services within the infrastructure in Brinnington for each of the segments. The discussions were recorded, transcribed and translated into a report for circulation after the event. The report contained ideas for the development of new services targeting each segment.

The second workshop, in early May 2008, focused on ways to communicate with the target groups, and generated ideas for the creative proposition, branding, media, incentives and relationship building. The resulting report formed the creative brief for design agencies. The draft intervention plans, developed as a result of the first community consultation meeting, were also discussed and agreed.

PHASE 3: KEY FINDINGS

○ The services were developed so that access was as easy as possible. Suggestions included texting rather than telephoning to make initial contact, extended the hours of services and enabling women with children to access a service with childcare facilities.
○ Localising the creative design was the key to successful communications. It was important to promote the services as something that local people had called for.
○ It was recommended that local residents were used to feature in the communications campaign, which was guided by the proposition that 'Brinnington is giving up smoking'.
○ It was recommended that local humour, language and locations were used in the visual material.

PHASE 4: COMMUNICATIONS PRE-TESTING

The creative brief was sent out to tender, and five creative themes were returned for testing in a series of single-gender focus groups in August 2008. Each of the themes was discussed and tested in detail. As the chosen creative concept was slightly contentious, two further pre-test focus groups were held to confirm the final concept boards. Council and PCT senior managers, leaders and organisations operating in Brinnington were also engaged to ensure the rationale underpinning the use of the creative concept was understood and its use was supported.

PHASE 4: KEY FINDINGS

- ○ The 'Lose the Fags' concept was agreed at the creative pre-testing stage, but concerns were raised as to whether parents would find the strap line 'give smoking the two fingers' offensive or upsetting to children. In British culture a two-fingers hand gesture is seen as offensive by most people (see Figure 4.1).
- ○ The photographs were therefore taken in a way that clearly portrays the 'two fingers' pose as a smoker holding an invisible cigarette. Smoke was also added to the photos so that, even though the cigarette was missing, it was obvious what the pose meant.
- ○ The word 'Brinny' (a local nickname for Brinnington) was intended to be used as the keyword in the text-for-help service, but pre-test research found negative connotations with the word, due to the derogatory way it is sometimes used. 'Brinny' was replaced with 'lose fags' as the keyword.

PHASE 5: CONCEPT TESTING

Finally, with a fully developed intervention plan, communications plan and creative concept, the full intervention concept was discussed in detail with users of the Lapwing Centre and Children's Centre. No further changes were made.

A communications strategy was subsequently developed to underpin the promotion of new and existing services. This includes:

- ○ Interactive promotional material, which encourages smokers to text or free-phone a central contact point for advice, support or signposting to appropriate services.
- ○ Consistent word-of-mouth promotion via community groups and clubs in Brinnington and regular 'road shows' in community centres.
- ○ Engagement with key reference groups to promote the 'Lose the Fags' services and create a multitude of referral pathways.

The development of the 'Lose the Fags' brand was a key component of the project. The brand was co-created with the Solutions Team and chosen from several suggested by the creative agencies in response to the brief based on the research. It portrays very 'local' humour, indicating that people in Brinnington are giving smoking the 'two fingers'. It suggests that Brinnington residents are in control – it is their choice to lose the fags.

 STAKEHOLDER ENGAGEMENT

The 'Lose the Fags' project involved numerous stakeholders. It was recognised immediately that the stakeholders involved in this project were not a homogeneous group. Therefore, early on in the project, a stakeholder engagement plan was prepared using the matrix shown in Figure 4.2 (illustrated at an early stage of the project) to identify who were the most powerful and most interested (and least powerful and least interested) stakeholders. The arrows indicate the direction of desired travel, achieved through an internal marketing strategy.

Key stakeholders were identified as the PCT (particularly the executive), the Department of Health, service-delivery partners (the Children's Centre and Lapwing Centre), voluntary groups within Brinnington and the local press. A marketing communications plan was developed so that these groups could be included in the development of the project. A newsletter was sent to a database each month and key stakeholders were invited to a team meeting every other month to discuss the daily running of the project.

Figure 4.1   'Give Smoking the Two Fingers'

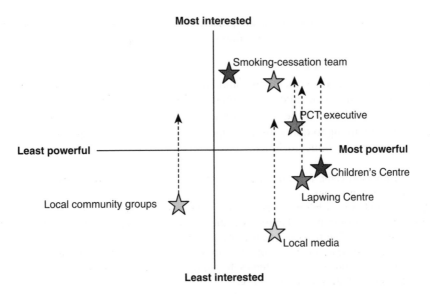

Figure 4.2   **The stakeholder management matrix**

In addition, stakeholder events were held to showcase the project. These were held before the launch of the project, to share insights from the research phase, at a press launch of the project and two-thirds of the way through the first 12 months, to offer interim findings and showcase key learning from interventions.

 INTERVENTION MIX

PRODUCT
INTERVENTIONS FOR MEN

The core product (benefit promised) was convenient stop-smoking support in a familiar environment, i.e. the Lapwing Centre gym in Brinnington. Fitness instructors were trained as smoking-cessation advisors and were able to deliver vouchers for NRT, which could be exchanged at the local pharmacy.

The actual product (the product or service you develop to deliver the core-product benefits) was a new stop-smoking service designed just for men at the Lapwing Centre, rather than attempting to quit smoking without support.

The augmented product (the features that encourage and support uptake of the actual product or service) included:

- Advice on an ad hoc basis: Fitness staff members are approached by male customers as a result of seeing promotional material.
- Easily available advice: Clients can return regularly and at extended hours (from 7.00 a.m. until 9.00 p.m.) with or without using the gym or other facilities this helps men get access around their working day.
- Brief intervention at induction: Probing questions and signposting for smoking cessation support have been incorporated into the standard induction questionnaire.
- Marketing communications and PR aimed at men: Communications materials across Brinnington signpost clients to the Lapwing Centre for stop-smoking advice.

Fitness instructors are incentivised to proactively approach gym customers (mostly men) who smoke to offer their smoking-cessation service.

INTERVENTIONS FOR WOMEN

The core product was convenient stop-smoking support in a familiar environment, i.e. at the Children's Centre with childcare facilities for pre-school-age children.

The actual product was the service at the Children's Centre for stop-smoking support rather than attempting to quit without support or not attempting to quit.

The augmented product included:

- A stop-smoking clinic for drop-in/one-to-one appointments, delivered by a central stop-smoking team member.
- Support staff at the Children's Centre, who have been trained as Level 2 smoking-cessation advisors and are incentivised to promote the sessions to members of the community groups who meet at the Centre, as well as parents of nursery children.
- The free crèche, which enables mothers with pre-school-age children to attend the sessions.
- Marketing communications materials to signpost parents (particularly mothers) to the Children's Centre stop-smoking service.

Figure 4.3   Trained fitness staff at a local gym

An exchange or cost/benefit (price) analysis solution to 'Lose the Fags' research identified key costs to other target audiences and addressed them through the exchange shown in Table 4.1.

MONITORING AND EVALUATION

The evaluation plan for 'Lose the Fags' has four strands, each described below.

1 PRE- AND POST-INTERVENTION SERVICE REGISTRATION RATES

Access rates of local stop-smoking services are the primary evaluation data required. However, the standard measure for NHS supported quit attempts (which is that the person should have quit for four weeks)[3] will be used to compare the intervention with other smoking-cessation interventions and 26 weeks will also be examined for the evaluation. The percentage of quits that are successful at four weeks will be compared with data from before the 'Lose the Fags' project was launched to gauge any change. There are no comparative measures for longer-term success, as this data was not collected prior to the launch of the intervention.

---

[3] Clients of NHS stop-smoking services are contacted four weeks after their declared quit date to gauge the success of their quit attempt.

Table 4.1   The Exchange Offered

Cost	Barrier Reduction/Benefit
Psychological cost of going to a 'new' clinic or group (lack of self-esteem and self-confidence).	Services in well-known locations using known staff, trained as smoking-cessation advisers, to deliver the services.
Time cost of visiting stop-smoking services in work hours (for men, particularly).	Service at the Lapwing is available until 9 p.m.
Psychological cost of telephoning the stop-smoking nurse to make an appointment.	Texting service is available so contemplators can simply text a word and their name to a number at minimal financial cost (less than 10p) and then receive a phone call to discuss next steps.
For women, the effort cost of having to find childcare to visit a stop-smoking group.	Crèche facilities are available at the Children's Centre during the stop-smoking meetings.
Psychological cost for men of asking for help and advice to give up smoking.	The service based at the Lapwing Centre enables men to feel they are just 'going to the gym', which is free of a stigma, rather than seeking out smoking-cessation advice.
Psychological cost of Brinnington residents feeling like they have yet more 'outsiders' coming to tell them how to live their lives.	Brand and intervention co-creation with the community to encourage feelings of ownership of 'Lose the Fags'.

2 POST-INTERVENTION QUALITATIVE
Qualitative research was undertaken after 'Lose the Fags' had been in place for 12 months to explore how the intervention has impacted Brinnington's smokers.

3 PRE- AND POST-QUANTITATIVE: AWARENESS AND EXPERIENCES OF QUITTING IN BRINNINGTON
A quantitative market-research company was commissioned to deliver a statistically significant pre–post survey questionnaire. The questionnaire, to be delivered in Brinnington and a control area, captured the impact of 'Lose the Fags' work plus detailed smoking and demographic data.

4 QUALITATIVE SERVICE DELIVERY EVALUATION
For internal use only, a two-stage qualitative research programme has also been implemented to gather implementation evaluation data. Service-delivery staff were interviewed half-way through the first 12 months and also at the end of the first 12 months. The purpose was to feed back to the PCT comments from the service-delivery teams, key partners and stakeholders which were used to improve the sustainability of the intervention.

FINDINGS

The total number of quit attempts in Brinnington increased by 47 per cent from 149 in the year before the intervention (2008/9) to 220 during 2009/10. In contrast, the number of quit attempts made in the two other areas of relatively high deprivation in Stockport did not increase.

The number of successful quits also increased from 60 in 2008/9 to 84 in 2009/10. However, the overall percentage of quits that were successful decreased slightly from 40 per cent in 2008/9 to 38 per cent in 2009/10, reducing the impact of the programme. Feedback from providers suggests that whilst the programme prompted more people to act on their desire to stop smoking, people were struggling to maintain a quit attempt as a result of increasingly challenging personal circumstances.

At least 519 residents received a brief intervention and signposting to services from the project team. The greatest single contribution was made by the Lapwing Centre who incorporated questions about stopping smoking into their induction programme and offered 'Lose the Fags' support to 123 new members.

At least 111 people made a direct approach to a new or existing service as a result of the 'Lose the Fags' initiative. The most productive element of the communication strategy was the roadshow which resulted in 25 requests for smoking-cessation support. Another 22 requests were made initially by text or free phone.

Of the 111 who made a direct request for support at least 82 went on to make a supported quit attempt with the support of a new or existing service. The largest number (21) made an attempt with the new Children's Centre service. The new Lapwing service, the existing GP service and the existing quit for life group were equally popular with between 16 and 18 new participants each.

LESSONS LEARNT

The following three key lessons around community engagement and working in partnership were learnt:

1   The intervention has been a triumph of co-creation and partnership working, with numerous community organisations having a genuine stake in the intervention. From the outset, the project team focused on building strong links with volunteers and workers, and on developing an intervention which would fit into Brinnington alongside existing services, so it would be readily accepted by the target audience.
2   This community partnership approach also brought problems, in that when management changed at the Children's Centre, the new 'Lose the Fags' intervention was changed, causing problems with delivery. However, the 'Lose the Fags' team reacted fast by having more team meetings and increasing communication between partners. It was also difficult for the fitness instructors and Children's Centre staff to adopt smoking cessation into their existing roles, and considerable support was required to provide them with the necessary skills and confidence to deliver the 'Lose the Fags' intervention. The support of the PCT's smoking-cessation team made this possible.
3   The project was designed to be sustainable because existing, established community organisations were engaged in its development and have adopted smoking cessation as part of their core-service offer; the 'Lose the Fags' project has provided a strong brand to support all the community efforts. Gradually, quitting smoking is becoming a social norm in Brinnington.

CHAPTER RECAP

This chapter has shown how developing genuine partnerships at a community level, instead of a tick-box or going through the motions engagement approach, can help to develop a sustainable project.

In the next chapter we will learn how clear segmentation of target audiences enables responsive, tailored interventions to be developed.

SELF-REVIEW QUESTIONS

1   The scoping research identified that self-esteem; perceived self-efficacy and confidence were all very low amongst Brinnington's young mums. When developing a behaviour change intervention, how might you respond to a similar lack of self-esteem/low confidence in your target audience?
2   Stakeholder engagement and community work was vital in this project's success. What strategies would you employ to engage with, and keep engaged, community leaders?
3   The Stages of Change theory were used when selecting the target audience: 'contemplators'. Based on the insights generated from the scoping research, what other behavioural theories do you think could be applied to this project?

REFERENCES

Banister, E. and Burgess Allen, J. (2007). Stockport Adult Health Survey, NHS Stockport.

Brinnington Area Profile, available from Profiling Stockport, Profiling Stockport https://interactive. stockport.gov.uk/profile/. Accessed June 2010.

Indices of Multiple Deprivation. (2007). Communities and Local Government. Available from http:// www.communities.gov.uk/communities/neighbourhoodrenewal/deprivation/deprivation07/. Accessed June 2007.

Neighbourhood Renewal Area Residents' Survey. (2007). Neighbourhood Renewal, Stockport Council.

Stockport's Neighbourhood Renewal Strategy, Priority 1 Areas: Brinnington, Adswood & Bridgehall, Lancashire Hill & Heaton Norris and the Town Centre. Stockport Council, January 2009.

Stockport Stop Smoking Service Health Equity Profile statistics 2009, available from Public Health Directorate, Stockport NHS.

Prochaska J. O., Norcross J. C. and DiClemente, C. C. (1994). *Changing for Good: The Revolutionary Program that Explains the Six Stages of Change and Teaches You How to Free Yourself from Bad Habits*. New York: W. Morrow.

5 SEGMENTING TARGET AUDIENCES

VIGNETTE: TAKE CHARGE, TAKE THE TEST

KEY WORD: SEGMENTATION

The US Centers for Disease Control and Prevention implemented a one-year social marketing project in Cleveland (OH) and Philadelphia (PA) to increase HIV testing in African American women at high risk of infection. Launched in 2006, the 'Take Charge, Take the Test' project promoted HIV testing and information seeking through HIV telephone hotlines; a dedicated HIV website; community partnerships; events; and print, radio and outdoor advertising.

The project underwent a very detailed process to segment the market. The following were considered for each segment: size, HIV incidence rates, risk behaviours, testing behaviours, ability to reach, ability to influence, and potential to influence others.

Findings demonstrated that African American women aged 18–34 were found to constitute a high percentage of the overall African American populations (54 per cent), and African women represent 67 per cent of all AIDS cases in adult females in the US.

Upon evaluation of all the available target audience data, single, Africa American women aged 18–34 years, with some colleague education or less, who earned US$30,000 or less per year, who resided in certain zip codes where prevalence of HIV was high, and who had unprotected sex with men, were chosen as the target segment.

For the full case study, go to: www.thensmc.com.

This vignette features a project where segmentation was used to identify a target audience that was high risk, but also reachable.

ABOUT THIS CHAPTER

When starting a project, often the problem you are looking to address seems unmanageable. However, by many people changing small things, the impact can be great. In this chapter you will learn:

- ○ How a government behaviour-change initiative that worked with individuals and the community to bring about small behavioural changes had a big overall impact.
- ○ A new approach to segmenting your audience.
- ○ Ways to evaluate to demonstrate success, ensuring continuation of the programme.

CASE STUDY: TRAVELSMART: AN INTERNATIONAL APPROACH USING SOCIAL MARKETING TECHNIQUES TO CHANGE TRAVEL BEHAVIOUR

Ewen MacGregor, BehaviourChangeSolutions.com, and Colin Ashton Graham, Consulting Behavioural Economist

PROJECT OVERVIEW

TravelSmart is a unique and innovative travel-demand management approach, which has been developed and implemented by the Department of Transport in Perth, Western Australia. It aims to reverse the trend of increasing use of private motor vehicles by encouraging alternative sustainable transport options such as walking, cycling and public transport.

The programme is an example of a successful government behaviour-change initiative that demonstrates, by working with individuals and the community, that small behavioural changes made across the population can make a big difference overall. The approach has now spread world-wide with similar projects in Australia, Europe and North America.

BACKGROUND

The publishing of the Perth Metropolitan Transport Strategy (MTS) (Department of Transport, 1995) and the TravelSmart (TS) ten-year plan (Department of Transport, 1999) (alongside similar plans for freight, cycling and public transport) saw deliverable programmes established to implement travel-demand management in Perth. Perth led the world in this integrated approach to travel-demand management.

Travel-demand strategies can be used in conjunction with pricing policies, regulation and investments in mass transit and facilities for walking and cycling (TravelSmart works with or without infrastructure investment). TravelSmart is often coordinated by state, regional or national governments in partnership with local government and the private sector.

TRAVELSMART HOUSEHOLD PROGRAMME

The core TravelSmart tool is the deployment of community-based social marketing techniques at an individual household level. This involves asking the households what information they need in order to reduce their car use – for example, information about the times, routes and costs of bus or train services, or the locations of bicycle routes. The TravelSmart Household programme was created as a response to the growth in car use and declining public-transport use. It is an innovative behaviour-change approach that helps Perth residents reduce the cost of their car use, their impact on the environment and increases levels of physical activity. The TravelSmart approach is proven to increase the use of public transport, walking and cycling (Brog et al., 2002).

Following a pilot project in 1997, the programme has now been delivered to other suburbs across the Perth metropolitan region reaching more than 400,000 residents. The programme is successful because there is significant potential for change with a convenient sustainable transport option available for almost half of all car trips made.

INTERNATIONAL EXAMPLES OF TRAVELSMART (PERSONAL TRAVEL PLANNING)

TravelSmart, also known as Personal Travel Planning or TravelSmart Communities, has now been deployed to more than 1.7 million households in projects across Australia, Europe and North America (see Table 5.1). Recent innovations in Western Australia have extended the scope of the services to include demand management of travel, energy, water and waste under the public brand Living Smart. The Living Smart approach deploys an extended coaching relationship with households over a period of around ten months to facilitate multiple behavioural changes.

TravelSmart contributes to the establishment of new social norms and helps to build communities that are more able to use alternatives to the car. It works best when there are opportunities for people in a locality to use other modes of transport. In preparing for a behaviour-change programme of this kind it is important to research the barriers and benefits of the different transport modes available, to work out how best to communicate with the target audience, and to collect data on transport usage before and after involvement in the programme to see how effective it has been.

Table 5.1 International application of travel-demand management (Personal Travel Planning)

Country	Target Number of Households
Australia	700,000
UK/Europe	1,000,000
USA/Canada	30,000

Note: Includes multi-modal projects and those with a public-transport-only focus.

PROJECT RATIONALE

Perth is one of the most car-dependent cities in the world with 84 per cent of all trips under-taken by car (Parliament of Australia, 2009). Both local-government and state-wide surveys placed traffic congestion in the top two priority issues, behind only crime, for government to address (RAC, 2008).

From a database of cities around the world, Perth (in 1995) ranked:

- Third highest in road infrastructure length per capita
- Fourth highest in car ownership
- Sixth highest in Central Business District parking spaces per job.

Should those trends in car use and urban growth have continued it would have resulted in car traffic in Perth increasing, resulting in extreme congestion, poor air quality and loss of community amenity (Department of Transport, 2006). However, the government consulted widely with the population and the results indicated two-thirds of the population were in favour of reducing car dependency and increased spending on public transport (Department of Transport, 2003).

 ## AIMS AND OBJECTIVES

There are six main aims of the Perth TravelSmart project:

1 Reduce greenhouse gas emissions
2 Improve air quality
3 Maximise the use of public-transport services and walking/cycling facilities
4 Reduce traffic congestion
5 Improve health
6 Make Perth a better city to live in.

The objectives included:

- People living within the Perth Metropolitan Region will:
  o Consistently consider their travel options before using their cars.
  o Realise they can significantly reduce traffic and associated problems through small changes to their travel behaviour.
- Organisations such as employers, schools and institutions will increasingly accept responsibil-ity for how their staff and customers travel and will be empowered through training and funding to implement their own TravelSmart programmes.
- Organisations with similar objectives to TravelSmart will share resources and work together to achieve a better modal balance.
- Community groups will be advocates for and participate in TravelSmart initiatives. They will be informed and supported in their work to promote and deliver travel-demand management initiatives.

SCOPING RESEARCH

To explore the degree to which private car travel is discretionary, the Department for Transport conducted in-depth research into the viability of alternatives to the car and barriers to change for specific trips made by a sample of individuals in the community.

This research revealed that Perth has public-transport services, bicycle networks and walkable developments that were sufficient to provide a realistic alternative for up to half of all car trips made. Walking, cycling and public transport have the potential (based on existing travel patterns and ignoring network-capacity constraints) to increase their mode share in Perth from around 20 per cent to almost 60 per cent of trips.

KEY INSIGHTS

The following insights were identified:

- A combination of providing local information with motivational interviewing techniques (counselling) can affect travel-demand management.
- Up to half of all car trips in Perth were (theoretically) replaceable by walking, cycling or using public transport.
- Around one-fifth of all car trips within Perth (22 per cent) were replaceable by public transport, more than one-quarter (26 per cent) of the car trips are replaceable by bicycle and 21 per cent by walking (figures not cumulative because one car trip can be replaced by multiple other mode choices).
- Many of the barriers to using sustainable transport alternatives were related to either lack of information on the alternatives or related to subjective perceptions such as using an alternative to the car for travel. Hence the programme approach of targeting information and reducing the barriers in regards to perceptions of alternatives.

In addition to the above insights, the following were determined to be actionable:

- The TravelSmart programme is based around robust research both local and international that indicated potential for change.
- Direct communication with individuals empowers significant behaviour change because it:
  - o Engages the participant in selecting information for themselves (capacity building rather than advising).
  - o Facilitates a 'social contract' between the service provider and the household.
  - o Allows programme resources to be directed to participants who are open to behaviour change.

BARRIERS

As demonstrated in the above section, community barriers around lack of detailed knowledge regarding access to local services, misperceptions regarding the comfort, convenience and travel time of the alternatives to car travel, etc., were identified. In addition to these barriers, institutional barriers were also identified. These included:

- *Funding.* Securing funding from the main project partners that range across health, environment and transport portfolios is difficult given lack of leadership from any one portfolio.
- *Ensuring local government buy-in.* Local government are essential partners in making the TravelSmart household programme relevant to households (local ownership).
- *Supportive bus operator.* A supportive bus operator in the intervention suburb is important to ensure that new customers experience good services when they first switch to public transport.

HOW DOES TRAVELSMART WORK?

Voluntary Behaviour Change is a rapidly developing area of research and practice, blending approaches from public health (e.g. coaching, motivational interviewing) and localised (community-based) social marketing.

TravelSmart engages residents, both at the individual and collective level. Powerful interventions tap into the social behaviours of individuals using community-based social marketing techniques that can create conversations that in turn change behaviour. Figure 5.1 shows how the 'tools' of behaviour change can be applied to establish the desired behaviour as a social norm and to help people to experience the behaviour and to form new attitudes. This approach breaks the nexus that 'attitudes do not predict behaviour' by nudging behaviours that trigger supportive attitudes.

HOUSEHOLD SEGMENTATION PROCESS

TravelSmart establishes a dialogue with households in the intervention suburb. Depending on the response to an initial contact, households are taken through a process that provides information and motivates them as to how to replace car trips with walking, cycling and public-transport trips.

Following direct contact (by telephone or door-to-door) with the target households (every contactable household in the participating suburb) each household is then segmented into one of three groups: those not contactable or not interested in the service (the 'N group'); those who currently use alternatives to the car on a regular basis (the 'R group'); and those interested in information to assist them to make changes (the 'I group'). The 'R group' is

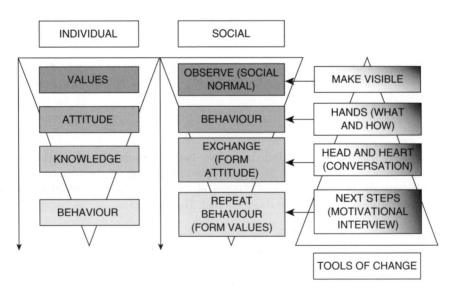

Figure 5.1 Behaviour change model: applying the tools of change to individual decision-making frameworks

Reproduced with kind permission from Colin Ashton-Graham

further divided into those with further information needs (e.g. public-transport users who would like to take up cycling) and those without information needs.

The 'R without' group households are provided with incentives to thank them and encourage them to continue to use sustainable transport alternatives for some of their journeys.

The 'I group' and 'R with' group receive the most intensive level of programme intervention. These households receive a service sheet (list) of information on train, bus, cycling, walking and smarter car use. Motivational interviewing techniques are used through direct contact with the household. Households choose very specific information on their local transport options. Residents can also sign up for a personalised journey plan, a home advice session on walking, cycling or public-transport use and receive incentives to encourage them to try new ways of travelling other that the car. The information that they request is then delivered using bicycles with trailers, demonstrating commitment to change and the programme philosophy.

Figure 5.2 represents the segmentation process and is an example from the South Perth project.

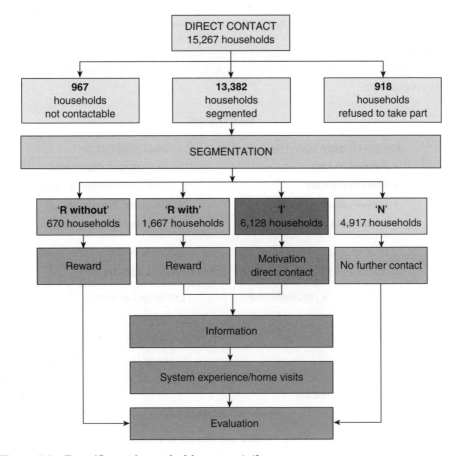

Figure 5.2   TravelSmart household segmentation process

Reproduced with kind permission from Socialdata Australia

STAKEHOLDER ENGAGEMENT

The TravelSmart programme recognises that building the capacity of stakeholders is key, and uses their influence to help their customers change their travel behaviour. This tried and tested technique recognises that changing travel behaviour is also dependent upon favourable community and organisational cultures and many stakeholders have an important role in helping to removing barriers to using the travel alternatives. (See Figure 5.3.)

TravelSmart builds the capacity of stakeholders including local governments, employers, schools and institutions to influence travel behaviour in their respective settings in the following main ways:

- Providing seed funding support (e.g. contributory grants for local governments to employ TravelSmart Officers) and resources (information and promotional materials)
- Education and training support
- Developing learning networks so that stakeholders can share experiences and learn from each other
- Linking policies, strategies, projects, programmes and partners.

In line with best practice for managing partnerships and volunteer contributions, TravelSmart deploys recognition and reward for stakeholder contributions through its annual awards programme.

PARTNERS:

Non-government authorities:
- **Millennium kids**
- **Heart foundation**
- **Conservation council**
- **Sustainable transport**

State government:
- Transport department
- Public-transport authority
- Health department
- Physical-activity taskforce

Individual capacity
- **Households**

Stakeholder capacity
- **Local government**
- **Schools**
- **Workplace**
- **Institutions**

Local government:

Other states:

Private sector:
- Bus operators
- Employers

Australian government:
- **AGO department of environment and Heritage**

Figure 5.3   TravelSmart stakeholder map

MARKETING MIX

The marketing mix of public-transport services is more complicated than for consumer products because the individual decision-making process involves complex situational and personal factors that are different for the same individual at different times of day and for different journey purposes – one size does not fit all.

PRODUCT

The core product (beneficial outcomes promised) being promoted is a mix of health, convenience and financial benefits resulting from using public transport, walking or cycling (or a combination), as well as a reduction in pollution and traffic congestion in Perth.

The input product is a personalised service (to correct information failure) in order to facilitate a reduction in car use (for short journeys in particular) in favour of cycling, walking and public transport. Given community attitudes towards both car use and ownership the messages are intended to focus on 'smarter car use' and not 'restricting car use'.

A range of augmented products and services has been developed, identified and or promoted as part of the TravelSmart programme:

- 'Individual' pocket bus timetables with actual bus times and destinations for every bus stop in every intervention suburb.
- Free TravelSmart guides detailing the bus (showing the closest bus stop), cycling and walking routes. They also highlighted many local facilities, including shops, health centres and schools.
- Prompts or messages to remind people to use public transport at the point of decision-making; for example, key-rings bearing several TravelSmart call to action messages to intervene at the point of decision (when the householder reaches for the car keys!).
- Improvements in public transport (a new public bus fleet and services have been introduced as part of the Public Transport Plan).
- Modern electric trains with air conditioning and expansion to the rail network including the new Mandurah to Perth railway line.
- Perth Cycle Network: Perth has a high-quality cycling network that was developed through consistent investment over 25 years.

PRICE

The price elasticity of public transport and car use is low because non-monetary costs dominate the decision. Non-monetary costs or barriers such as user 'safety and security' and the perception that public transport is inconvenient and takes up more time were identified as important. These costs or barriers were addressed in a variety of ways:

- Co-benefits, such as financial savings of using your car less, improved health and lower stress travel experiences are promoted.
- The government addressed 'safety and security' concerns by introducing security guards on trains.
- People often over estimate journey time of using alternatives to the car and underestimate car-journey time and other costs such as car-parking time and fees. TravelSmart access guides

and walking information also address the issue of journey time by showing typical journey times of walking and cycling in local areas.

○ For households that had already expressed an interest in using public transport (not current users), but lacked confidence to access the service, a bus driver would visit the household to explain the system and address the barriers and benefits of using the service.

PLACE

TravelSmart or Personal Travel Planning techniques can be applied in many places, including residential households, schools, workplaces and major destinations such as universities and hospitals. Evidence suggests that the greatest project success is achieved where there are good levels of sustainable transport services and good access to local services such as health, education and retail. More recently the creation of Transit Orientated Developments and Liveable Neighbourhoods in Perth are creating local communities or 'places' that will make promoting and choosing alternatives to the car more attractive.

PROMOTION

The Perth household programme uses an individualised approach of promotion by segmenting the audience and tailoring information and advice specific to the segments needs. A number of follow-up motivational phone calls to engage and encourage participation are conducted.

KEY CHANNELS

Due to budget limitations and limited evidence of mass-media campaignsdirect influence upon travel-demand management, the main channels used to promote the programme are either free or relatively cheap. Examples of this are the participating bus companies placing adverts on buses running in the area, adverts in local newspapers, libraries and displays in local shopping centres.

In terms of programme-delivery phase, telephone and face-to-face contact are used to promote the household programme. The high level of brand awareness within a participating suburb has been shown through evaluation to help with message recall and gains a higher response rate in terms of participation in the programme.

Media stories from 'typical families' making changes were published in local free papers (delivered to most households in Perth) and this was another way of encouraging change and keeping the messages alive for longer following the implementation phase of the programme.

MONITORING AND EVALUATION

The TravelSmart household programme behaviour changes were measured by before and after travel-diary surveys of households in the intervention area; these changes were validated against the pubic-transport electronic ticketing data and Perth cycle-route monitoring data.

Substantial actual and potential financial benefits to state government have been identified and estimated in a number of areas:

- ○ Increased public-transport fare revenues and reduced operating costs
- ○ Improved health and fitness due to increased physical activity
- ○ Reduced users' and others' exposure to air pollutants
- ○ Reduced greenhouse-gas emissions
- ○ Improved road capacity reducing need for improvement
- ○ Reduced road trauma.

The principal evaluation frameworks, each of which is useful in different stakeholder contexts, were:

- ○ *Socio-economic*: to guide the overall allocation of resources to achieve the most beneficial outcomes for society.
- ○ *Public-sector finance*: to assist in the assessment of the impacts of the programme on public-sector expenditure requirements.
- ○ *Private (user)*: to demonstrate the value to the individual.

The Perth metropolitan public-transport system has a fully integrated electronic smart ticketing system. This system allows detailed analysis by suburb and bus routes, thus enabling detailed before and after intervention analysis of behaviour change. In addition, a control suburb is also measured to enable external influences to be taken into consideration during the evaluation.

FINDINGS

TravelSmart or personal travel-planning programmes targeting households have consistently delivered reductions in car trips of 10 per cent or more, reduced distances travelled by car as well as increases in walking, cycling and public transport use. These results are achieved without restrictions being placed on the amount that people travel or use their cars.

So far in Perth the state government has worked with 418,500 residents since 1999, at a cost to the state of under $36 (AUS) per resident (approx £23.00) and the programme is continuing under the LivingSmart banner. If you take into account the reductions in the public and private costs of car use that it has achieved, the programme saves $30.00 for every dollar it costs. Increases in scale of the project have further positive impacts on results and cost effectiveness; On average, each programme participant produces 225 kg less carbon dioxide from their travel each year.

A common dataset exists for eight of these projects (representing 143,000 residents), including travel data for 6,000 households, 14,000 persons and 48,000 trips.

The combined dataset (of projects conducted between 2000 and 2003) shows the WA TravelSmart programme has achieved on average a 10 per cent reduction in car trips and 13 per cent reduction in car kilometres across the suburbs in which it has been delivered. This is an average of 72 fewer car trips per person per year with reductions in car trips transferred to more walking, bicycle and public-transport trips.

Project benefits have proven to be sustainable, with lower levels of car use recorded in South Perth four years after the initial TravelSmart household pilot was delivered. Table 5.2 demonstrates typical TravelSmart household project results.

Trip details	Percentage change	Change per person year
Car trips	10% reduction	72 trips/year reduction
Car km travelled	13% reduction	750 km/year reduction
Walking trips	26% increase	33 trips/year increase
Cycling trips	58% increase	12 trips/year increase
Public-transport trips	18% increase	11 trips/year increase

Table 5.2   TravelSmart household programme results
Source: Bell Pottinger Public Relations

There are multiple outcomes or benefits of these behavioural changes for the individual, the community and government, which represent a model for triple bottom-line accounting.

The annual evaluation outcomes of the programme to date (for 418,000 Perth residents) include:

- 10 million fewer car trips
- 100 million reduction in vehicle kilometres
- 30,000 tonnes reduction in greenhouse-gas emissions (equivalent of taking 6,000 cars off the road)
- 1.6 million extra hours of physical activity
- 1.4 million extra public-transport trips. (Kerr and James, 1999).

LESSONS LEARNT

The TravelSmart household programme in Perth is now recognised world-wide as a leader in the field of sustainable transport use and behaviour change:

- *Policies and strategies:* The Perth programme used both a strategic and operational approach to encouraging behaviour change. The programme was underpinned by a visionary approach to the integration of transport, environment-related strategies and policies with stated behavioural goals. The numerous cross-sectoral benefits of TravelSmart have been demonstrated through evidence and research, leading to leveraging of strong cross-government agency policy support of the TravelSmart programme.
- *Transit-orientated developments:* More recent programmes have focused around transit-orientated developments (high population density developments orientated towards public transport, walking and cycling) with excellent results.
- *Public-transport, walking and cycling facilities and services:* The success of the Perth TravelSmart programme has been in part due to the good standard of public-transport services and extensive cycling and walking networks. Perth has a modern fleet of buses and electric trains with air conditioning and accessible for customers with reduced mobility.

○ *Multi-skilled Committed Team:* Experience has shown that a multi-skilled dedicated team increases the success of the programme. Outsourcing of programme aspects such as the 'face to face' delivery of the programme enabled improved cost effectiveness and efficiency.

○ *Programme Innovation:* The Perth TravelSmart programme encouraged a culture of innovation, with many new ideas gaining widespread use in similar programmes in other counties around the world.

○ *Partnerships and Intersectoral Approach:* Identifying and influencing opinion leaders (as authoritative and credible sources of information) and encouraging, developing and maintaining partnerships to implement TravelSmart contributes the success of the programme in many settings.

○ *Small Change, Big Difference:* The TravelSmart programme results (both in Perth and internationally) show that small behavioural changes made across the population can make a big difference overall. The approach and technique is transferable and has recently been applied to other household sustainability issues (LivingSmart), such as saving water, energy and recycling, with promising results.

CHAPTER RECAP

This chapter used insights gathered plus a robust segmentation model to develop products and services to meet the target audience's needs.

In the next chapter we see how the use of behavioural themes can help you gain a deep understanding of your target audiences.

SELF-REVIEW QUESTIONS

1 The TravelSmart team worked hard to ensure they had full stakeholder buy-in. For the stakeholders in this case study, what techniques would you use to gain buy-in?

2 This project used a community-based social marketing approach. Figure 5.1 shows the different 'tools of change'. How could you use those tools for a project you are working on or a project you know about?

REFERENCES

Brog, W., Erhard, E. and Mense, N. (2002). Individualised marketing: Changing travel behaviour for a better environment. Available at: www.socialdata.de/info/IndiMark.pdf. Accessed August 2010.

Department of Transport, Western Australia. (1995). Perth Metropolitan Transport Strategy. Available at: www.transport.wa.gov.au/tsmart_mts.pdf. Accessed August 2010.

Department of Transport, Western Australia. (1999). TravelSmart 10 Year Plan. Available at: www.transport.wa.gov.au/14974.asp#plan. Accessed August 2010.

Department of Transport, Western Australia. (2003). Changing Perth for the better: Dialogue with the city. Available at: www.transport.wa.gov.au/2276.asp. Accessed September 2010

Department of Transport, Western Australia. (2006). Working paper: TravelSmart Household program: Frequently asked questions in travel demand management and dialogue marketing. Available at: www.transport.wa.gov.au/ts_faqs.pdf. Accessed September 2010.

Kerr, I. and James, B. (1999). Behaviour change in transport: Benefit–cost analysis of individualised marketing for the city of South Perth. Available at: www.transport.wa.gov.au/tsmart_cost_benefit.pdf. Accessed September 2010.

Parliament of Australia. (2009). Senate Standing Committee on Rural and Regional Affairs and Transport Inquiry: Investment of Commonwealth and state funds in public passenger Transport. Available at: www.aph.gov.au/senate/committee/rrat_ctte/public_transport/submissions/sub186.pdf. Accessed November 2010.

RAC. (2008). How much is traffic congestion costing us? Available at: http://rac.com.au/About-Us/RAC-eNews/2008/December-08/How-much-is-traffic-congestion-costing-us.aspx. Accessed September 2010.

6 USING THEORY TO DEVELOP EFFECTIVE INTERVENTIONS

VIGNETTE: 'GIVE IT UP FOR BABY'

KEY WORD: REINFORCEMENT THEORY

Asking pregnant women to stop smoking is a difficult challenge – especially if they find quitting stressful, and will be alienated from their peer group if they become a 'non-smoker'. 'Give It Up For Baby' counteracts these barriers, by offering an incentive of £12.50 per week in supermarket vouchers, for every week a woman demonstrates she is smoke-free (via a carbon-monoxide test).

This uses the principles of Reinforcement Theory, which proposes that behaviour can be shaped by controlling the consequences of that behaviour, either by rewarding good behaviour, or by punishing bad.

'Give It Up For Baby' uses positive reinforcement (financial reward), at fixed interval schedules (once a week), so that the target group learns that there is a direct relationship between a particular behaviour (stopping smoking) and getting a reward. Importantly, this reward means that mothers can adopt a no-smoking behaviour which, though different to her social group, does not isolate her because her group accepts that changing behaviour for a financial reward is legitimate.

In one year, 55 mothers quit in Dundee and a total of 140 had quit across Tayside using 'Give It Up for Baby'.

This case study is available in full at: www.thensmc.com.

This vignette shows how a theory-based understanding of behavioural triggers and motivations was used to inform programme design and development.

ABOUT THIS CHAPTER

As we saw in Chapter 1 and 2, understanding behavioural theory and using it to guide and interpret target-group insight is a key approach in social marketing. In this chapter we look at a city-wide intervention focused on helping people lose weight. Behavioural theory helped in the understanding of what would move and motivate people to change and how to diffuse innovation in terms of a social norms shift through a population in the most rapid way possible.

CASE STUDY: LIVERPOOL'S CHALLENGE: USING SOCIAL MARKETING TO ADDRESS OBESITY

Jane Thomas, Liverpool Primary Care Trust

Further information is available on the 'Liverpool's Challenge' website at www.centralliverpoolpct.nhs.uk/Your_PCT/media_centre/Background_information/Factsheets/Liverpools_Challenge_factsheet.aspx.

PROJECT OVERVIEW

With the increase in 'lifestyle' diseases linked to poor diet, obesity and lack of exercise, the NHS and UK government face a significant challenge. This chapter examines the development and impact of a social marketing programme – 'Liverpool's Challenge' – to reduce obesity in Liverpool, a large city in the north-west of England that has higher than average social disadvantage and a worse than average health profile. Recognising that government campaigns promoting healthy eating and exercise tended to have limited success, Liverpool Primary Care Trust (PCT), the local health commissioning body social marketing team focused on developing insights into the factors that motivate people to change their habits. They found that, while most people were aware of the benefits of a healthier diet and were keen to lose weight, they found it difficult to stick to a long-term regime and often felt isolated and therefore unmotivated. The subsequent social marketing programme that was developed formed relationships with the target audience using Customer Relationship Management (CRM) techniques more commonly used in the commercial sector, to provide people with ongoing support and feedback within the framework of a city-wide challenge to residents to pledge to lose weight.

INTRODUCTION

Obesity shortens average life expectancy by nine years (UK National Audit Office, 2002) increasing the risk of many diseases including diabetes, heart disease and cancer. Obesity-related illnesses are estimated to be responsible for approximately 30,000 deaths in the UK each year (Department of Health, 2008). In 2008, the government published 'Healthy Weight, Healthy Lives: A Cross-Government Strategy for England'. From this have come a number of initiatives, aimed at increasing physical activity and improving diet, notably the 'Change4Life' social marketing programme, launched in Autumn 2008 (the 'Change4Life' programme is a case study in this book – see Chapter 19).

Liverpool, like many UK cities, has seen a significant rise in obesity in recent years. In the city, an estimated 40 per cent of the adult population is overweight and 20 per cent obese (Liverpool Public Health Intelligence Team, 2008). It is estimated that obesity results in over 130,000 sick days every year in Liverpool. The NHS in Liverpool spends £5 million a year on treating obesity-related problems, which goes on to cost the city's wider economy an additional £15 million a year. If current trends continue, up to half of all children and one third of adults will be overweight or obese by 2020.

Liverpool PCT launched its 'Healthy Weight: Healthy Liverpool' strategy in April 2008, with the objective of stopping the rise in obesity by 2010 and ultimately reducing the level of obesity in the city from 2010. The PCT already ran two programmes, 'Active City' (2008) and 'A Taste for Health' (2008), both of which aimed to increase take-up of exercise and healthy eating. 'Liverpool's Challenge', devised and managed by the Trust's social marketing team, was another strand of that long-term strategy and directs the public towards these existing programmes.

Qualitative research was commissioned by Liverpool PCT's social marketing team to develop insights into the target audience and discover:

- Attitudes towards dieting and exercise.
- Factors influencing the likelihood of getting involved, staying motivated, barriers and competition.
- Reactions to programme proposals.
- Overall appraisal of programme proposals (such as the most/least motivating elements, appropriate media channels, etc.).

Group discussions were conducted amongst Liverpool residents, drawn from various life stages designed to reflect the target audience for the campaign, as follows:

- Female 'Family'
- Female 'Late'
- Male 'Family'
- Male 'Pre-Family'
- Female 'Pre-Family'
- Male 'Late.'

All belonged to lower economic households and were 'overweight' and interested in doing something about their weight. Within each group was a mix of 'slightly overweight', 'very overweight' and 'obese'.

The research showed that people aspired to lose weight and tried to eat a healthy diet and exercise more but struggled to change their habits.

'I should do more really.' (Male, Pre-Family)

'I've been on a diet for most of my life (37 years).' (Female, Family)

'I eat quite sensibly, but I don't exercise at all.' (Male, Late)

These comments suggested that people were aware of the benefits of healthy eating and exercise and that there was a perceived need for the PCT's 'product' (that is, healthy eating). Where they 'fail' is in starting and sticking to a long-term diet and exercise plan – so while people stated that they wanted information, the insights suggested that simply providing advice would not be sufficient to achieve behavioural change.

The main barriers for not eating healthily and exercising more regularly were given as lack of time, shift-work patterns and cost. The perception that it is expensive to eat healthily. This suggested that interventions needed to demonstrate that these barriers could be addressed by showing, for example, that exercise can be integrated easily into a daily routine or through providing low-cost recipes. Group members made various comments about how having the support of friends, family and peers would positively influence a lifestyle change:

> 'All in the same boat regardless of how much you want to lose.' (Female, Pre-Family)

> 'You need a good friend to go to the gym with. You're not as motivated otherwise.' (Male, Pre-Family)

> 'I need someone steering me to do it.' (Female, Family)

> 'It's difficult on your own.' (Female, Pre-Family)

This indicated that people would be more likely to succeed if they felt they were part of a community of people sharing the same challenges and aiming towards similar goals. This tied in with the view, mentioned later, that regular positive reinforcement would be beneficial. Respondents also mentioned the recent 'Capital of Culture' – a European arts-based festival that took place in Liverpool the preceding year – as something that had brought the city together, and expressed support for an event or series of activities that could do the same.

One theme that emerged was that people wanted advice to be provided by sources that were credible to them. This indicated that programme messages and voices that did not patronise or preach would help to achieve 'buy-in'. Another topic from the research was the need for simple and accessible advice. This suggested that making it as easy as possible for residents to start making lifestyle changes would help to reduce the barriers to entry. Residents stated that they would rely on some form of ongoing contact. The type of support residents wanted to receive to keep them motivated included:

- More 'simple' (but healthy) recipe ideas
- Alternative diet and exercise regimes to prevent participants from losing interest
- Updates on events in the local community
- News or some means of monitoring how the 'challenge' as a whole was progressing
- Relevant incentives.

It was evident that participants needed regular contact, with new stories and ways of measuring their progress against other people. There was strong support for a rallying cry to call residents to action.

> 'You want to prove you can do that.' (Male, Late)

> 'We can do it as a city.' (Female, Late)

The sense of being part of a community was evidently enhanced by the idea of working together as a city to meet a challenge.

USING THEORY AND INSIGHTS TO DEVELOP THE PROGRAMME

Insights from the research led to the development of 'Liverpool's Challenge', a 15-month programme that took the form of a challenge to people in Liverpool to collectively pledge to lose a million pounds (in weight). Several behavioural theories were used to inform the design of the programme. The first, Locke and Latham's 'Goal-Setting Theory' (1990), helped to develop the concept of the challenge as a means of motivation. The theory suggests that people need clear and specific goals and the programme tried to achieve this through creating a simple proposition – 'join Liverpool's Challenge and we will help you to lose weight'.

The second theory consulted was the 'Health Action Process Approach' (Schwarzer, 2008, 1996). The insight research showed that the target audience had the intention ('volition') to change their behaviour but that the motivation element was lacking. The programme therefore attempted to ensure that the elements required for people to undertake the desired behaviour were in place through providing support, regular motivational messages and information.

The 'Diffusion of Innovation' theory (Rogers and Everett, 1962) was also used in the design of the programme. Recognising that different individuals adopt new behaviour at different rates, the programme took a phased approach that mirrored the anticipated take-up by different groups. For example, at the point at which the 'early majority' was expected to come on board, some campaign activities were stepped up in order to maximise the potential penetration of this large group. The phased approach was also linked to times of year at which people would be most likely to embark on a weight-loss programme (Figure 6.1).

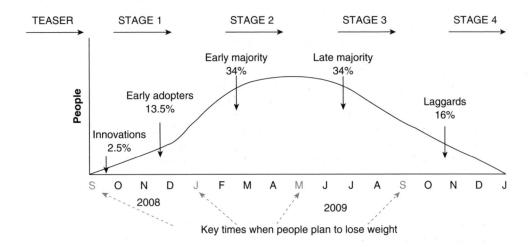

Figure 6.1   Diffusion of Innovation model

PROGRAMME OBJECTIVES

The programme's objectives were defined in terms of behavioral change, awareness and changes in knowledge. All objectives were SMART – specific, measurable, achievable, relevant and time-specific:

- To support the target audience to eat more healthily, exercise more and lose weight by the end of 2009.
- To raise awareness of the Challenge and encourage the target audience to sign-up and engage with the campaign.
- To provide the people of Liverpool with the (local) knowledge and skills needed to lead a healthy lifestyle by eating healthier foods and exercising regularly.
- To increase the number of people engaging with the Taste for Health and Active City programmes.
- To make information and support available from Taste for Health and Active City more accessible.

Interim objectives to the end of February 2009 were also set. These were:

- To get half a million pounds (of weight loss) pledged by end February 2009.
- To generate unprompted public awareness of the campaign of 10 per cent.
- To generate prompted public awareness of 50 per cent (verbal).
- To generate prompted public awareness of 60 per cent (visual).
- To get 50 per cent of the public exercising more.
- To get 50 per cent of the public eating more healthily.

Objectives would be measured through benchmark research and ongoing measurement of programme database analysis, as well as telephone and face-to-face interviews:

- Measure awareness of the Liverpool Active City and Taste for Health programmes and subsequent levels of engagement with different information and service offerings.
- Record a baseline measurement of BMI and monitor changes across the period of the campaign.
- Record a baseline measurement of dietary habits that can be re-measured at a number of intervals during the campaign to determine whether there has been any impact upon behaviour.
- Determine whether there are any correlations between level of engagement with the campaign and changes in BMI and dietary and exercise behaviours.
- Measure self-reported health benefits as a result of participation in the Challenge.
- Compare differences in awareness, attitudes and behaviours towards a healthy diet and an active lifestyle between people who engaged with the campaign and those who did not.
- Measure awareness of the overall Challenge campaign (including effectiveness of different campaign tactics in encouraging engagement) and of key messages communicated.

TARGET AUDIENCE SEGMENTATION

The target audience for the campaign was people aged 18 years and older residing or working in the Liverpool Primary Care Trust area who are classed as overweight or obese – see Figure 6.2. The campaign was city-wide but some interventions focused on the areas of greatest obesity: advertising frequency was increased in these areas and additional promotional teams were sent in to sign up participants on-street.

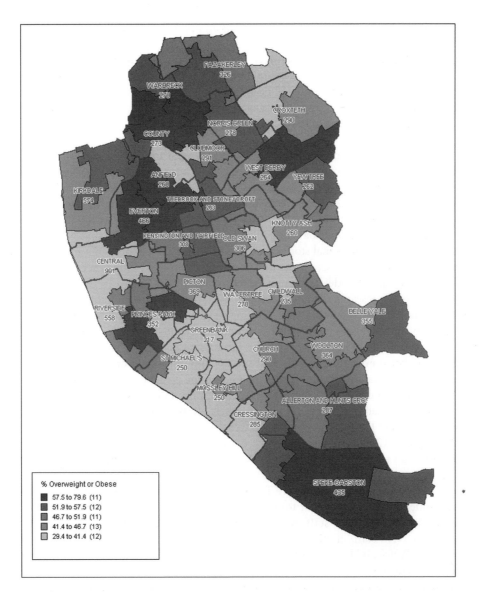

Figure 6.2   Percentage of interviewees whose BMI was classified as overweight or obese

Source: NWPHO 2007 Lifestyle Survey

The Challenge launched with a campaign that saw over £560,000 worth of press and £1 million broadcast coverage to create high levels of awareness and a sense of something 'big' happening in the city. An outdoor advertising teaser campaign with the strapline 'We've got one million pounds to lose' generated curiosity prior to the launch, which took the form of a city-centre day-long event, with the Million Pound Tanker providing a hook and visual focus for the media as well as an opportunity for the public to sign up and meet with healthcare professionals.

People pledging entered a community in which they were supported at every turn – from receiving regular CRM packs containing informative and motivational material, to one-to-ones with health professionals. Each pledger had their own account on which they could record their progress and people were kept informed of the campaign progress through the website, Challenge tower and motivation packs.

Liverpool PCT negotiated media partnerships with the *Liverpool Echo* and Radio City, the two largest media outlets in Liverpool, chosen because of their extensive reach and fit with the target audience. Coverage was extensive, with the *Liverpool Echo* running tenfull pages featuring campaign events and two front-page features. There was a weekly mention on the 'diary' feature, regular 30-second trailers, interviews, live broadcasts which saw presenters pledging and a day-long focus on the Challenge. Participants were shown a regular stream of motivational stories – people of all ages, obese residents and those who just had a few pounds to lose, people who, for health reasons, couldn't exercise vigorously and those who started undertaking more intensive activities.

As the scoping research demonstrated that the target audience did not need to be convinced of the benefits and desirability of losing weight. The highest costs were rather associated with sticking with a weight-loss programme and becoming more active. The programme tried to address these issues by showcasing people – often those who had, in their words, 'tried everything' – who had successfully lost weight and demonstrating the barriers that they had overcome. Stories focused on the positive aspects of the experience, such as people reporting that they did not feel hungry following a healthy eating plan; people making small but effective changes to their lifestyles; and people adopting exercise routines as part of their day-to-day life.

'Liverpool's Challenge' tried to make it as easy as possible for people to find out about and sign up to the campaign (see Figure 6.3). The extensive media campaign was designed to create 'ambient' awareness of the Challenge. There were many points of access across the entire Primary Care Trust area at which people could to sign up to the programme – at roadshows that toured communities in the city, online, by freephone, by some Boots pharmacy staff, with Challenge promotional teams across the city or at work for NHS staff, employees of Liverpool City Council, Merseyside Fire Service, Merseyside Police and local transport companies, via the Health at Work programme or employer roadshows.

Programme messages focused on showing the ease and convenience of participation. Incentives such as gym passes and swimming lessons encouraged taster sessions, and people were given advice on topics that the insight research had shown to be important to them, such as exercising at home and healthy eating for busy lifestyles. Stories featured free resources such as personal health trainers, community food workers, guided walks and cycle hire.

There was a strong focus on showing that eating healthily and exercising did not have to be expensive, with features on 'credit crunch cooking', 'grow your own veg' and shopping on a budget. People were encouraged to make small changes to their daily routines, rather than embarking on drastic new regimes that would be difficult to sustain. Overall, the

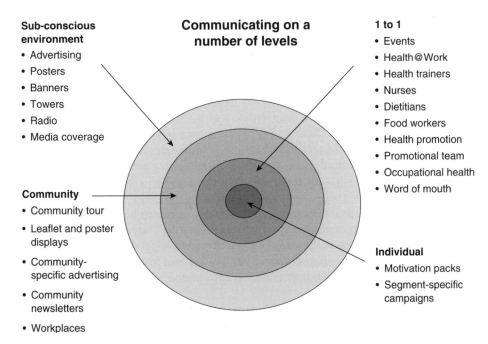

Sub-conscious environment
- Advertising
- Posters
- Banners
- Towers
- Radio
- Media coverage

Community
- Community tour
- Leaflet and poster displays
- Community-specific advertising
- Community newsletters
- Workplaces

Communicating on a number of levels

1 to 1
- Events
- Health@Work
- Health trainers
- Nurses
- Dietitians
- Food workers
- Health promotion
- Promotional team
- Occupational health
- Word of mouth

Individual
- Motivation packs
- Segment-specific campaigns

Figure 6.3 Communications channels

Source: Liverpool Health Challenge Report, 2009.

programme tried to generate a positive 'buzz' about being a part of the Challenge that would help to minimise the cost of participation in the public's minds.

KEY MESSAGES

- *You're not alone* – case studies online, in the media and in the CRM motivational packs showed people 'just like me' who had pledged and were successfully losing weight. A Facebook group was set up. Celebrities such as local actress Claire Sweeney, who had recently undertaken a weight-loss challenge for a television programme, and comedian Johnny Vegas, who lost five stone, supported the programme.
- *It's easy to eat well* – healthy, low-cost recipes were published in the motivational and starter packs. Case studies showed people who had lost weight with the help of Community Food Workers. Dieticians provided face-to-face advice to people attending the 'Million Pound Tanker' roadshow (featuring a converted milk tanker) and Community Food Workers gave cookery demonstrations at road shows. Participants were also directed towards resources provided by the existing 'Taste for Health' programme.
- *It's easy to become more active* – fitness workers demonstrated easy exercises, including those that could be done at home. Ideas for building in exercise to daily routines and low-cost activities, such as local walking, cycling and running groups, were publicised in the motivational and starter packs. The services of personal health trainers were publicised in motivational packs. The existing 'Active City' resource was promoted throughout.
- *We're just like you* – friendly, approachable, local health professionals were on hand at sign-up events and road shows to provide practical and accessible help and support.

◌ *Keep going* – regular motivational and case studies appeared in the CRM packs, online and in the press. The growing number of pounds pledged appeared on the website, the side of the Million Pound Tanker and on a *Blue Peter*-style 'pledgeometer' in the city centre.

The Million Pound Tanker was a mainstay of the programme, taking the message out to local communities as it toured the city. Inside the converted tanker, visitors were taken through a series of simple interventions with friendly healthcare professionals who weighed and measured them and provided advice based on the results. Outside the tanker in the 'food zone' and 'exercise zone' community food workers, local community groups and fitness advisers gave interactive cookery and exercise demonstrations, enabling people to have a 'taster session' that would encourage them to sign up to a local activity.

Each community event was localised, run by people from within the community such as health trainers and community food workers, and featuring performances by local community groups. The 'experiential' nature of the tanker was designed to engage people with the Challenge brand and begin to develop a relationship with them. Local celebrities lent their support throughout, attending 'tanker' events, providing quotes for the press and attending photocalls.

A television advert featured people taking part in the Challenge, discussing their reasons for signing up. Advertising was also taken on Facebook and Google adwords were used. Staff throughout Liverpool PCT were involved in the delivery of the campaign, in particular those working on the existing award winning 'Liverpool Active City' and 'Taste for Health' initiatives. Staff were consulted during the production of newsletters and other information, providing exercise advice, recipes and editorial feedback.

People pledging entered a community in which they were supported at every turn – from receiving regular CRM packs containing informative and motivational material, to one-to-ones with health professionals. Each pledger had their own account on which they could record their progress and people were kept informed of the programme progress through the website, Challenge tower and motivation packs.

EVALUATION AND RESULTS

Benchmarking research was carried out at the programme start and a number of methods are being used to measure changes in awareness, engagement, behaviour, social norms and self-reported wellness throughout the 12 months duration of the programme.

Three waves of telephone interviews are being conducted amongst participants to find out about their diet, weight loss, general health, sense of well-being, and the usefulness of Liverpool's Challenge materials and support. 200 were carried out in November 2008; and 240 were carried out in March 2009.

Three waves of 300 each face-to-face street interviews were undertaken to assess awareness and impact of the programme. The first and second phases were carried out in October 2008 and March 2009.

The interim results indicated that the programme had achieved the interim targets (see Table 6.1).

Table 6.1 **Liverpool's health challenge interim targets and results**

Interim target	Result
To get half a million pounds (of weight loss) pledged by end February 2009	503,907 pledged by 24 February 2009
To generate unprompted public awareness of the campaign of 10%	13% spontaneous local awareness of programme (compared with Weight Watchers 3%)
To generate prompted public awareness of 50% (verbal)	54% verbally prompted awareness of programme
To generate prompted public awareness of 60% (visual)	72% visually prompted awareness of programme
To get 50% of the public exercising more	67% claim to be exercising more
To get 50% of the public eating more healthily	69% claim to be eating more healthily

 LESSONS LEARNT

Initial indications suggest that:

- Developing media partnerships helped to leverage significant coverage which in turn led to high levels of public awareness.
- Employing a 'teaser' campaign generated significant media and public interest.
- The use of CRM techniques resulted in 84 per cent of participants opting in to receive future communications from the PCT, providing the trust with a new corporate asset – a database of a significant segment of the local population.

CHAPTER RECAP

The use of theory to help develop interventions and insights is a strong feature of this programme. Knowing about behavioural theory and applying it, as we saw in Chapters 1 and 2 helps to ensure that subsequent planning and implementation is more effective. This story from Liverpool also demonstrates the value of a social marketing programme linked to a clear set of goals and supported by a broad coalition from a wide range of organisations. The use of in-depth customer insight resulted in the development of an effective city-wide approach to assisting people to lose weight. In the next chapter we will take a look at how a project took a strategic look at changing a system to create change and save lives.

SELF-REVIEW QUESTIONS

1   Make a list of the behavioural change theories and models you are aware of. Take a look at the 'GSR' review of behaviour-change models and select at least two other models that you feel help you understand the behaviour change challenges you face. You can find the GSR review at: www.civilservice.gov.uk/Assets/Behaviour%20change_practical_guide_tcm6-9696.pdf
2   This case study demonstrates the power of social group action and the power of fostering new social norms. Think about a problematic behaviour change issue that you are concerned with. Ask yourself what major social norms reinforce the behaviour and then consider what you might need to do to change this social norm.
3   This case study used a campaign approach to creating awareness and then a change in the targeted population perception and behaviour. List some of the possible limitations of such an approach and some of the strengths.

REFERENCES

Liverpool Public Health Intelligence Team, Liverpool Primary Care Trust, (2008).

Liverpool Active City at: www.liverpoolactivecity.co.uk. Accessed 2008.

Liverpool Health Challenge Report. Liverpool PCT. Liverpool, (2009).

Locke, E. and Latham, G. A. (1990). *Theory of Goal Setting and Task Performance*. Englewood Cliffs: Prentice Hall.

North West Public Health Office, Annual Lifestyle Survey, (2007).

Rogers, C. and Everett, M. (1962). *Diffusion of Innovations*. Glencoe: Free Press.

Schwarzer, R. (2008) Modelling health behaviour change: How to predict and modify the adoption and maintenance of health behaviours. *Applied Psychology: An International Review*, 57(1): 1–29.

Taste For Health: www.tasteforhealth.com. Accessed 2008.

UK Department of Health. (2008). *Healthy Weight, Healthy Lives: A Cross Government Strategy for England*. London: Department of Health.

UK National Audit Office. (2002). *Tackling Obesity in England*. London: NAO.

7 INROADS INTO AFRICA: ENABLING LOCAL SERVICES

VIGNETTE: COLALIFE

KEY WORD: SUPPLY CHAIN/'PLACE'

In the world of social marketing and behaviour change, the 'Promotion' P often steals the spotlight. However, in social marketing, as well as commercial marketing, the 'Place' element of the marketing mix is vital – the products and services need to be in the right place, at the right time.

At nearly every social marketing conference, someone will talk about Coca-Cola and how easy it is for anyone, wherever they are in the world, to buy a Coke. Coca-Cola has managed to reach our 'hard to reach' audiences – they manage to reach the most deprived communities. Social marketers can use this reach to help them also reach 'hard to reach communities, for example: ColaLife is a purely voluntary campaign, with the aim of getting Coca-Cola to leverage its world-wide distribution channels to provide social products that help sustain life and improve public health. How? They have created innovative packaging – 'Aidpods'. The AidPod is a wedge-shaped container that fits between the necks of the bottles in a crate of Coca-Cola. It makes use of unused space to get simple medicines, such as oral rehydration salts, and other social products like water purification tablets to the places that Coca-Cola gets, i.e. virtually everywhere!

With the help of these Aidpods and Coca-Cola's distribution channels, ColaLife hopes to achieve the following three goals:

1 Reduce child mortality in developing countries (= UN Millennium Development Goal No. 4).
2 Improve maternal health (= UN Millennium Development Goal No. 5).
3 Combat HIV/AIDS, malaria and other diseases (= UN Millennium Development Goal No. 6).

To find out more, go to: www.colalife.org/.

This vignette reveals the importance of working collaboratively with the private sector to extend reach and impact into what some public and NGO organisations would consider to be hard to reach communities.

ABOUT THIS CHAPTER

As we discussed in Chapter 1, behaviour-change programmes require a set of clear, measurable and realistic behavioural objectives that can be achieved within the timescales of the specific programme. This chapter describes a programme that started out on a small manageable scale and, as funding increased, the programme has been rolled out to other countries. In this chapter you will learn:

- ○ How to generate insight when no or little funding is available for research.
- ○ Ways to engage and communicate with international government departments in order for them to see the added value in your programme.
- ○ How using both the Design and Support forms of intervention, as set out in Chapter 1, can bring about changes in behaviour and improve service delivery.

CASE STUDY: RIDERS FOR HEALTH: CREATING A SUSTAINABLE HEALTH SERVICE TRANSPORT INFRASTRUCTURE IN AFRICA

Clare Pickett and John Bromley, the NSMC. With acknowledgement to Emma Howard and Matthew Hann, Riders for Health

This case study appears in full on the National Social Marketing Centre's ShowCase resource (www.thensmc.com).

PROJECT OVERVIEW

'Riders for Health' (Riders) began its work in the late 1980s and became a non-governmental organisation (NGO) in 1996. Their programmes aim to support African health systems and improve the delivery of healthcare in rural Africa. They do this by providing specially designed and highly systematic transport management services for a large number of partners, including ministries of health (MoH) and NGOs.

With poor vehicle maintenance systems, vehicles in Africa fail well before their intended mechanical lifespan, and unnecessary repairs are prohibitively costly or simply not undertaken. This means that vehicles can be unavailable to health professionals after just a few months. Riders' work dramatically reduces fleet maintenance costs. They ensure that vehicles and motorcycles do not break down and that they are readily available for healthcare usage.

Riders operate using a cost-recovery model charging an accurately calculated usage fee to governments and healthcare agencies. This means that Riders' programmes are sustainable and can provide a long-term service to support effective healthcare delivery, as well as ensuring MoH and governments can budget effectively for transportation costs.

Across Africa, Riders employ over 250 people, maintain more than 1,400 vehicles and enable health workers to improve access to healthcare for over 10 million people (OC&C, 2005).

PROJECT RATIONALE

> All the donated drugs in the world won't do any good without an infrastructure for their delivery. (Dr Margaret Chan, Director-General of the World Health Organization, Nov, 2006)

Currently, more than 26,000 children under the age of 5 die every day across the developing world from preventable or treatable diseases including measles, diarrhoea and malaria (UNICEF, 2007). Millions of people across Africa remain deprived and isolated from healthcare resources due to distance, terrain, poverty and lack of transport (World Bank, 2006). As such, lack of reliable transportation constrains the performance of health delivery organisations and therefore restricts the uptake of health technologies.

In addition to the often poor transport infrastructure such as a lack of paved roads, many vehicles break down in Africa after a very short time period. This is due to a widespread misunderstanding of the precise needs and nature of vehicle maintenance in hostile conditions and harsh terrain, allied to an acute and extremely damaging shortage of vehicle maintenance infrastructure in Africa (Rammohan, 2010). The outcome is often that precious resources are wasted, healthcare goals are not reached and isolated communities are not provided with services.

 ## AIMS AND OBJECTIVES

In 2009, Riders developed a five-year strategic plan which focused on up-scaling operational growth, in both existing and new country programmes, to enable their partners to improve access to healthcare for a further 10 million people in Africa by 2013. The objectives are to:

1   Enable local healthcare providers to reach 20 million people living in the poorest rural African communities
2   Operate in at least eight countries in sub-Saharan Africa
3   Manage 4,000 vehicles for health-focused partners
4   Conduct in-depth research with Stanford University to prove conclusively the impact of reliable, outsourced transportation on the delivery of healthcare.

 ## IDENTIFYING THE TARGET AUDIENCES

At the heart of Riders' mission, and key to the delivery of healthcare across Africa, are the public-health workers who perform outreach healthcare. This is the *primary target audience* for behaviour change and the users of Riders' maintenance and training service.

The *secondary target audience* are the employers of the healthcare workers (i.e. the primary target audience's employers) who are national MoH, NGOs and other healthcare agencies, whom Riders term their 'partners'. All the health workers who use the motorcycles Riders manage in Africa are employed by the national MoH or other agencies, not by Riders. It is these groups that must make the decision to use Riders' programmes, and with whom Riders tries to engage most closely. Riders then develop specific tailor-made programmes to meet the needs of each partner, having segmented them on the basis of size and financial capacity.

SCOPING RESEARCH

In 1986, Riders' three co-founders, Andrea Coleman, Barry Coleman and Randy Mamola, were using motorcycle sport to raise money for another international development organisation, Save the Children. Two years later, Randy Mamola, a successful motorcycle racer, was invited to visit the fruits of this fundraising. He travelled with Barry Coleman to Somalia, where they found motorcycles intended for healthcare delivery terminally damaged after very short operational lives.

On subsequent trips, Andrea and Barry Coleman saw healthcare vehicles, including motorcycles and ambulances, at clinics just piled up and broken, often for want of a US$3 part. No one knew how to carry out the regular maintenance that would keep them working. At these clinics nurses would tell them that without these vehicles people living in rural villages could not be reached. Many were trying to serve their communities either with shared unreliable and unsafe motorised transport, or with inappropriate and out dated means for the distances, such as donkey cart, bicycle or even on foot.

They discovered that there was an assumption held widely throughout the community that vehicles in Africa always failed because the environment was too harsh. To people with an expert knowledge of motorcycle engines, this made little sense. They knew that transport affects everything and that without effective transportation, treatments and healthcare support could not reach areas most in need. But further to this, and contrary to popular belief, they also knew that an appropriate vehicle in Africa would work perfectly over a long life if it was maintained properly.

The solution was to put in place a system of maintenance and supply of replacement parts, so that a vehicle would run properly for its intended lifespan. It was with this purpose in mind that Riders was formed.

In 1989 Barry Coleman worked as a consultant to the Save the Children Fund and the World Health Organization, examining motorcycle use/maintenance arrangements in the Gambia. This research formed the basis of a new training/maintenance system and it was with this in mind that Riders was formed and grew.

Between 1990 and 1996 Riders worked as part of a larger development agency. Techniques for maintenance and training were developed and refined, while Riders also began to build an organisation in the UK to fundraise and generate world-wide support for this new initiative in Africa. Also during this period Riders carried out large-scale testing of training techniques in Uganda and opened its first national programmes in Lesotho and Zimbabwe.

Research and insight were gained from observation of people working in development and trying to achieve their outreach healthcare goals, as well as from international public health data. As well as invaluable, this method was advantageous as it enabled Riders to conduct their research and insight work on a relatively low budget. Riders' system for charging an accurate fee for the cost of running a vehicle requires analysis of a lot of complex technical and cost data (for example the costs to replace parts, how frequently the parts need to be replaced, etc.). As such, this phase also required Riders to build an expert and in-depth knowledge of how vehicles respond to the challenging terrain of Africa over certain distances. It was on this wealth of knowledge and understanding that the strength of the Riders' preventative maintenance system (known by Riders as 'zero-breakdown') was born.

KEY INSIGHTS

Riders' Executive Director spent a lot of time working with colleagues in Africa investigating vehicle use and maintenance arrangements in various regions. Key insights from time spent in Africa and research with the target audiences included:

○ *Failure to prioritise transport*: Transportation was very much seen as an add-on, not as a priority. Transport was never factored into the costings of healthcare – the costs of drugs were calculated, plus the costs of healthcare workers, but not transportation costs. In rural Africa the majority of people do not have the means to travel to access healthcare. To ensure healthcare coverage (including vaccinations and attendances at births) health workers must be able to travel to communities. However, as transport is often a hidden cost for healthcare, it is rarely budgeted for. They also found that as a result of this inefficient transport system, money and resources were often wasted as they did not reach their intended beneficiaries. This key insight – not just that transportation is required but that it must be cost effective and accurately costed – underpins Riders' preventative maintenance system on which all their programmes are based.

○ *Lack of mechanical expertise*: Where transport was being provided there was no system of maintenance to support it. Donor organisations often provided motorbikes and cars but not the knowledge to run and maintain them, resulting in their often rapid breakdown.

○ *Lack of training*: Vehicles were often supplied to health workers to use without any training – people who had never even ridden bicycles were given motorcycles. This often resulted in accident and injury, putting a health worker out of action and depriving a community of a health worker.

○ *Time pressures*: One of the main challenges to managing disease in Africa – particularly HIV – is detection of the disease itself, via testing of the population.

 STAKEHOLDER ENGAGEMENT

Riders' work is based on effective partnerships with a number of key stakeholders. First, as they provide a service to health ministries, they work very closely with key partners in government. Secondly, although Riders programmes are designed to be self-sustaining in the long term, initially they do require the support of funders. This funding comes from both those who fund Riders directly and the country's MoH.

Finally, Riders receives support from a wide range of organisations and individuals in the UK, Europe and the USA who also provide support to Riders programmes. Key supporting partners range from Dorna (who own MotoGP), the FIM (Fédération Internationale de Motorcyclisme) and motorcycle manufacturers like Ducati, to a number of grant-giving trusts and foundations such as the Bill & Melinda Gates Foundation, the Schwab Foundation for Social Entrepreneurship, the Venture Partnership Foundation, the Elton John Aids Foundation, the Skoll Foundation, and United Nations agencies such as UNICEF.

Riders use a variety of ways to engage with these stakeholders, understanding that they are not a homogeneous group. (See Figure 7.1.) Stakeholder engagement methods include:

○ Carrying out formal reporting commitments
○ Providing tailored updates and impact information
○ News and information through a newsletter, including use of video material
○ Production of a detailed annual report
○ Regular telephone calls or personal meetings, both with in-country programme teams and the UK office
○ Direct contact with co-founders where appropriate
○ Invitations to go on-site visits.

Figure 7.1 Stakeholder engagement

BARRIERS

The barriers to delivering healthcare in Africa provide the context for Riders' work and can be divided into physical and political barriers.

○ *Physical barriers:* The roads in rural Africa are often very bad or even non-existent. Without the appropriate vehicle, health workers cannot travel between rural communities and cannot provide healthcare on a predictable basis. Physical barriers also present difficulties to running any kind of organisation within many African cities and especially rural towns. There are often power (electricity) restrictions as well as a weak telephone infrastructure.
○ *Political barriers:* Working with any government can be a difficult process. It can be bureaucratic, time consuming and slow moving. African MoH have limited resources, which is particularly challenging as it means they are naturally risk averse. Thus, Riders must persuade those in power to invest in programmes such as theirs which may cost more in the short-term but which will promise long-term financial (as well as non-financial) gain.

 MARKETING MIX

The marketing mix has evolved since the programme was set up.

PRODUCT

○ The *core product* (the benefit promised) is access to healthcare for those across Africa who are in need.

○ The *actual product* (the product or service you develop to deliver the core product benefits) is the use/purchase of Riders' models/services.
○ The *augmented product* (the features that encourage and support uptake of the actual product or service); for example the cost-per-kilometre (cpk) calculator.

PREVENTATIVE MAINTENANCE SYSTEM

Riders knew and understood that replicating the transportation infrastructure that existed in the developed world would not be possible. So Riders set about designing their own appropriate, sustainable and innovative infrastructure, in which to manage vehicles able to deliver healthcare across the harsh conditions of the African terrain. Drawing on their knowledge from the world of motorcycling and the scoping research, Riders' founders developed their preventative maintenance system for managing the vehicles, people and money involved in the delivery of healthcare and other vital services. The system incorporates

○ training in driving skills
○ daily preventive routine maintenance procedures – supported by Riders' technicians who provide regular servicing.

The foundation of the system is Riders' unique cost-per-kilometre (cpk) calculator, which gives the true costs of running any vehicle in any given environment. This calculation involves regularly monitoring information on fixed costs such as management and logistics and also on variable costs such as fuel and replacement parts. These costs are averaged by the calculator and distributed over every kilometre travelled during a given time span. This information was gathered during the initial scoping phase and is updated on an ongoing basis.

Together with learning from their work with their customers and partners in Africa, the accuracy of the cpk calculator has allowed Riders to reformulate their successful system into four distinct financial models suitable for different kinds of scale and partnership.

PROFESSIONAL SAMPLE COURIER (PSC)

Insight gained during the scoping research demonstrated the need for effective medical sample testing. This led to the PSC service which incorporates not only the management of reliable vehicles (motorcycles have been found to be the most appropriate and cost-effective) but also the employment of specialist, highly trained and disciplined motorcycle couriers to collect and deliver the specimens and return the results on a timely basis.

INTERNATIONAL ACADEMY OF VEHICLE MANAGEMENT (IAVM)

Riders understands that no development in Africa can be sustainable in the long term unless it is managed by local people. So in 2002 Riders established the IAVM in Harare, Zimbabwe. Training over 1,200 delegates in safe motorcycle riding and driving, basic maintenance and comprehensive fleet management to date, these courses allow skills in vehicle management to be passed on so that a culture of preventive maintenance can be built across Africa. (See Figure 7.2.)

Figure 7.2   Skills in vehicle management being developed with the local community

PRICE

Cost is a major factor for both target audiences. For the primary target audience, the public-health workers, the cost can be accounted for in *non-monetary* terms. This is through time taken to learn the new skills to look after their vehicles as well as the risk of using them in rough and hazardous terrain. However, this has proved not to be a severe barrier. The benefits of having a reliable vehicle are obvious to them and they respond positively to the training and preventative maintenance.

For the secondary target audiences (the MoH, NGOs and healthcare agencies who employ the public-health workers) the cost incurred is *monetary*. The various models that Riders offers are not free but require purchase and vary in price depending on size, capacity and the funding available. However, in the long term the savings are considerable as Riders' systems means that their resources are effectively and efficiently managed.

By outlining these costs up front, so that governments or organisations can budget over the full life span of their vehicle, it is likely to introduce a new line to a client's budget. In the short term the costs may be higher, but in the long term costs will be much lower and the programme will be successful. However, the potential clients must overcome this psychological barrier regarding costs.

PLACE

Riders' maintenance programmes are based on 'outreach servicing'. Regardless of distance or destination, wherever a programme operates and requires Riders' services, a technician will travel to at an arranged time and place to carry out maintenance. This ensures that each vehicle is serviced at the right time and that health workers suffer minimum down-time because they do not have to transport their vehicle to the nearest workshop. The benefit of this is that public-health workers do not have to travel far in order to replace a part or, worse, wait for a donation from an aid agency. This sustainable solution saves time, money and lives.

PROMOTION

A range of media channels, PR events and communications tools are used by Riders to build support and promote their mission:

- *Media channels*: Riders promote their services through a variety of networks and by word of mouth. They do not rely on spending money on heavily promoting their transport models as they tend to focus the money they receive through fundraising and donation on their front-line services with the communities in Africa. For every £1 spent by Riders, 79p is spent on their work, 19p is invested in raising funds to enable them to develop their work and reach more people as well as administration and running costs, and 2p is spent on governance. As part of the motorcycling community and the social-entrepreneur community they are able to share their vision and promote their products. Furthermore, belonging to the international community of social entrepreneurs gives Riders the opportunity to raise the issue of transport and development on the global agenda at events like the World Economic Forum, the Global Philanthropy Forum and the Clinton Global Initiative.
- *PR events*: Since 1990, Riders has organised an annual fundraising event in order to further support the work in Africa. On the Thursday before the British Grand Prix the stars of MotoGP come together to help support Riders for Health which is the official charity of MotoGP. 'Day of Champions' is the only place where you can see all the stars of MotoGP when they appear on stage in the famous Day of Champions auction. Day of Champions now attracts around 5,000 visitors and is one of the highlights of the British motorcycle-racing calendar.
- *Online communication*: Riders maintain a comprehensive website of their work and services which is updated regularly. They also offer a free subscription to a newsletter. Riders work can be followed through Twitter and Facebook (www.riders.org/).
- *Other media*: Riders have been credited on several high-profile television programmes, news-papers and magazines including Trans World Sport, the London *Times*, BBC *LifeLine*, CNN documentary, PBS documentary and *Time* magazine. In 2007 Riders became one of three charities supported by Charley Boorman and Ewan McGregor through their TV bike adventure *Long Way Down*.

MONITORING AND EVALUATION

Throughout Riders' history the demands of funders have required them to report and evaluate their progress, and the organisation has also conducted its own careful scrutiny and impact assessments on an increasingly formal basis. It is only through such feedback and learning that the programmes have been able to develop over time. However, until recently their monitoring and evaluation had not been a core activity of the organisation. As the demands of partners increases and as the capacity of the organisation grows to meet it, Riders has been able to establish a more formal monitoring and evaluation function within the organisation.

Where previously Riders did not have the funding for evaluative work, they have now established a monitoring and evaluating (M&E) department from scratch in the UK support centre, and have begun to recruit and train local Monitoring and Evaluation officers in their programmes. They have established health-related baseline and ongoing data collection in three country programmes – Lesotho, the Gambia and Zambia – with some health-related monitoring also being carried out in Kenya and Zimbabwe.

2009 was the first year of Riders' new five-year strategic plan. The strategy is based on the replication of the programmes being carried out, hand-in-hand with rigorous monitoring, as well as evaluation of the work with advocacy for both the practical impact of Riders' systems and the benefits of contracting-out vehicle management for healthcare delivery. Working with Stanford University's Global Supply Chain Management Forum, Riders aim to demonstrate that their work results in a 45 per cent increase in health workers productivity, a 30 per cent increase in coverage of key healthcare interventions and an 80 per cent improvement in efficiency and effectiveness of vehicle-fleet management.

FINDINGS

The international business consultancy OC&C carried out a pro-bono 'due diligence' report on Riders' activities in Africa in 2005 and found that Riders 'provides sustainable development benefits by creating self-sustaining, indigenised organisations to maintain health worker vehicles'.

The benefits to Riders' work are far reaching:

- *Economic gains:* Riders has dramatically reduced the fleet-maintenance costs associated with health-worker outreach in Zimbabwe and the Gambia, with a 62 per cent reduction in annual motorcycle-fleet maintenance cost per thousand people reached by health workers in Zimbabwe. Riderssystem vastly increases the number of health workers that can be kept mobile on a given budget. In an area in Zimbabwe where Riders operates, there are around 90 per cent more health workers using vehicles than in areas where it is not. This means that Riders enables more health workers to become mobilised, allowing them to reach even the most isolated villages.
- *Health benefits:* Because the health workers can reach the rural communities with healthcare and can provide people with the education they need to prevent disease, malaria deaths have decreased 21 per cent in Zimbabwe, compared with a 44 per cent increase in a neighbouring region where Riders was not operating. (See www.riders.org/downloads/binga1.pdf.) The mobility afforded by Riders enables health workers to diagnose and treat more patients. In 2002, one year after Riders began operating in the Gambia, there was a 261 per cent increase in diagnoses of diarrhoea, a 75 per cent increase in diagnoses of acute respiratory infection and a 55 per cent increase in the diagnosis of malaria, as compared to the previous year.
- *Social advances:* By providing training for health workers, technicians and fleet managers, the team at the IAVM helped to improve the knowledge and skills needed to keep vehicles on the road. Riders only employ nationals of the countries in which they work and the health workers that they support are employed by the MoH in those countries. This means that Riders is helping to build a sustainable solution and does not reply on volunteers, people on 'gap years' or Western expatriates. This means that the skills and knowledge that Riders brings stays in the country. Riders programmes have empowered women in the countries where they work. Roughly 15 per cent of health professionals trained to ride motorcycles by Riders have been women. The programme directors in Zimbabwe, the Gambia and Lesotho are all women.

LESSONS LEARNT

Riders has developed its system and models continuously over the years, always striving for excellence and improvement. Most recently, Riders has implemented an organisation-wise system for project management that incorporates lessons learned into all areas of work and operations.

Lack of resources has historically meant that Riders has not been able to engage in as much formal in-depth market research or feasibility planning as they would have liked, although that is changing as the organisation grows and has more funds to use for these vital precursory stages of the work.

CHAPTER RECAP

This chapter has shown how, even when there is no budget for research, insights can be generated by the project team simply experiencing the problems and issues for themselves.

In the next chapter we will understand the importance of evaluation. No project is 100% effective – there are always elements which work well and those that work less well. Therefore, it is important to evaluate, so we can make the necessary changes.

SELF-REVIEW QUESTIONS

1 Riders receives support from a wide range of organisations and individuals, detailed in this chapter. How would you engage with these different stakeholders and what exchange would you offer them?
2 Think of an example of a social marketing project. How could you do research on a shoestring and what type of data collection methods would you use?
3 Assuming you have little or no money to spend on the promotional aspect of your project, make a list of five low/no-cost ways of promoting your programme.

REFERENCES

OC&C Strategy Consultants. (2005). *Due Diligence Report on Riders' Operations in Africa.* Available from: www.riders.org/downloads/OC&C%20report.pdf. Accessed August 2010.

Rammohan, S. (2010). *Riders for Health – A Fleet Leasing Model in the Gambia.* The Stanford University Global Supply Chain Management Forum April 2010. Available from:www.gsb.stanford.edu/scforum/research/documents/RidersforHealthCaseStudy-FleetLeasingintheGambia.pdf. Accessed August 2010.

Riders for Health (2009). *Because Africa Needs Reliable Transport.* Riders for Health Press Information Sheet. Available from: www.riders.org/downloads/Riders_press_info_2009.pdf. Accessed August 2010.

Riders for Health website. (2010). Accessed August 2010. www.riders.org.

Roberts, P., Shyam, K. C. and Rastogi, C. (2006). *Rural Access Index: A Key Development Indicator* . The World Bank, March. Available from www.worldbank.org/transport. Accessed August 2010.

UNICEF (2007). *The State of the World's Children 2008: Women and Children – Child Survival*. Available from: www.unicef.org/sowc08/docs/sowc08.pdf. Accessed August 2010.

WHO (World Health Organization). (2006). Available from www.who.int/mediacentre/news/releases/2006/pr66/en/index.html. Accessed August 2010.

WHO (World Health Organization). (2009). Newborns: Reducing mortality. WHO Fact Sheet No. 333. Available from www.who.int/mediacentre/factsheets/fs333/en/index.html. Accessed August 2010.

8 BEING HONEST ABOUT THE CHALLENGES

VIGNETTE: 'ANN SMOKERS': SMOKING-CESSATION SERVICE TASTER SESSIONS

KEY WORD: BUILDING SUPPORTIVE ENVIRONMENTS

It is fair to say that, though effective, stop-smoking services can labour under an unattractive image in many people's minds. As part of a comprehensive project to reduce smoking prevalence in Portsmouth, in the UK, NHS Portsmouth City Primary Care Trust worked with local smokers to develop innovative solutions to overcome entrenched service-delivery issues identified through scoping research.

In the UK, Ann Summers is a national retail chain selling women's lingerie. As part of their sales strategy they hold lingerie parties in people's homes. The party concept was used to improve awareness of local stop-smoking services was the 'Ann Smokers Party', which borrowed elements from the Ann Summers party model, such as the pyramid hosting and incentives schemes. Smokers attending the event were led through a range of games and activities, which gave them the information required to choose the most appropriate stop-smoking service for them locally, in a non-judgemental, sociable and supportive environment. The idea was piloted with positive feedback and the PCT are currently building their capacity to deliver public-health messages in this novel way, to ensure that mainstream services are promoted and networked via supportive 'peer' engagement events.

For further information, go www.uscreates.com.

This vignette illustrates how the provision of mainstream support services on its own is not enough. In order for users to select appropriate services and access them, a whole-systems approach is required, which creates a supportive and confidence-building environment in which information can be shared and decisions can be made.

ABOUT THIS CHAPTER

As discussed in Chapter 1, no project is 100 per cent successful, nor does it completely fail. There are always elements which work better than others. That is why evaluation is vital – you need to know what worked, but also what didn't work as well, and why that was the case. In this case study, the authors speak honestly about what worked and what did not work. The interventions were launched just as swine flu hit the UK, so this case study also acts as a useful reminder that social marketing is delivered in complex environments, where financial and political determinants can change quickly.

In this chapter you will learn:

○ The importance of understanding what aspects of your project were most successful.
○ How to generate baselines and gather outcome data on a small, local scale.
○ The importance of checking assumptions about health professionals' knowledge, attitudes and behaviours.

CASE STUDY: BEING BREAST AWARE: EMPOWERING WOMEN FOR EARLY CANCER DETECTION

Denise Ong, the National Social Marketing Centre; Gideon Smith, NHS Tameside and Glossop; Debbie Bishop, Tameside Metropolitan Borough Council

This case study appears in full on the National Social Marketing Centre's ShowCase resource (www.thensmc.com).

PROJECT OVERVIEW

This project, which aimed to promote breast awareness, was jointly funded by National Health Service (NHS) Tameside and Glossop and Tameside Metropolitan Borough Council (MBC).

NHS Tameside and Glossop serves a population of just over 250,000 living in the largely industrial Tameside areas and the adjacent town of Glossop, situated in the north-west region of England. The 2001 census identified 96 per cent of the population as white British and 4 per cent as black or minority ethnic. Compared with the rest of England and Wales, Tameside and Glossop have a lower proportion of AB and C1 and a higher percentage of people in groups C2 and D.[1]

The project was piloted in the Ashton Hurst ward of Tameside, which is among the 10 per cent most deprived communities in NHS Tameside and Glossop and experiences particularly low breast-screening uptake and breast-cancer survival rates.

PROJECT RATIONALE

In line with the rest of England, breast cancer is the most common cause of death from cancer amongst women in Tameside and Glossop. Although the incidence of breast cancer in the region is no higher than the national average, survival rates are lower due, in part, to late presentation (Tameside and Glossop Primary Care Trust, 2006). Early detection of breast cancer can lead to simpler, more effective treatment and improvement in survival rates. The NHS Breast Cancer Screening Programme provides free screening every three years to women aged between 50 and 70. However, breast screening uptake in NHS Tameside and Glossop is showing a downward trend, and as at 31 March 2007 coverage of

---

[1] National Readership Survey social grade classifications: A (upper middle class); B (middle class); C1 (lower middle class); C2 (skilled working class); D (working class).

women aged 53–70 in NHS Tameside and Glossop was just 61.3 per cent, compared to 73.8 per cent in England (NHS Information Centre, 2008).

Whilst breast-screening programmes are an important method of detecting cancer, self-awareness and understanding of what clinical signs to look for also have an important role to play. In 1991, the UK Department of Health (DH) abandoned systematic breast self-examination and replaced it with a policy that encourages women to be breast aware from age 18. This has been encapsulated by the NHS's breast-awareness five-point code: know what feels normal for you; look and feel; know what changes to look for; report any changes without delay; and attend full breast screening if aged 50 or over (UK Department of Health, 2006).

To increase awareness of the five-point code and the number of women who are breast aware, NHS Tameside and Glossop and Tameside MBC collaborated with the National Social Marketing Centre (NSMC) on a social marketing programme to increase breast awareness in women aged 35 to 50.

 AIMS AND OBJECTIVES

The aims of the project were to increase the number of women aged 35 to 50 in Ashton Hurst who:

- Were aware of the five-point code
- Had the self-confidence to be 'breast aware
- Were examining their breasts regularly for any changes.

 IDENTIFYING TARGET AUDIENCES

The target audience was initially defined as women aged 35 to 50, living in the top 10 per cent of deprived communities in Tameside and Glossop. This age group was targeted to increase the possibility of early detection in younger women who are not yet eligible for free breast screening, and to increase interest in and uptake of breast screening once they reach 50. Late presentation is a particular issue amongst more deprived women. One of the most deprived areas was selected for the pilot The area also had particularly low breast-screening uptake and breast-cancer survival rates.

Further segmentation using Mosaic[2] highlighted that within Ashton Hurst, the key lifestyle groups with a sizeable population that fit the demographic segmentation were: G, Municipal Dependency; D, Ties of Community; and H, Blue Collar Enterprise.

Key common characteristics of the three groups were:

- They lead generally unhealthy lifestyles.
- They can tend to lead passive lives – a significant proportion do not take deep responsibility for their own futures.
- The focus of their lives is very local.
- They are a homogeneous market, without markedly distinct individual needs and preferences.
- As consumers, they focus heavily on price, reliability and convenience, and are more influenced by straightforward benefit-based advertising, than by sophisticated lifestyle imagery (although they do value face-to-face contact).

---

[2] MOSAIC is a lifestyle segmentation tool that classifies all consumers in the UK into 61 types, aggregated into 11 groups.

○ They are unlikely to be influenced much by issues such as healthy ingredients, social/environmental responsibility or ethics.

○ They are receptive to the following communications channels: TV, posters, telemarketing and drop-in centres.

Insights gathered during scoping allowed the audience to be segmented into three distinct groups according to their behaviour:

○ Group 1: Do not check their breasts and are least likely to present to a health professional if an abnormality is detected.

○ Group 2: Might check their breasts, but not consciously or regularly, and only likely to present to a health professional if a lump is detected.

○ Group 3: Check breasts regularly and are likely to present to a health professional if an abnormality is detected.

Interventions were developed to target groups 1 and 2, but efforts were made to identify and use group 3 to spread their knowledge and behaviour throughout the community.

SCOPING RESEARCH

The scoping stage of the project comprised desk-based research, primary research with the target audience and interviews with key stakeholders.

Desk-based research was carried out in summer 2008 to provide an overview and analysis of existing secondary research and what is known from the evidence base of social marketing and other work relating to breast awareness, cancer and screening. The research focused on gathering information about the target audience, current UK policy and examples of good practice. However, the evidence base around breast awareness, particularly among women aged under 50, was scant. Research that did exist suggested that breast awareness is affected by a host of psychographic factors, including self-efficacy, confidence, body image and embarrassment.

To establish a baseline of local knowledge, awareness and behaviour around breast awareness, a street survey was carried out in summer 2009 in Ashton Hurst (intervention area) and South Denton (comparison area), which had been matched for age structure, deprivation and rural/urban mix. A face-to-face questionnaire was implemented with 185 women aged between 35 and 50 across the intervention and control areas.

To further explore local women's knowledge, behaviour and attitudes around breast awareness, and their barriers and motivators for being breast aware, primary research was conducted with women aged 35 to 50 living in Ashton Hurst and South Denton. This involved two focus groups with six to eight members of the public, and 15 women were interviewed, either individually or as part of a friendship pair.

Twenty in-depth interviews were also conducted with key stakeholders (such as GPs, nurses, and a range of other health professionals and community workers) to explore if and how service improvements could be made to increase breast awareness.

ACTIONABLE INSIGHTS

The findings from the street survey and qualitative research were largely consistent: women are aware of the dangers of breast cancer, but few regularly examine their breasts or feel confident they are doing it correctly and know what changes to look for, other than lumps. Barriers to breast awareness include a fear of finding breast cancer and a fatalistic view that early detection will not make much of a difference to the outcome. Most women have not been offered advice on breast awareness by their GP or nurse.

While women are unlikely to visit a mobile unit or stand, or attend workshops, they are amenable to receiving health messages in the community from non-health professionals and in non-health settings, such as in community centres or the workplace. Poster advertising, direct mail and articles in local newspapers were regarded as the most effective media channels.

The baseline survey and primary research with women found that, although many women are aware of the dangers of breast cancer and claim to check their breasts, most only check infrequently and feel they are probably doing it incorrectly. The majority of women associate breast awareness with finding lumps, and few are aware of other changes to look out for.

While most women are concerned about breast cancer, the barriers to being breast aware are varied and include: not seeing the benefits; not knowing what to look for; lack of confidence in their ability to self-examine; fear of finding cancer; having a fatalistic view; and not wanting to bother their GP.

Nurses seem to have an accurate understanding of what it means to be breast aware and report giving lifestyle advice, including about being breast aware. GPs seem to have a more basic understanding and do not routinely offer lifestyle advice. Health trainers[3] also have a potential role to play as they engage directly with people to offer advice on a wide range of lifestyle issues, but not specifically on being breast aware.

Interestingly, none of the professionals interviewed were spontaneously aware of the breast-awareness code, but were very positive about it when it was described to them. Although the nurses interviewed have a good understanding of what it means to be breast aware and report giving women advice about being breast aware, most of the women involved in the research had not received advice from their GP or nurse about breast awareness. However, women are amenable to receiving health messages in the community from non-health professionals and in non-health settings. Since some women worried about bothering their GP, and many considered the practice nurse the most appropriate person to give breast-awareness advice, nurses and community workers, rather than GPs, were particularly encouraged to proactively provide advice and support around breast awareness.

In light of these insights, the team arrived at an approach that mixed communication and community-based and service-led initiatives to ensure the target audience were made aware of the importance of breast awareness and were also prompted and facilitated to change their behaviour. There was a clear need to promote the breast-awareness five-point code consistently to the target audience and service providers to give women a full understanding of how to check, what to look for and why to act fast.

---

[3] Health trainers are a NHS scheme which trains up local community members to help their local residents to develop healthier behaviour and lifestyles in their own local communities. They offer practical support to change their behaviour to achieve their own choices and goals, such as stop-smoking support.

Four creative concepts for community-based initiatives were tested using focus groups with members of the target audience. The creative concept that clearly struck a chord with the audience was 'Breast Expert'. Using images of strong and confident women, 'Breast Expert' focused on the flexibility and ease of becoming breast aware, and showed that getting to know your breasts gives you a sense of empowerment and control.

There was also a need to engage with health and community professionals to reach the target women with clear and consistent messages around breast awareness.

 ## STAKEHOLDER ENGAGEMENT

STEERING GROUP

This project was jointly funded by NHS Tameside and Glossop and Tameside MBC. Members of the PCT's public-health team and the council's health-improvement team were responsible for steering the project and securing internal resources for development and delivery.

Chosen as one of ten social marketing learning demonstration sites, the project received guidance and support from the NSMC. The NSMC also provided funding for independent outcome evaluation, which was carried out by the London School of Hygiene & Tropical Medicine (LSHTM).

Members from these organisations formed the core project team and met regularly throughout the project to plan and coordinate work.

Healthcare professionals and community workers, such as GPs, practice nurses, Macmillan cancer nurses, health visitors, health trainers and community development workers, had an important role to play as key influencers of the target audience. Engagement activities included:

- Interviews in the scoping phase.
- A stakeholder workshop during the development phase to test creative concepts and intervention ideas.
- A launch event during implementation to brief stakeholders on the project and gain their buy-in.
- Face-to-face and written communication during implementation to coordinate, monitor and encourage progress.
- Interviews following the implementation phase to gather process evaluation data.

OTHER STAKEHOLDERS

Prior to implementation, the community development team approached local venues, such as schools, places of worship, library, pubs, hairdressers, stop-smoking service and dental practices, to distribute campaign posters and leaflets.

As funders of the learning demonstration sites scheme, the Social Marketing and Health-Related Behaviour team at the UK Department of Health (DH) was provided with periodic written updates of the project and invited to attend annual networking events. The final outcome evaluation report was sent to the team and a policy briefing sent to the DH cancer team.

During implementation, the PCT and Council communications team liaised with local press and media (for example, local newspapers) to promote the campaign and its activities.

INTERVENTION MIX

The strategy involved a mix of communication, community-based and service-led initiatives. This combination aimed to ensure that, not only would the target audience be made aware of the importance of breast awareness, but they would also be prompted and facilitated to change their behaviour.

- Community-based initiatives helped to strengthen the message and ensure the information reached the target audience. A free 'well woman' event, with a particular focus on breast awareness, was co-delivered with other local health and community stakeholders. Efforts were also made to identify and recruit breast-aware 'community champions' from the local population, who could help spread the message through peer networks.
- Service-led initiatives aimed to encourage health professionals to systematically and opportunistically influence and support women to become breast aware. Breast awareness materials and training sessions were offered to practice nurses, health trainers and community-development workers. These efforts are ongoing, with the longer-term aim of building breast awareness into service delivery to ensure its systematic inclusion in all relevant primary-care appointments. One prospective option is inclusion in GP contracts to ensure that breast awareness is routinely raised and discussed during cervical screening and family planning appointments.
- Communication initiatives provided women with a compelling case for regularly checking their breasts and reporting any changes to their GP as soon as possible. They also provided women with the information they needed to check their breasts and identify the changes requiring further investigation, as well as where to go for extra help and support.

PRODUCT

The core product (i.e. benefit promised) was early diagnosis, which results in simpler and more effective treatment and increased survival rates.

The actual product (i.e. the product or service you develop to deliver the core product benefits):

- Becoming a breast expert.
- Information leaflet and website, clearly outlining what changes to look out for and what to do if you notice any changes.
- Free 'well woman' events where women could find out more about breast awareness and other health and well-being issues.
- Community group proactive advice service.
- Opportunistic GP advice sessions.

The augmented product (the features that encourage and support uptake of the actual product or service) included:

- Training materials and workshops for nurses, health trainers and community development workers to encourage consistent delivery of messages and support to women around breast awareness.
- Free fun events.

PRICE

The main perceived 'costs' of being breast aware are non-monetary, namely the time and effort required to regularly self-check and to attend an appointment with a health professional if any changes are spotted. There are also the emotional costs of feeling uncomfortable with breast self-examination (particularly for minority ethnic women), worries about bothering their GP and fear of finding cancer.

PROMOTION

Being breast aware was promoted as something women could easily incorporate into their everyday routines, such as when bathing, moisturising or getting dressed.

Messages about breast awareness were delivered to the target group at their home (e.g. through direct mail from the PCT), in the local community (e.g. 'well woman' event at Hurst community centre, poster advertising in various local venues) and in health settings (e.g. discussions in a GP appointment).

Communication efforts emphasised the flexibility and ease of becoming breast aware and empowered women as 'breast experts' who can take control of their own health. Nurses, community workers and community groups were engaged to proactively offer advice and reassurance to their clients/members about breast awareness, and women were encouraged to speak to their practice nurse or a community worker about breast awareness if they preferred not to see their GP.

The local 'well woman' event was promoted as a free, fun event just for women and was held at a central community centre from early afternoon to evening. Along with health and well-being advice, attendees were offered freebies (e.g. goody bag, prize draw, refreshments), pampering (e.g. massages and manicures) and fun activities (e.g. yoga and pilates).

Strong and consistent messaging around breast awareness was key for this project, given the lack of women's understanding of the benefits of being breast aware, how to self-check and what changes to look out for.

KEY MESSAGES USED IN THE COMMUNICATIONS

- Early breast-cancer diagnosis results in simpler and more effective treatment and increased survival rates.
- Take control of your health – being breast aware significantly reduces your risk of dying from breast cancer.
- It's quick and easy to be breast aware and can be incorporated into your everyday routine.
- Being breast aware gives you peace of mind.

The campaign and its messages were promoted through a variety of activities, including:

- Face-to-face at health and community venues and local events.
- Poster advertising in outdoor, health and community settings.
- Information leaflet distributed to pharmacies, GP surgeries, pubs, hairdressers and other community venues.
- Direct mail to all women aged 35 to 50 on the PCT practice list.
- Local PR.
- A breast awareness website linked to the PCT and council websites.

See Figures 8.1 and 8.2.

Figure 8.1 **Breast Expert poster 1**

MONITORING AND EVALUATION

The outcome evaluation was independently carried out by the London School of Hygiene and Tropical Medicine and consisted of three components:

1 Prospective case-control study: To assess progress made by the project in achieving its aim of raising breast awareness among women aged 35 to 50 in Ashton Hurst. This comprised two waves of fieldwork – a baseline 'pre' survey (completed in April–June 2009), followed by a 'post' survey (completed in June–July 2010), conducted in Ashton Hurst and South Denton. The sample included around 100 women aged 35 to 50 in each of the two areas, and at both stages.
2 Qualitative research with key stakeholders: To explore the extent to which operational plans proposed were carried out, gauge acceptability of the interventions and examine factors that may have enhanced and/or hindered progress. This involved in-depth face-to-face interviews with eight stakeholders who were involved in the scoping, development and implementation of the campaign, and were held in July–August 2010.

Figure 8.2   Breast Expert poster 2

3   Qualitative research with target women: To explore women's experiences of the interventions, how useful they found them, and what effect (if any) they had on their breast awareness. This involved in-depth face-to-face interviews with 11 women in Ashton Hurst who had been exposed to at least one of the interventions. These were completed July–August 2010.

FINDINGS

A key objective of the campaign was to increase women's knowledge of the various symptoms to look out for, and promote the breast-awareness five-point code. When asked what the term 'breast aware' meant to them, the majority of post-survey respondents had some knowledge and understanding of it: 42.5 per cent of respondents said it was about checking or regularly checking your breasts for changes, 20 per cent said it was about looking for lumps and other changes, and around 15 per cent said it was about being aware of your breasts more generally (rather than looking specifically for symptoms). However, 10 per cent of respondents said being breast aware was about looking for lumps (without mentioning other symptoms).

Most women who reported checking their breasts were looking for lumps when they examined and were not so vigilant about other symptoms, like changes in breast appearance or feeling. However, compared to pre-survey results, a greater proportion of respondents to the post-survey mentioned looking for 'lumps and other abnormalities', rather than looking for just lumps (pre: 49 per cent; post: 61 per cent).

Another key objective of the campaign was to boost women's confidence in their ability to self-examine (i.e. that there is no one right way to check). Compared to results gathered before the campaign, the intervention area saw a drop in the proportion of women who were 'not at all confident' of noticing a change, and compared to the comparison area, a greater proportion of respondents reported being 'very confident' of noticing a change (29 per cent compared to 24 per cent in the comparison group, post- intervention).

According to the post-survey, 40 per cent of respondents in Ashton Hurst (compared to 31.5 per cent in South Denton, the control area) had seen, heard or received something about breast awareness during the campaign period. Of these, 25 per cent said the information prompted them to examine their breasts more regularly and 41.7 per cent (compared to 31.8 per cent in South Denton) said the information made them clearer about what is normal for them and what changes to look for.

From the scoping research, it had been recognised that, in order to achieve a sustainable behaviour change, health professionals had to be involved and actively promoting the five-point code. An increase in women reported being offered advice in breast awareness by their general practitioner or practice nurse (24.2 per cent to 31.4 per cent). However, an increase was also recorded in the comparison group (20.9 per cent to 27.4 per cent).

 ## LESSONS LEARNT

The key lessons learnt can be separated into what worked well and what worked less well.

WHAT WORKED WELL

- A strong history of joint working between the PCT and the council, which established a shared function for public-health commissioning, allowed extra local funding to be secured to supplement the initial £18,000 funding for the project.
- The local community events were well attended and more women felt they were able to be breast aware.
- Costs were kept down by using existing resources as much as possible. For example, community-development workers and their networks, specialist cancer nurses, and internal support mechanisms (e.g. PCT and Council communications teams and their own design and print suppliers) were used to capitalise on resources that required no extra cost.

WHAT WORKED LESS WELL

- Despite efforts to engage GPs and nurses in the campaign, clinician involvement during the project was disappointing due to various reasons, and training planned for practice nurses by a Macmillan cancer nurse had to be postponed to late 2010. Sufficient lead-in time needs to be built in and senior level buy-in secured from the start to gain active involvement from GP staff.
- Despite the planned efforts aimed at health professionals, the campaign launched at an unfortunate time. The launch coincided with swine flu hitting the UK, therefore all NHS staff time was diverted onto swine flu.
- Feedback from stakeholders and target women highlighted the importance of family and social networks as key avenues for encouraging women to become breast aware. In addition to print and online media, providing information and the option to discuss any issues or

concerns in person would greatly increase women's confidence to self-examine and spot any changes. Greater use of word-of-mouth and face-to-face communication would help to motivate and support women to become breast aware, without requiring the expenditure of paid-for advertising.

CHAPTER RECAP

Despite the acknowledgement that there are always elements which are more successful than others, people are often reluctant to publicise and talk openly about what didn't work as well. However, understanding what didn't work and why is often as valuable to others looking to do similar projects as just being told about the successes. In this case study, due to the generation of a baseline, and the ongoing monitoring and evaluation throughout the campaign period, it could be clearly determined what elements worked well and which did not.

In the next chapter we will learn how opinion leaders can be used to influence social norms, and reach traditionally 'difficult to engage' target audiences.

SELF-REVIEW QUESTIONS

1 This project was evaluated in three components: pre- and post-street surveys; face-to-face stakeholder interviews; and telephone interviews with target women. What kinds of questions would you consider asking in each component?
2 Enhancing confidence and empowering women were important components of this project. What additional methods and interventions would you have developed to empower women and move them to become breast aware?
3 As discussed in the lessons learnt, clinician involvement during the project was disappointing. What might some of the reasons for poor engagement have been, and how might you have addressed these?

REFERENCES

NHS Information Centre. (2008). Breast Screening Programme 2006–2007 Data Tables. Available at www.ic.nhs.uk/statistics-and-data-collections/screening/breast-cancer/breast-screening-programme-england-2006-07-ns. Accessed on 1 October 2010.

Tameside and Glossop Primary Care Trust. (2006). Public Health Annual Report 2005–2006. Available online at: www.tamesideandglossop.nhs.uk/upload/documents/corporate/annual%20reports/Tameside%20Public%20Health%20Report%202005%20-%202006.pdf. Accessed 1 October 2010.

UK Department of Health. (2006). Be breast aware. [Online] Available online at: www.dh.gov.uk/prod_consum_dh/groups/dh_digitalassets/@dh/@en/documents/digitalasset/dh_062743.pdf. Accessed 1 October 2010.

9 REACHING THE 'HARD TO REACH'

VIGNETTE: RED CARD

KEY WORD: HARD TO REACH

Red Card: Equipping girls to sideline risky behaviour

To prevent the spread of HIV/AIDS and give girls the confidence to say 'no', the Academy of Educational Development (AED), a non-profit global organisation, turned to the signal football referees use to kick aggressive players out of a game – a red card. Red Cards are now the tool Malagasy girls use as an ice breaker to start conversations on sensitive topics and to stop risky and inappropriate behaviours at school, parties, their homes, and on dates. As part of a larger health-communications programme, called C-Change, funded by USAID, Red Cards have been distributed to 1.5 million young women across the country.

To kick off the initiative, AED ran television spots showing teenage girls in common, but difficult, situations. For example, one spot features a boyfriend who won't listen to a girl's polite, but insistent, refusals to drink alcohol at a party. Not knowing what else to say, she draws a Red Card from her pocket, shakes her head with confident disapproval, says, 'I told you three times I just want a soda; why won't you listen to me?' and leaves.

As the initial series of four spots was airing, dozens of two-hour training sessions were held in schools and clubs and with sports teams so that girls could practise using the Red Card.

Within a couple weeks, women were saying they don't go anywhere without their Red Cards. The rates of violence against women decreased instantly too.

For more information, and a full evaluation of the programme, go to: www.aed.org.

This vignette features a project where brand awareness and positive attitudes towards the programme were crucial, and it became normalised to use the Red Card. This chapter describes an innovative programme which works with hard-to-reach groups, where the social norm is to smoke, to try and normalise a tobacco-free culture.

ABOUT THIS CHAPTER

When starting a project, it is often difficult to gain consensus from the whole project team and key stakeholders on who actually the target audience should be. The phrase 'hard to reach' is frequently used to refer to those living in greatest poverty. However, these people may not be the 'hardest to reach' group. In this chapter you will learn:

- ○ To think 'outside the box' when identifying who your hard to reach audience actually is.
- ○ How taking a segmentation approach, using psychographic variables, can help you prioritise and reach your target audience effectively.

CASE STUDY: PSYCHOGRAPHIC MARKET SEGMENTATION TO REDUCE SMOKING AMONG YOUNG ADULTS IN BARS AND NIGHTCLUBS

Pamela M. Ling, University of California San Francisco; Jeffrey W. Jordan, Rescue Social Change Group

PROJECT OVERVIEW

Whilst overall smoking prevalence is decreasing in the USA, young adults (aged 18–26 years) continue to have a high smoking prevalence. A social marketing programme, 'Commune', was established to try to reduce smoking prevalence in young adults. Commune was implemented in San Diego, California, with funding from the Public Health Trust, the Flight Attendant Medical Research Institute and the Tobacco-Related Disease Research Program through grants awarded to the University of California, San Francisco (UCSF) Center for Tobacco Control Research and Education.

Rescue Social Change Group (RSCG), a US-based social marketing company with a focus on youth and young adults, implemented all programme activities. The programme was evaluated independently by the University of California San Francisco Center for Tobacco Control Research and Education.

This project began in July 2007 and this case study includes activities and outcomes up to 30 August 2010. As of 1 December 2010, this programme was still in place. The programme operated with a combined intervention and evaluation budget of US$250,000 per year.

PROJECT RATIONALE

Young adults (aged 18–26 years) continue to have a high smoking prevalence in the US, even in states like California where smoking rates have dropped dramatically (California Department of Health Services, 2006). However, smoking-prevention efforts have almost entirely concentrated on primary prevention amongst adolescents, despite the fact that the process of smoking initiation takes several years, extending well into young adulthood (Pierce et al., 1991; Gilpin et al., 2001; Everett et al., 1999). In fact, many experimenters and occasional smokers either quit smoking or progress to become established smokers during young adulthood (Ling and Glantz, 2002a; Wechsler, 1998; Rigotti et al., 2000; Lantz, 2003).

Young adults are the youngest legal targets of tobacco marketing, and tobacco companies have extensive experience of developing campaigns tailored to different groups of young adults that promote attractive smoker identities within social environments such as bars and nightclubs (Sepe et al., 2002; Katz and Lavack, 2002; Sepe and Glantz, 2002). Previously, secret tobacco industry documents containing thousands of pages of market research on young adult smoking behaviours informed the industry's development of marketing campaigns targeted to 'psychographic' segments (segments based on common attitude and lifestyle profiles) of the young adult population (Ling and Glantz, 2002b). Tobacco advertising targeting young adults aims to create positive smoker images, identities and social norms for smoking (Ling and Glantz, 2002a). In complementary efforts, tobacco companies also work to affect the social context of smoking to keep both smoking behaviour and the industry 'legitimate' parts of society (McDaniel et al., 2006; Holm Group, 1998).

Bar and club attendance and exposure to marketing in these venues are strongly associated with smoking (Gilpin et al., 2005). A study of young adults in California reported approximately 33 per cent of all young adults go to bars and clubs at least sometimes, and bar and club goers had over three times greater odds to be daily smokers and over three times the odds to be social smokers (Gilpin et al., 2005). Since bars and clubs attract young adults at higher tobacco-use risk, these are environments that should be considered for tobacco prevention and cessation messages. To date, most interventions addressing young adult smoking occur in colleges or health centres, rather than social environments (Berg et al., 2009; Hughes et al., 2009; Copeland et al., 2009; Klatt et al., 2009; McDermott et al., 2008; Thomas et al., 2009; Riley et al., 2008; Tevyaw et al., 2009).

Like the tobacco industry's promotion efforts (Hendlin et al., 2010), this programme focuses on the most socially successful young adults who set trends for the rest of the community, and who tend to be the ones others look to for cues about social norms, i.e. 'Trendsetters'. The Commune programme was developed to reach high-risk young adult populations by utilising the tobacco industry's market-segmentation principles and implementing strategies the tobacco industry uses to sell cigarettes to young adults. The Commune programme was strategically designed to counteract aggressive marketing in bars and nightclubs, reinforce non-smoking environments, and de-normalise tobacco use, in order to reduce smoking among young adults in social settings.

 ## AIMS AND OBJECTIVES

The aim of Commune is to reduce tobacco use amongst trendsetting young adults within a specific subculture known as 'hipsters'[1] in San Diego, California, using a specialised proprietary form of social marketing developed by Rescue Social Change Group known as 'Social Branding'.

---

[1] 'Hipsters' is a term commonly used in the US to describe people, mostly young adults, who reject mainstream fashion and music trends, as well as mainstream bars and nightclubs, in favour of smaller, boutique fashions, bars and local musicians. Rather than frequent a megaclub, Hipsters prefer smaller environments that feature performances by local bands that are followed by DJs who play underground music. While they reject mainstream corporations, they do not reject the tobacco industry and have a high prevalence of tobacco use. The hipster's desire not to be mainstream often results in this group of young adults being trendsetting amongst young adults. This subculture has even been mentioned by name within tobacco-industry documents as an important target for their marketing practices.

The following is the objective of the 'Commune Social Branding' programme. The target market is defined as young adults aged 18–26, who identify with the hipster subculture, are concerned about their social status amongst peers and live in San Diego:

○ Decrease the number of young adult hipsters who have smoked cigarettes in the past 30 days by 10 per cent over two years.

 FORMATIVE RESEARCH

Unlike traditional health interventions targeting demographic groups, tobacco marketing efforts focus on 'psychographic' groups defined by common attitudes, beliefs, lifestyle activities, values and social circles (Ling and Glantz, 2002b). Counter-engineering these strategies, Commune development involved innovative psychographic market segmentation based on formative research and the Social Branding model. Formative research utilised mixed-method qualitative and quantitative strategies.

First, during exploratory research conducted with 219 club-and-bar goers, we measured socio-cultural group affiliations using pictures and bar/club preference ratings. We also measured level of social concern, demographic characteristics, smoking-related attitudes and tobacco use. We identified four major social-cultural segments among young adults attending bars: Mainstream (52 per cent) Lesbian, Gay, Bisexual and Transgender (20 per cent), Urban (21 per cent) and Hipsters (17 per cent). Hipsters were a small but high-risk group that resisted traditional health messaging and had the highest current smoking prevalence (50 per cent). Multivariate logistic regression controlling for demographics showed 'hipster' affiliation was significantly associated with current smoking (OR 2.36 95 per cent CI [1.13, 4.92]).

Social concern was defined as how much the respondent prioritises social success within his/her social network. This measure of social concern consists of a short series of items where respondents select the best self-descriptor from a series of binary choices, such as 'Center of Attention/Lay Low' and 'Partier/Studier', which reflect self-identification as a social leader. In addition, respondents report attitudes, such as whether they have considered being an entertainer or actor, which may reflect desire or power to influence others, and intensity of their social behaviour reflected by the frequency of going out at night, and how late they stay out. Responses to these series of questions generate a raw score for the Social Concern Index, and respondents scoring above the 75 per cent percentile are defined as having high levels of social concern. A linear dose response relationship can be observed between the social concern index and current smoking. For example, social concern was significantly associated with current smoking ($p < 0.001$), with increased odds of 20 per cent for each point increase on the social concern index score (OR = 1.20 [1.14, 1.26]). In addition, having a social concern score in the top quarter percentile of all survey respondents was also significantly associated with smoking (OR 2.86 [1.50, 5.44]).

The intercept survey also served as a screen to recruit participants for the qualitative components of the formative research process. Formative qualitative research (focus groups and key informant interviews) was used to assess the values, beliefs and attitudes of young adults attending bars and nightclubs. Nine socio-cultural-specific focus groups were conducted. In focus groups, Hipsters were consistently identified by all participants and were perceived to have the highest smoking prevalence. We also discovered hipsters preferred bars and clubs in a local neighbourhood called North Park, and were more likely to be established regular or daily smokers. These smokers had low levels of perceived threat, highly valued personal freedom, highly valued the creative arts, perceived their community as tightly-knit and had negative attitudes towards capitalism.

During the focus groups, exercises were conducted to encourage participants to talk about associations and beliefs about themselves that they may not normally be comfortable expressing. By providing participants with pictures of unknown others, and asking them to describe these individuals, the researchers were able to explore subconscious associations and beliefs. During these exercises, participants expressed that many individuals began smoking to fit into a particular social group and that pictures of individuals associated with the hipster subculture in particular were more often perceived to be smokers. Participants also suggested that some young adults would smoke as a strategy to stand out in their peer group and be perceived as more socially adept. Smoking was believed to start in social environments and to be perpetuated by friends who were already established smokers. While those established smokers would not verbally encourage smoking, social situations in which smoking occurred would make those not smoking feel uncomfortable and out of place. The combination of a positive image of smoking, desire to be socially accepted or 'cool', and frequent situations where friends would be smoking were qualitatively associated with smoking within the hipster subculture.

Following the formative research, a survey of 1,198 young adults attending hipster bars/clubs identified through a venue-based random sampling method, confirmed the high smoking prevalence within the hipster subculture. In this sample, 56 per cent of respondents were smokers, and respondents who were most strongly affiliated with the hipster subculture had a smoking prevalence of 61 per cent. The general young adult population in California has a smoking prevalence of 18 per cent. Hipsters with high levels of social concern had a smoking prevalence of 77 per cent. Based on this research, the target audience for the 'Commune Social Branding' programme was selected as young adults age 18–26 who identify with the hipster subculture in San Diego, California, and prioritised hipsters with high levels of social concern.

ACTIONABLE INSIGHTS

Formative research showed the negative health effects of smoking were largely irrelevant to the hipster target population, or were regarded as common knowledge. For example, compared to a national sample, the San Diego hipster trendsetters were more likely to agree smoking was useful to control stress or to socialize, but also more likely to agree that second-hand smoke is dangerous, perhaps as a result of California's longstanding media campaign emphasising the dangers of second-hand smoke (Ling et al., 2008). However, hipsters had solid convictions about social justice, were anti-corporate and strongly supported their local arts community. To increase message relevance to the target market, Commune anti-tobacco messaging emphasised the behaviours of the tobacco industry that are at odds with the values and worldview of the hipster subculture.

AUTHENTICITY

○ The hipster community was self-described as tightly knit and sceptical of the general public. Outsiders from different subcultures or people perceived to be 'trying too hard to fit in' were easily identified among the group and maligned. With this in mind, we determined that social leaders from the target market needed to be involved in the messaging process.

SOCIAL JUSTICE

○ Hipster young adults tend to be politically liberal and outspoken about their support of social-justice issues. This finding led us to focus on disseminating messages regarding the tobacco industry that focus on issues such as global warming and deforestation, political corruption, inhumane animal testing and world hunger, among other social-justice issues.

RESISTANCE TO CONVENTIONAL HEALTH MESSAGES

○ The target market was extremely sceptical of overt anti-tobacco messages. A nihilistic philosophy seemed to be prevalent among the group, thus making the perceived health threats irrelevant. This finding suggested that disseminating health messages would not progress our overall efforts, and could potentially hurt the brand's ability to communicate non-health-oriented anti-tobacco messages effectively.

CORPORATE BEHAVIOUR

○ Hipster young adults were highly distrustful of large corporations. This presented the team with an opportunity to expose the manipulative marketing efforts of the industry.

LOCAL ARTS COMMUNITY

○ Young adults who identify with the hipster subculture value creativity and highly support the local arts community, which includes music, fashion, painting, photography, graphic design and multi-media. The arts are perceived as an opportunity for eclectic self-expression.

ADDITIONAL KEY FINDINGS

○ It was found that there were few non-smoking opinion leaders among the target audience, though many smokers wanted to quit. Unfortunately, however, there was little interest in existing traditional cessation resources such as calling the state quit line, and few had access to regular medical care for smoking-cessation assistance, thus making it more difficult for these leaders to quit smoking successfully. This suggested a need for a tailored smoking-cessation programme for hipsters.

 STAKEHOLDER ENGAGEMENT

A core component of the Social Branding model is the engagement of peer leaders, as perceived by those at highest risk. Amongst hipsters, local artists, musicians and fashion designers were perceived as leaders. In addition, local bar tenders and bar managers were some of the most socially connected. In order for culture change, and then subsequently behaviour change, to occur, these stakeholders had to be genuinely engaged in the programme, and they had to authentically redistribute the message themselves. These leaders were engaged in multiple ways, including ongoing message development, performance opportunities at events, opportunities to participate in cessation groups and other strategies that are part of the Social Branding model.

In order to engage funders and university leadership, the programme strategy had to be founded on a comprehensive logic model that also informed the evaluation. Here, the Social Branding model provided behaviour change principles that were used to implement the strategy and measure changes in attitudes and perceptions that were theorised to lead to behaviour change. By explaining programme process in terms of behaviour-change theory and presenting research findings that documented progress on a predefined logic model, funders and university leadership were successfully engaged in this non-traditional public-health programme.

BARRIERS

A competition analysis was performed to identify potential barriers. The primary competitor for the Commune programme is the tobacco industry. When Commune began, the industry was actively promoting smoking to the hipster population through bar and club nights and special events. While the industry has a significantly larger budget than Commune, we found that the industry's promotions to this subculture were largely shallow and impersonal. There appeared to be a critical opportunity to compete with the industry in an environment where the public-health community had been largely absent. In addition, the public-health community lacked tailored interventions for young adult subcultures to match tobacco-industry tailored advertising. In contrast, Commune is intentionally targeted to the hipster subculture with significant tailoring based on hipster values to counter tobacco marketing efforts in bars and clubs.

Tobacco industry marketing capitalises on pro-tobacco attitudes expressed by hipsters who enjoy smoking and believe it should be a part of their culture. These attitudes are also more common among smokers in general, and since hipsters had a high (over 50 per cent) smoking prevalence, pro-smoking attitudes were more common in this community. Thus we expected to encounter many young adults in this community who did not want to quit and did not want to see their culture become anti-tobacco. Because this subculture has been associated with smoking for many years, pro-smoking young adults may resist the Commune programme strenuously. In order to discourage this, it was important for Commune to establish authenticity within the hipster community first, and to gradually increase its anti-tobacco messaging strength, being careful not to attack smokers.

Finally, we anticipated the Commune programme would encounter some barriers from the public-health community itself. Few public-health programmes have ventured into bars and clubs, often believing that public health's presence in these environments would condone or encourage the other unhealthy activities not being addressed by the present programme, such as binge drinking. In order to demonstrate to public-health officials that pro-health messages within bars would not encourage alcohol consumption, the evaluation also measured drinking and binge drinking behaviours, even though these were not part of the intervention's objectives.

 METHODS MIX

Formative research revealed that, prior to addiction, the perceived value of tobacco use for this population is social benefit. Hipster young adults associate smoking with their identity and believe that smoking makes them more rebellious, trendsetting, social and artistic. An anti-tobacco message would need to strip smoking of these perceived benefits and associate the same benefits with a tobacco-free lifestyle.

The marketing mix was then developed to address this key insight.

PRODUCT

As defined by the Social Branding model, Communes product is an anti-tobacco brand, which embodies an anti-smoking message that is specifically appealing to the targeted segment of hipster young adults. If the message is the product, then the product includes the following product features:

○ Hipster Values: Smoking does not align with the values of the hipster culture because the tobacco industry is socially irresponsible.
○ Social Status: Socially well-known hipsters in the community are more often choosing to be smoke-free or quit today than ever before.
○ Social Norms: The majority of hipsters support a tobacco-free lifestyle.
○ Behavioural Function: Hipsters enjoy socialising more without smoking.

Since the product was intangible, each component of our marketing mix would have to reinforce the product features described above to associate social benefits with being tobacco-free.

While the primary product, the Commune brand, was intangible, a few secondary, tangible products were created to support the behaviour change. First, every month a new local artist created a poster that featured an anti-tobacco message (see figure 9.4): 100 of these posters were printed, numbered and signed by the artist for distribution at events and throughout the community. Second, each month a local fashion designer created a t-shirt that also included an anti-tobacco fact: 30 of these shirts were manufactured and sold at events as well as distributed to influential local young adults. Finally, in order to assist regular smokers who were ready to quit, a bar-based cessation group was piloted. Occurring twice within the reported time period, the groups met weekly for 8–12 weeks at a local bar and received support from Commune staff and tobacco-cessation counsellors. Monetary incentives were provided for reductions in tobacco use and quitting. Each week, participants who reduced their carbon-monoxide level on a breathalyser device were given $5 and those who successfully quit by the end of the group were given $20. A group-tracking chart was also used to follow each participant's progress and to support and celebrate tobacco-use reductions in the overall group. (See Figure 9.1.)

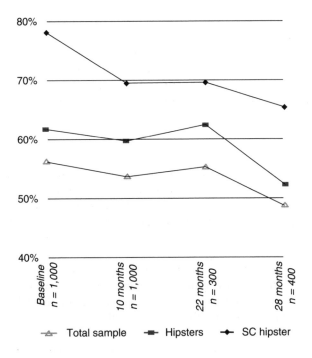

Figure 9.1   30-day smoking prevalence

PRICE/EXCHANGE

In consideration of price, the product was designed to lower the social cost of a tobacco-free lifestyle for the target population. Prior to Commune, a hipster young adult would have to pay the high social cost of going against the norms of his or her peer culture to live tobacco-free. However, by associating the product with the values of the culture, Commune made a smoke-free lifestyle more socially affordable. The Commune message removed a social barrier to becoming smoke-free, and introduced a social benefit. To make a smoke-free lifestyle socially valued, Commune introduced itself to the population as an events promoter.

As part of the Social Branding model, Commune hosted an event every month at a different bar or club. Each event included participation from local community leaders, such as bands, artists and fashion designers, to establish the Commune brand as a social leader. Once Commune had successfully included community leaders and attracted a large audience at a few events, the brand earned the necessary leverage to be able to introduce a tobacco-free lifestyle as socially acceptable and even desirable, which in turn reduced the 'price' of living smoke-free.

PLACE

The distribution, or 'place', of this product was a critical component of the programme. Smoke-free messages are typically distributed through brochures at health centres, mass media or health fairs. None of these distribution channels effectively reached hipster young adults.

While bars and clubs seemed like the ideal places to deliver the product, there was a concern about message resistance, since young adults frequent these venues expecting to socialise. The programme ran the risk of looking like an unwelcome intruder if the attendees did not expect anti-tobacco messaging. For this reason, Commune events were hosted each month on a Wednesday night (a night that is not typically busy) so that young adults attending the event would also be choosing to expose themselves to the message.

PROMOTION

Multiple strategies were used to promote the product. At the events, the MC or host would present the message on stage throughout the night. The featured bands and DJs would be asked to reinforce the message during their performance through announcements, and message cards reinforcing the current anti-tobacco fact were distributed. Finally, trained brand ambassadors communicated the message throughout the event by conversing with patrons.

Following each event, monthly mailings were designed that included the artist's poster and interviews with different local leaders, discussing both their own trades (such as being a designer or band) as well as their opinion of tobacco use and the industry. This mailer was sent between events to reinforce the message regularly.

Brand ambassadors continued messaging efforts outside of events. Trained by the programme's staff, these local, non-smoker leaders were empowered through customised Social Branding training, to help them develop the belief that they have the ability to influence their peers. Once empowered, they are given examples of how to provide culturally-tailored anti-tobacco messaging in social environments. They were offered t-shirts designed by local fashion designers that present anti-tobacco messaging in a fashionable and culturally relevant way. Brand ambassadors are offered new shirts every few months for continuing to support Communes message (See Figure 9.3).

MONITORING AND EVALUATION

Dr Ling and her colleagues from the University of California San Francisco Center for Tobacco Control Research and Education designed a random venue-based sampling strategy to gather cross-sectional samples of young adults who are likely to frequent the targeted bars/clubs. The evaluation began with a baseline sample of 1,000 young adults (age 18–26), followed by another 1,000-person sample after ten months of intervention. Beginning at 22 months after launch, 300–400 young adults are surveyed every four months, totalling 1,000 subjects per year. The baseline, ten-month follow-up, and three 400-person follow-up samples have been gathered (22, 28 and 32 months). Figures 9.1 and 9.2 show findings from each data point for the following three groups: the total sample; the subgroup of young adults who most strongly identified as hipsters; and the subgroup of young adults identified as hipsters and measured to have high social concern (labelled: SC Hipsters).

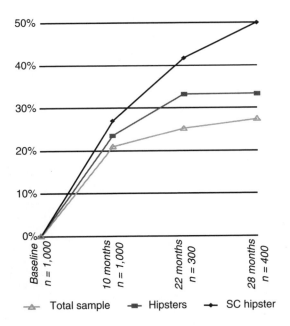

Figure 9.2   Exposure to commune

Campaign exposure was measured using Commune brand recognition, liking Commune, having attended an event and visiting the website. Brand exposure by all measures has increased over time, even though intervention activities and costs have remained stable. Hipsters and high social concern hipsters report higher levels of exposure than the rest of the sample (Figure 9.2). Liking Commune was measured using a five-point Likert scale, and more than half of those exposed to Commune reported liking Commune (either 'I like it' or 'I really like it'), with more hipsters and high social concern hipsters liking Commune than the general sample.

Compared to baseline, a significant decrease in current (past 30-day) smoking was observed in the total sample attending hipster bars from 56.3 per cent to 48.8 per cent at the 28-month follow up (p = 0.006, OR = 0.74 95 per cent CI [0.60, 0.92]). Among those who identified most strongly as hipsters, we observed a significant decrease in smoking from 61.6 per cent at baseline to 52.3 per cent at 28 months (p = 0.01, OR = 0.68 95 per cent CI [0.51, 0.91]). Among the hipsters with highest levels of social concern, we observed a 16 per cent decrease in smoking from 78.1 per cent to 65.4 per cent at 28 months (p = 0.07, OR = 0.53 [0.27, 1.06]). Both campaign exposure and decreases in smoking prevalence were largest among the hipsters with highest levels of social concern. We also observed an unexpected significant decrease in past-month binge drinking from 78.5 per cent to 69.6 per cent at 28 months (p < 0.001, OR = 0.63 [0.49, 0.80], compared to baseline).

Figure 9.3   T-Shirts for brand ambassadors

FINDINGS

The 'Commune Social Branding' programme set out to influence a subculture where smoking is perceived positively and is the norm. Despite these barriers to entry for an anti-tobacco programme, Commune has shown that a programme can not only conduct messaging in this community but can become a trendsetter. Communes events have grown to capacity, selling out local bars and clubs on nights when they are usually empty. Local cultural leaders eagerly await their chance to participate in a Commune event, leading to event partners being booked three months in advance. These accomplishments make it possible for Commune to deliver anti-tobacco messages in an authentic and effective manner, simply through events and direct mail. Other, more expensive and mainstream marketing channels, such as TV commercials, would have not been perceived as authentic to this subculture. With this approach, a subculture with a high concentration of tobacco use has been exposed to anti-tobacco messaging.

Figure 9.4   Poster created by local artist

Source: Jeff Jordon, Rescue Social Change Group. http://rescuescg.com

In 28 months, brand awareness, positive attitudes towards the programme and perceived social authority of the brand continue to grow. More importantly, tobacco use has been significantly reduced, with the largest reductions amongst the highest at-risk group, the high social concern hipsters. With continued efforts, the programme has the potential to cause change amongst a group of people that has been missed by most other anti-tobacco programmes.

 LESSONS LEARNT

Bars and clubs are important venues for interventions for young adults. Young adults attending bars and nightclubs are less likely to be reached by traditional methods, and they

report very high levels of both tobacco and alcohol use. Young adults in these venues are exposed to aggressive tobacco marketing, with little or no presence from public-health efforts.

Psychographic segmentation is a highly effective way to identify groups at the highest risk, and thus to use resources most efficiently. While this programme was successfully designed to reach the hipster subculture directly, this strategy was based on lessons learnt from other programmes. Formative research showed that programmes designed to reach the general adult or youth population were being ignored by this group. The success of Commune demonstrates the promise of culturally tailored interventions for young adults.

Interventions tailored to reflect the values of a subculture and the motivations of those who prioritise social success are able to reach those at the highest risk and change their behaviour. While identified as a potential concern by some health officials, interventions to decrease cigarette smoking among young adults in bars do not appear to increase alcohol use. Consequently, more interventions should focus on bars and clubs based on the high-risk behaviour prevalence in these environments.

CHAPTER RECAP

This chapter demonstrates the effectiveness of using a psychographic segmentation approach. This approach helped to identify and reach a high-risk group, and therefore use resources effectively.

In the next chapter we will see how all elements of the marketing mix can be combine to create effective, multi-faceted interventions.

SELF-REVIEW QUESTIONS

1   There are a number of factors which should be considered when deciding upon your primary segment; for example, size of segment, at risk, reachability, ability to influence. This project identified the hipsters as their target segment, due to their being high risk. Thinking about a project you have worked on or read about, what factors did they consider when prioritising their target segment?
2   Think about your own geographical area. What types of promotional activities and channels would you do to appeal to the hipster segment?

REFERENCES

Berg, C. J., Lust, K. A., Sanem, J. R., Kirch, M. A., Rudie, M., Ehlinger, E., Ahluwalia, J. S. and An, L. C. (2009). Smoker self-identification versus recent smoking among college students. *American Journal of Preventive Medicine*, 36(4): 333–6.

California Department of Health Services, Tobacco Control Section. (2006). 18–24 year old smoking prevalence. Available from: www.cdph.ca.gov/programs/tobacco/Documents/CTCP18-24YrOld06.pdf. Accessed 18 February 2007.

Copeland, A. L., Kulesza, M. and Hecht, G. S. (2009). Pre-quit depression level and smoking expectancies for mood management predict the nature of smoking withdrawal symptoms in college women smokers. *Addictive Behaviors*, 34(5): 481–3.

Everett, S. A., Husten, C. G., Kann, L., Warren, C. W., Sharp, D. and Crossett, L. (1999). Smoking initiation and smoking patterns among US college students. *Journal of American College Health*, 48(2): 55–60.

Gilpin, E. A., Emery, S. L., Farkas, A. J., Distefan, J. M., White, M. M. and Pierce, J. P. (2001). *The California Tobacco Control Program: A Decade of Progress, 1989–1999*. La Jolla, CA: University of California San Diego.

Gilpin, E. A., White, V. M. and Pierce J. P. (2005). How effective are tobacco industry bar and club marketing efforts in reaching young adults? *Tobacco Control*, 14(3): 186–92.

Hendlin, Y., Anderson, S. J. and Glantz S. A. (2010). 'Acceptable rebellion': Marketing hipster aesthetics to sell Camel cigarettes. *Tobacco Control*, 19(3): 213–22.

Holm Group, Philip Morris. (1998). Sunrise Social Acceptability Survey Tracking I. (University of San Diego, California: Legacy Tobacco Documents Library). Available from: http://legacy.library.ucsf.edu/tid/fkj05c00. Accessed 17 February 2007.

Hughes, J. R., Cohen, B. and Callas, P. W. (2009). Treatment seeking for smoking cessation among young adults. *Journal of Substance Abuse Treatment*, 37(2): 211–13.

Katz, S. K. and Lavack, A. M. (2002). Tobacco related bar promotions: Insights from tobacco industry documents. *Tobacco Control*, 11(S1): 92–101.

Klatt C., Berg, C. J., Thomas, J. L., Ehlinger, E., Ahluwalia, J. S. and An, L. C. (2008). The role of peer e-mail support as part of a college smoking-cessation website. *American Journal of Preventive Medicine*, 35(S6): S471–8.

Lantz, P. M. (2003). Smoking on the rise among young adults: Implications for research and policy. *Tobacco Control*, 12(S1): 60–70.

Ling, P. M. and Glantz, S. A. (2002a). Why and how the tobacco industry sells cigarettes to young adults: Evidence from industry documents. *American Journal of Public Health*, 92(6): 908–16.

Ling, P. M. and Glantz, S. A. (2002b). Using tobacco-industry marketing research to design more effective tobacco-control campaigns. *Journal of the American Medical Association*, 287(22): 2983–9.

Ling, P. M., Neilands, T. B. and Glantz, S. A. (2008). Using psychographic segmentation to identify high risk young adult smokers. In FAMRI (Flight Attendant Medical Research Institute) (ed.), FAMRI Annual Scientific Symposium, Boston, MA, 10–14 May. Miami, FL: FAMRI.

McDaniel, P. A., Smith, E. A. and Malone, R. E. (2006). Philip Morris's Project Sunrise: Weakening tobacco control by working with it. *Tobacco Control*, 15(3): 215–23.

McDermott, L., Dobson, A. and Owen, N. (2008). Smoking reduction and cessation among young adult women: A 7-year prospective analysis. *Nicotine & Tobacco Research*, 10(9): 1457–66.

Pierce, J. P., Naquin, M., Gilpin, E., Giovino, G., Mills, S. and Marcus, S. (1991). Smoking initiation in the United States: A role for worksite and college smoking bans. *Journal of the National Cancer Institute*, 83(14): 1009–13.

Rigotti, N. A., Lee, J. E. and Wechsler, H. (2000). US college students' use of tobacco products: Results of a national survey. *Journal of the American Medical Association*, 284(6): 699–705.

Riley, W., Obermayer, J. and Jean-Mary, J. (2008). Internet and mobile phone text messaging intervention for college smokers. *Journal of American College Health*, 57(2): 245–8.

Sepe, E. and Glantz, S. A. (2002). Bar and club tobacco promotions in the alternative press: targeting young adults. *American Journal of Public Health*, 92(1): 75–8.

Sepe, E., Ling, P. M. and Glantz, S. A. (2002). Smooth moves: Bar and nightclub tobacco promotions that target young adults. *American Journal of Public Health*, 92(3): 414–19.

Tevyaw, T. O., Colby, S. M., Tidey, J. W., Kahler, C. W., Rohsenow, D. J., Barnett, N. P., Gwaltney, C. J. and Monti, P. M. (2009). Contingency management and motivational enhancement: A randomized clinical trial for college student smokers. *Nicotine & Tobacco Research*, 11(6): 739–49.

Thomas, J. L., Gerber, T. A., Brockman, T. A., Patten, C. A., Schroeder, D. R. and Offord, K.P. (2008). Willingness among college students to help a smoker quit. *Journal of American College Health*, 57(3): 273–80.

Wechsler, H., Rigotti, N. A., Gledhill-Hoyt, J. and Lee, H. (1998). Increased levels of cigarette use among college students: A cause for national concern. *Journal of the American Medical Association*, 280(19): 1673–8. [Published erratum appears in *Journal of the American Medical Association*, 281(2) (1999): 136.]

10 USING A FULL INTERVENTION MIX

VIGNETTE: 'DON'T JUST SAY THEY MATTER'

KEY WORD: MARKETING MIX

'Don't just SAY they matter' addresses ethically based health inequalities in New Zealand. It aims to increase cervical screening amongst New Zealand's Maori and Pacific women by creating an understanding of the importance of screening, whilst enhancing the screening service in order to improve uptake. The two-phase programme launched in September 2007 and is ongoing until 2010. Phase One aims to start conversations about cervical screening, while Phase Two aims to motivate women to be screened.

The project used a variety of methods and interventions: health-education resources were developed for priority ethnic audiences; training was given to health promotion and screening staff to provide them with an opportunity to contribute to the campaign and to develop their capability to support interventions at a local level; an 0800 advice line was launched; and media relations and creative materials, featuring a clear call to action, supported clear behavioural goals.

The project achieved positive results against baseline screening uptake:

- Pacific 12.7 per cent increase
- Maori 6.8 per cent increase
- Asian 6.7 per cent increase
- Other 2.7 per cent increase.

This case study appears in full on ShowCase at: www.thensmc.com.

This vignette shows the value of using a variety of methods to reach your target audience, and not solely relying on communications.

ABOUT THIS CHAPTER

In this case study we will explore how a large multi-faceted programme was developed around a set of strategic objectives and then sustained over time to bring about a measurable reduction in deaths and injury on the roads. A key feature of the 'THINK!' programme was its full mix of interventions. It used all of the de-CIDES domains: Information, Education, Design, Support and Control. As well as its sustained media and educational programme interventions were coordinated with policing control interventions, road design and traffic-calming measures such as an increased use of speed cameras, support services such as road-safety training and driver re-education and outreach services also helped the programme deliver its results.

CASE STUDY: 'THINK!', DEPARTMENT FOR TRANSPORT ENGLAND. HOW ONE WORD HELPED SAVE A THOUSAND LIVES

Fiona Seymour from the UK Department for Transport (DfT) and Leo Burnett.

This case study appears in full on the National Social Marketing Centre's ShowCase resource (www.thensmc.com).

PROJECT OVERVIEW

This case study details how the DfT in the UK developed a comprehensive marketing and communications programme aimed at reducing the number of deaths and injuries on the roads. This broad programme of action was developed under the unifying 'THINK!' brand. This coordinated, systematic and sustained programme of action went beyond communications to encompass a wide range of solutions to help save over a thousand lives and prevent 90,000 injuries. This represents 3,494 people who are alive and uninjured today who wouldn't have been without 'THINK!' (Burnett, 2010).

The monetary value of this programme to society was £4.2billion, of which 'THINK!' would need to have accounted for just 2.2 per cent to pay back its full costs. 'THINK!' has actually had a greater contribution than this, it is estimate that, for every £1 spent on 'THINK!' The campaign has saved society £9.36 (Burnett, 2010). In addition to this value for money and cost effectiveness' one of the most important achievements of the 'THINK!' Programme is that it has been absorbed by many of its target audience as their campaign; it has entered into the mass-population consciousness so that the programme is owned by its target audiences and is sustained and promoted by them as well as the 'THINK!' Coalition.

PROGRAMME RATIONALE

Road safety has long been a government priority in the UK. The first conviction for speeding occurred in 1896[1]; drink driving was made illegal in 1930[2]; and the Driving Test was formally introduced in 1935[3]. Since the 1960s, changes to the design of our roads and vehicles, as well as significant investment in new policy initiatives and communications campaigns, have helped improve the

[1] The National Motor Museum Trust website Motoring Firsts – 'Who was the first person to be charged for a speeding offence?'

[2] In 1930 it became an offence to drive, attempt to drive or be in charge of a motor vehicle on a road or any other public place while being 'under the influence of drink or a drug to such an extent as to be incapable of having proper control of the vehicle'.

[3] The Driving Standards Agency website History of the British Driving Test – compulsory testing was introduced in 1935.

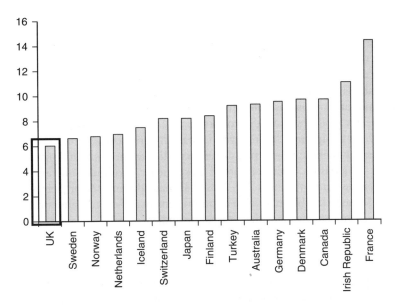

Figure 10.1 International comparison of road deaths per 100,000 population

Source: UK Department for Transport, 'Reported Road Casualties Great Britain 2001 Annual Report', Sept. 2009.

safety of our roads, despite increases in population, vehicles and traffic numbers. Indeed, by 2000, the UK was the safest country internationally in terms of road deaths per 100,000 population (DfT, 2009) (see Figure 10.1). However, from a social and economic perspective, crashes were still at an unacceptable level. In 1999 alone there were over 3,400 deaths and 39,000 serious injuries on UK roads. To put this into perspective, this represents six times the number of annual deaths from AIDS in the UK[4] – an astonishing loss to society. It has also been calculated that the benefits of avoiding all these casualties would be around £3 billion per year in 2000 (DfT, 2000). Therefore whilst the number of people 'killed and seriously injured' (KSI) had continued to fall, there was no room for complacency at the start of the new decade.

 AIMS AND OBJECTIVES

The government's first road safety strategy (from 1987 to 1999) aimed to reduce total casualties by a third, and succeeded in in successfully reducing the number killed by 35 per cent and those seriously injured by 49 per cent. Despite the declining number of killed and seriously injured, the new strategy in 2000 was based on a careful assessment of the potential for even greater reductions in KSIs over a ten-year period (Transport Research Laboratory, 2000).

On the basis of this assessment, specific targets for 2010 were set out compared with the baseline average for 1994–8:

- 40 per cent reduction in the number of people killed or seriously injured.
- 50 per cent reduction in the number of children killed or seriously injured.
- 10 per cent reduction in the slight casualty rate.

---

[4] AVERT, International AIDS charity data, www.avert.org

IDENTIFYING TARGET AUDIENCES

One of the key challenges facing the new strategy was audience fragmentation. The DfT has always been tasked with making the roads safer for all ages and all types of road user, from pedestrians, cyclists and motorcyclists to those driving and riding in cars and other forms of automobile. The principal segmentation that was applied by the DfT was one based on behaviour and form of road use. However, what was clear from road-casualty statistics was that there are key groups who are disproportionately at risk on the road and require special attention. These groups are: children, young male drivers, people who drive for work and motorcyclists. For example, young male drivers in particular are significantly over-represented in road-casualty statistics. Their mixture of inexperience, youthful exuberance and under-developed risk assessment ability (DfT, 2007) has made driving one of their biggest killers. The challenge was to be able to develop a comprehensive and coordinated strategy that was also capable of influencing all of these disparate audiences.

 ## STAKEHOLDER ENGAGEMENT

It was clear given, the many factors that impact on road safety and injury, that a single government department could not deliver the kind of step change in impact that the new targets demanded. Achieving the new targets meant considering the potential cumulative impact of local authorities, police forces, road-user associations and voluntary groups, car manufacturers and the individual road users themselves. There would also need to be a more holistic approach to the myriad issues that cause crashes, building on previous campaigns focusing on speed, seat belts, drink driving and child safety.

This presented a unique opportunity to create something that could unite all the disparate elements of existing interventions to make a sum greater than its parts. However this was easier said than done – the DfT needed a new approach that would be cost-efficient, practical, flexible, meaningful, inclusive and simple, and needed it to have real power to connect with and influence individual behaviour. There were no precedents in government for this kind of aspiration at the time, but the success of the whole strategy depended upon a uniquely effective solution.

BARRIERS AND COMPETITION

Making year-on-year reductions in road casualties becomes ever more challenging. Big reduction were achieved from measures like fitting seat belts to all cars and legislation to enforce there use, but, as the strategy has matured, it has had to address more diverse and intransigent problems. Three in particular influenced the new approach initiated in 2000. The first was audience segmentation as discussed above. The other two key challenges were issue proliferation (see Figure 10.2) and media complexity.

ISSUE PROLIFERATION

Road deaths and serious injuries are caused by a wide variety of factors. It is tempting to have a road-safety strategy that addresses as many as possible of these, but benefits are then dissipated as it become increasingly difficult to do enough on any particular issue to have an effect. By 2000, this was beginning to create a 'dis-economy' of scale that

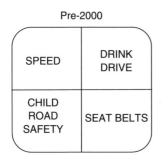

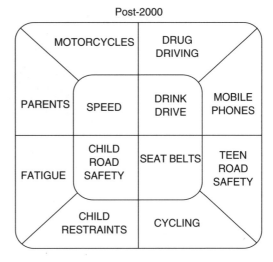

Figure 10.2   Issue proliferation

Source: Burnett, 2010.

threatened to overwhelm the DfT's existing approach, and was putting particular pressure on communications budgets.

ACTIONABLE INSIGHTS

The main challenge was to root the approach to change in a fundamental understanding of the underlying issues and causes that needed to be tackled. Given the everyday nature of road use, the single biggest catch-all danger to drivers and pedestrians is 'autopilot' behaviour in the road environment, which often militates against proper concentration and appropriate response. Available data made it clear that road users are responsible for far more crashes than can be attributed to factors outside of personal control (DfT, 2009); see Figure 10.3, which describes the proportional contributory factors in road accidents.

One of the many strengths of 'THINK!' is its use of target market research in developing individual elements of the programme. For example, one of the very successful sub-campaigns, called 'Moment of Doubt', was aimed at preventing men from drinking more than one pint if they were intending to drive. This campaign was aimed at men between the ages of 17 and 27.

The key insight derived from extensive research with this specific target audience about what might persuade them not to drink more than one pint was that this behaviour would have a high probability of leading to immediate and substantial negative consequences for them personally.

The 'Moment of Doubt' sub-campaign sought to create cognitive dissonance between the desire for another drink and a set of credible, relevant consequences. Six months after the launch, young men's perception that they would be caught by the police had risen from

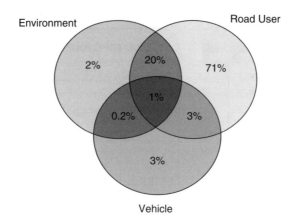

Figure 10.3 Proportional contributory factors in road accidents

Source: DfT, 2009.

58 per cent to 75 per cent. The number of people breathalysed during December 2007 rose by 6.4 per cent, while the number testing positive fell by 19.5 per cent. The number of deaths and serious injuries caused by drink driving fell for the first time in six years, from 560 in 2006 to 410 in 2007.

Specific research and insight programmes were commissioned for all subgroups and issues to help inform the DfT's segmented approach to meeting its targets, but the DfT also felt they needed a single unifying actionable insight that could break through the physical and emotional apathy around road safety and make individuals more self-aware on a day-to-day basis.

The key insight was that the DfT needed to be the voice of the road user's conscience, reminding them of the risk involved in their behaviour at every point in their journey.

This voice of conscience needed to be as relevant to primary-school children as to police and road-safety officers. In short, what was required was to make people think harder about their decisions on the road. In addition to activity directed at road users, there was also a need for a call to action and a unifying symbol for the multi-faceted programme.

It also needed to appeal and be meaningful to all the programmes stakeholders and partners at national, local and community level. One word, 'THINK!', was selected to create a powerful identity for the entirety of the road safety effort. This new brand was designed to work in three ways:

1   *Issues*: Drive efficiency, by creating coherence around previously separate road-safety issues. 'THINK!' acted as a relevant mnemonic, linking previously disparate road-safety issues and driving greater efficiencies.
2   *Stakeholders*: 'THINK!' united the wide variety of activities under a single banner. It gave stakeholders a common language and galvanised their efforts by creating a sense that absolutely everything they did was contributing towards the single-minded pursuit of better road safety.

3   *Individuals*: It prompted personal reappraisal of poor road-safety attitudes and behaviour. 'THINK!' also provided strategic and creative flexibility for effectively communicating to an increasingly diverse audience. In provoking consideration amongst individual road users about the consequences of their actions and, in doing so, it helped change behaviour. This has facilitated the use of a broad range of channels to deliver individual messages meaningfully.

 MARKETING MIX

The DfT set out an approach to achieve its road accident and death prevention targets, which can be summed up as the '3Es': Enforcement, Education and Engineering. This approach was designed to facilitate a more holistic way for all policy initiatives to work together to reduce deaths and serious injuries and encompassed all areas of the 3Es:

○   *Enforcement*: playing a significant role in the way we drive, as evidenced by the ongoing effect of drink drive legislation from the 1960s onwards.
○   *Education*: both in learning to drive and where communications reinforce correct road-safety behaviour whilst highlighting all that's unacceptable.
○   *Engineering*: through advancements in car and road engineering that can reduce the impact of collisions or even the risk of crashing altogether.

This is an example of what the Organisation for Economic Cooperation and Development (2008) calls a 'Safe System' approach to reducing road casualties – stressing the importance of shared responsibility for road safety amongst road users, designers and policy makers. Despite a long-term trend in casualty reduction (due to significant improvements in engineering; additional enforcement measures; and changes in road-user attitudes and behaviour), it was acknowledged that the new approach would need to be backed by additional measures in order to meet targets.

The 3Es approach adopted by the DfT led to an intervention mix focused on creating the right kind of physical environment to promote safe road use (such as speed cameras and traffic-calming measures), alongside measures to increase awareness and understanding, and measures to enforce behaviour and punish inappropriate and unsafe behaviour.

In marketing-mix terms, the DfT strategy used all modes of intervention depicted in the de-CIDES framework outlined in Chapter 1, and also all forms of intervention described in the Cost Value Matrix set out in Chapter 1.

In terms of product the 'THINK!' programme core product was clearly to reduce the number of injuries and deaths associated with road use and in so doing deliver a safer and more enjoyable travel experience. In terms of the actual product 'THINK!' delivered a range of interventions targeted at different segments of road users covering control, support, information, education and design solutions. For example:

○   *Information*: Rolling programmes of media advertising aimed at specific at risk road users such as young men. On road information systems such as electronic warning signs.
○   *Education*: In school road-safety education in all areas of England tailored for specific year groups and for other specific groups such as offender re-education programmes for traffic violation offenders as an alternative to fixed endorsements of their driving licence.
○   *Control*: Policy speed-enforcement action, including random speed and vehicle-safety checks and the increased use of speed cameras to deter speeding.

○ *Support*: Cycle training and safety checks, for cyclists and motorcyclists, advisory services to community groups about road safety and support service led by the community such as walking bus projects.[5]

○ *Design*: Road lay-out changes and redesign such as road bumps and road narrowing to slow traffic down in urban areas.

One of the other key strengths of 'THINK!' was that in addition to a full intervention mix it coordinated this mix at the local level with that at the regional and national levels as well. Staff working at all levels were briefed about national activity and national programme leads were briefed about local on the ground initiatives to support the national programme on a regular basis and in this way all efforts were better coordinated and mutually reinforcing.

PROMOTION

An increasingly complex media environment had developed in the UK in which message cut-through became more and more difficult. Road-safety communications had to 'compete' with a greater variety and volume of commercial messages. 'THINK!' embraced channel proliferation – including the growth of a digital media economy to deliver the task of influencing attitudes and behaviours.

The strategy to overcome this media proliferation and issue proliferation was to develop specific intervention programmes for each issue and target audience. The DfT also invested heavily in developing its web presence and use of interactive and social media channels as they developed over the course of the programme from 2000 to 2010. The DfT became a leader in the public sector in using interactive web-based media and channels and social networking to promote safe road use.

MONITORING AND EVALUATION

One of the key strengths of the 'THINK!' programme is its systematic, insight-led approach, combined with a strong focus on evaluation. Dealing as it does with road-traffic deaths and injury, the programme has the advantage that it can track impact in near real time, through the analysis of routinely collected road-accident data. In addition to this data, 'THINK!' collects and analyses specific information around attitudes, knowledge and behaviours, to track awareness and compliance rates amongst target audiences. The programme has also put in place evaluation mechanisms focused on measuring return of investment and value for money, which enable it to refine where it should focus its efforts to get best returns. This economic evaluation also helps defend the programme and justify ongoing expenditure.

FINDINGS

The 'THINK!' brand is very well recognised by the general public and more importantly by its target audiences as being trusted, thought provoking and helpful. The programme is also able to demonstrate significant positive change in attitudes and reported behaviour

---

[5] A 'walking bus' is a community scheme whereby children can come together in a supervised group by adults and walk to school and cross roads in a safe way. It reduces transport volume and gives children some exercise at the start and end of the day on the journey from home to school.

towards a range of road-safety behaviours including reducing speed, seat-belt wearing, drink driving and mobile-phone use.

In relation to the behavioural bottom line, there were 1,040 fewer deaths, 18,044 fewer serious injuries and 69,939 fewer slight injuries recorded in 2008 than during the 1994–8 average baseline set by the government as a target. This does not represent the cumulative total for reductions over the period, which are significantly higher (cumulatively there were 3,326 fewer deaths, 109,189 fewer serious injuries and 251,087 fewer slight injuries over the eight-year period 2000–8 versus the 1994–8 benchmark).

With regard to the impact of 'THINK!' on achieving programme targets, it has met or exceeded all three of its casualty-reduction targets, two years ahead of schedule. Compared to the baseline average (1994–8), it has achieved:

- 40 per cent reduction in KSI
- 19,084 fewer killed or seriously injured
- 59 per cent reduction in child deaths
- 4,053 fewer children reported killed or seriously injured
- 36 per cent reduction in slight injuries
- 69,939 fewer slight injuries.

However, one of the common criticisms of big national programmes like 'THINK!' is the difficulty of proving cause and effect, as improvements can often have more to do with trends than with direct programme impact. In order to separate out the actual impact that 'THINK!' has had, the evaluation strategy included the development of a forecast model that included an analysis of the impact of various elements of the total road-safety effort, such as new legislation and the introduction of more speed cameras.

It would clearly be wrong to argue that 'THINK!' delivered all 19,084 of the KSI decline or that it is responsible for the projected 2,682 additional KSI reduction versus the previous nine years – although this figure does give us an outer indication of 'THINK!'s possible effect.

The programme 'forecast model' concluded that even a conservative interpretation of the data indicates that 'THINK!' made up for a significant proportion of the 3,912 KSI gap. The forecast model analysed major policy initiatives and other factors, such as primary engineering which, the DfT have concluded, have had limited total effects. It can therefore be argued that the biggest single additional change to road safety after 1999 has been the introduction of 'THINK!'.

In addition to this attribution research, 'THINK!' was also subject to ongoing value for money analysis. The intention of the 'THINK!' programme is to save lives rather than create revenue, so traditional revenue or profit return on investment calculations were not deemed to be applicable. However, the cost of road casualties is high and any reduction will deliver huge savings to society as a whole.

In order to quantify the value from the reduction in road casualties, the DfT use a 'willingness to pay' (WTP) analysis. WTP analysis is used by the DfT to help with decisions regarding the level of public-safety provision and the benefit of new road schemes. This approach encompasses all aspects of the valuation of casualties, including the human costs and the direct economic costs (i.e. an amount to reflect the pain, grief and suffering and the lost output and medical costs associated with road crash injuries). Based on the difference between the number of road deaths in 2008 and the 1994–8 baseline average, 1,040 lives have been saved and there have been 18,044 fewer serious injuries and 69,939 slight injuries, saving society £5.1 billion or £4.2 billion if only KSIs are taken into account. This means that a reduction of only 418 KSIs is needed to cover all of 'THINK!' costs. As can be seen from the results above, this figure has been greatly surpassed.

In a world where 71 per cent of crashes are directly attributable to the road user, 'THINK!' has bolstered self-awareness on the road by acting as the voice of people's conscience. It joined up disparate road-safety issues for the first time under a single brand umbrella, driving efficiencies, and it has galvanised all stakeholders under one cause. In short, it has changed the road-safety landscape in the UK.

 LESSONS LEARNT

○ 'THINK!' is an example of how to develop a large national programme dealing with a complex issue, with many stakeholders and potential partners. The 'THINK!' brand was used as both a call to action for the public, and a way of building a comprehensive programme amongst many stakeholders and partners.
○ 'THINK!' demonstrates the need for programmes to be specifically targeted at a range of target audiences and behaviours when dealing with a complex issues such as road safety.
○ 'THINK!' demonstrates that a full mix of interventions is effective in bringing about sustained changes in social behaviours.
○ 'THINK!' is an excellent example of a large-scale programme that has been sustained over time.
○ 'THINK!' demonstrates the need for, and the usefulness of, a comprehensive evaluation strategy capable of tracking impact, change in behaviour and return on investment.

CHAPTER RECAP

In this chapter we have seen how the 'THINK!' programme used a full intervention mix alongside a multi-faceted and sustained promotional programme executed through national and local media and community and public-service staff to change attitudes and behaviour and save lives. By understanding both the causes of road deaths and people's attitudes towards road safety, the DfT was able to develop a sophisticated social marketing programme that produced not only impressive results but also was cost effective. In the next chapter we will explore another example of a project that put a lot of effort into ensuring that as well as a creative media push, local services were also ready to pull people into a better service.

SELF-REVIEW QUESTIONS

1 Think about a complex social issue, such as obesity or youth crime. List how design, control, education, information and support interventions could be used to reduce the problem.
2 Go to the 'THINK!' website (www.dft.gov.uk/think/) and review some of the targeted material on the programme. Ask yourself these two questions: Who is the specific audience? What specific behaviour is being targeted?
3 Review the 'Cost Value Matrix' in Chapter 1 and think of one form of road-safety action that would fit into each of the matrix quadrants.

REFERENCES

Burnett, L. (2010). How one word helped save a thousand lives between 2000–2008. Department for Transport IPA Effectiveness Paper. London: Department for Transport.

Department for Transport. (2000). *Tomorrow's Roads: Safer for Everyone*, Chapter 1: The direct cost of road accidents involving deaths or injuries is thought to be in the region of £3 billion a year. London: Department for Transport.

Department for Transport. (2007, Jan.). The good, the bad and the talented: Young drivers: Perspectives on good driving and learning to drive. Road Safety Research Report No. 74, S. Christmas. London: Department for Transport.

Department for Transport. (2009). Road safety strategy beyond 2010: A scoping study. Road Safety Research Report No. 105, J. Broughton, B. Johnson, I. Knight, B. Lawton, D. Lynam, P. Whitfield, O. Carsten and R. Allsop. London: Department for Transport.

Department for Transport. (2009). Reported road casualties: Great Britain 2001 Annual Report. London: Department for Transport.

Organisation for Economic Cooperation and Development. (2008). Towards zero: Ambitious road safety targets and the Safe System approach. Available online at: www.internationaltransport forum.org/jtrc/safety/targets/08TargetsSummary.pdf.

Transport Research Laboratory. (2000). The numerical context for setting national casualty reduction targets. Report TRL382, J. Broughton, R. E. Allsop, D. A. Lynam, and C. M. McMahon. Wokingham, UK: Transport Research Laboratory.

11 USING SERVICE 'PULL' TO COMPLEMENT CUSTOMER 'PUSH'

VIGNETTE: 'CLEANYOURHANDS', NATIONAL PATIENT SAFETY AGENCY

KEY WORD: SERVICE 'PUSH'

'Cleanyourhands' is a national initiative in England and Wales to combat preventable healthcare associated infection (e.g. MRSA), by encouraging healthcare staff to clean their hands at the right time, every time, during their care of patients. Campaign messages promote hand-cleaning behaviour but, importantly, this is physically enabled through provision of alcohol hand rub at the actual point of care.

This service element is the system change needed to make optimal hand hygiene possible, and to overcome traditional difficulties around access to hand-cleaning facilities. It also means patients can see healthcare staff cleaning their hands before every contact, giving them confidence in the care they receive. To support this service element, national hand-wash-supply contracts have been put in place, ensuring the NHS has access to high-quality products at reasonable prices, distributed via an effective delivery mechanism.

Results from the programme include a threefold increase in procurement of soap and alcohol handrub; alcohol handrub now available at point of care (by the bedside) in most wards in 94 per cent of hospital trusts; and declines in MRSA and MSSA bacteraemia.

A full case study is available on ShowCase, via www.thensmc.com.

This vignette makes the point that target audiences can be both 'pushed' and 'pulled' towards a desired behaviour, and that the 'pull' element is a crucial part of the interventions mix.

ABOUT THIS CHAPTER

As we discussed in Chapter 1, successful social marketing programmes combine a mix of methods that go beyond simple information-giving alone.

In this chapter you will explore:

○ How a social marketing team used messages to drive awareness of cancer symptoms and encourage early presentation to a doctor.
○ How the team also worked with health-service providers to ensure that screening and X-ray services were ready for increased demand, and actively pulling patients through the system.
○ How careful stakeholder consultation and support ensured that the joint 'push' and 'pull' strategy worked as a seamless whole.

CASE STUDY: EARLY DETECTION OF LUNG CANCER: KNOWING THE SYMPTOMS AND RESPONDING FAST

Dr Rupert Suckling, Deputy Director Public Health NHS Doncaster

This case study appears in full on the National Social Marketing Centre's ShowCase resource (www.thensmc.com).

PROJECT OVERVIEW

'Early Detection of Lung Cancer' was a programme developed in Doncaster, South Yorkshire, UK. Doncaster is the largest metropolitan borough in the UK and is the 40th most deprived local authority (2004). It has a registered population of 305,000, and is 97.7 per cent white, although this has shifted recently, with other important populations now including: approximately 600 asylum seekers (refugees); 4,000–6,000 gypsy/travellers; and around 2,800 prisoners. Over 41 per cent of residents live in the nationally most deprived fifth and 21,000 people receive incapacity benefit.

Initiatives to increase earlier diagnosis of lung cancer in Doncaster have been deployed in 2007, 2008 and 2009. This chapter describes the 2008 intervention, which ran between March and April 2008. A total budget of £187,500 was targeted at six communities, with a total population of 30,000.

PROJECT RATIONALE

Lung cancer is the most common cancer in the world, with 1.3 million new cases diagnosed every year (GLOBOCAN, 2002). The vast majority of lung cancers are caused by cigarette smoking (Biesalski, 1998). In the UK lung cancer is the second commonest cancer in men (after prostate cancer) and the third most common cancer in women (after breast and bowel). It is responsible for one in seven of all cancers (37,700 cases a year) (ONS, 2005). Lung cancer is more common in men, although the UK has one of the highest rates of female lung cancer in Europe (Cancer Research UK). Lung cancer is associated with deprivation. In 1993 the incidence of lung cancer was almost 2.5 times higher in the most deprived male groups than the least deprived groups, with the difference for women three times higher (Quinn, 2001).

The majority of lung cancers are non-small-cell lung cancer (NSCLC) and surgery is the main curative treatment. Early presentation and assessment for treatment is essential as there is a small window of opportunity where these patients can be offered curative treatment. Only 20–30 per cent of patients may be eligible for radical surgery (Carney et al., 2000), yet in England less than half of these people underwent surgery (between 7 and 17 per cent of patients diagnosed in 2000 had surgery for NSCLC) (UK National Audit Office, 2004). Five-year survival rates for people with Stage I (early disease) and treated with radical surgery are over 60 per cent and can be as high as 80 per cent for very early squamous cell carcinomas (Souhami, 2003).

Patients present with a variety of symptoms, usually relating to the primary tumour. These include dyspnoea (breathing difficulties), haemoptysis (coughing up blood) and chest pain. Loss of appetite, weight loss and general fatigue are also common. However, the presence of these symptoms already indicates established and possibly advanced disease. Some types of presentation are associated with a good prognosis. These include coincidental discovery, presentation with 'chest infection' and presentation with cough (Buccheri, 2004).

An urgent Chest X-ray (CXR) is the required initial investigation for symptoms suggestive of lung cancer (NICE, 2005). However, there is some concern that people do not have CXRs as often as might be clinically indicated. This is complicated by primary-care clinicians feeling that they should not refer too many people for CXR (following campaigns to reduce X-ray use), and also the fact that, in a population with very high levels of chest disease, they could easily swamp the local radiology department with extra referrals.

Doncaster has higher rates of lung-cancer incidence and mortality than the national average. The indirectly standardised registration rate (2001–3) for Doncaster was 139 (95 per cent CI 129–49) (NCOHD) with a standardised mortality ratio (SMR) for Doncaster from lung cancer in 2004 of 134 (NCOHD). So lung-cancer incidence is 39 per cent more common than nationally and mortality rates are 34 per cent higher.

Doncaster's lung-cancer survival rates reflect the national picture, with only 25 per cent of people diagnosed with lung cancer alive at one year, and 7 per cent at five years. The high mortality rate from lung cancer is a contributory factor to Doncaster's Spearhead status[1] and the impact of lung cancer is a key driver of health inequalities in Doncaster.

This early-detection programme was initiated as a consequence of high levels of lung cancer in Doncaster in areas of social disadvantage, combined with the clinical observation that early diagnosis improves prognosis. It was envisaged that encouraging members of the public to seek early detection, diagnosis and treatment would impact on mortality rates and quality of life. A feasibility pilot was undertaken in a small area of Doncaster (Carcroft), and indicated that a social marketing approach would be advantageous in driving awareness of symptoms.

---

[1] Spearhead areas are the fifth of English local authorities (defined by the 1997 Labour government) with the worst health and deprivation indicators compared to England.

AIMS AND OBJECTIVES

The programme aimed to improve life expectancy and reduce health inequalities in Doncaster's areas of highest deprivation, by encouraging early identification and diagnosis of people with Stage I or II lung cancer.

The project objectives were to:

○ Raise awareness of early symptoms of lung cancer – specifically a cough that lasts more than three weeks.
○ Change the target audience's behaviour and increase the number of people with potential symptoms presenting to prioritised GP surgeries.
○ Increase the number of chest X-rays undertaken in Doncaster by 20 per cent.
○ Increase the number of people diagnosed with Stage I or II lung cancer, i.e. early diagnosis.

IDENTIFYING TARGET AUDIENCES

The primary target audience was males aged over 50 from groups C2, D and E.[2] The secondary audience was the families of these men.

Consumer planning was carried out with local experts and the Yorkshire & Humber Public Health Observatory (YHPHO) and involved the following steps:

1 Identification of data for known lung-cancer sufferers in the Doncaster region, including deaths and admissions:

Age and sex variables captured in the file of lung-cancer deaths for Doncaster showed that 98.6 per cent of all lung-cancer deaths were amongst people aged over 50 years (NCOHD); with a male:female split of roughly 60:40 (NCOHD) (see Figure 11.1).

From this information, the team identified the primary target audience as males, aged over 50, with a secondary target audience of females aged over 50.

2 Profiling this data against deprivation indicators:

Lung-cancer admissions and mortalities were then mapped against deprivation, which revealed that the majority of lung-cancer sufferers resided in areas of deprivation, although there were pockets that did not follow this pattern (Yorkshire & Humber PHO). The six communities with the highest rates of lung cancer were identified as the target communities.

3 Cross-comparing this data against various geo-demographic classifications, to try and further enhance the profiles:

A variety of geo-demographic classifications were applied to the Male 50+ data to see if the profile could be enriched. Five classification systems were used:

○ Health ACORN[3]
○ ACORN[4]

---

[2] C2, D and E describe the lowest three social and economic groups in society from the A, B, C1, C2, D, E classification that is used in England.

[3] Health ACORN is a classification tool that enables health specialists to identify those types most at risk from specific conditions. This analysis allows managers to quantify demand for services and to inform these at-risk groups with relevant and targeted health advice. www.caci.co.uk/PublicSector.aspx.

[4] ACORN is a geo-demographic segmentation of the UK's population which segments small neighbourhoods, postcodes, or consumer households into five categories, 17 groups and 56 types. www.caci.co.uk/acorn-classification.aspx.

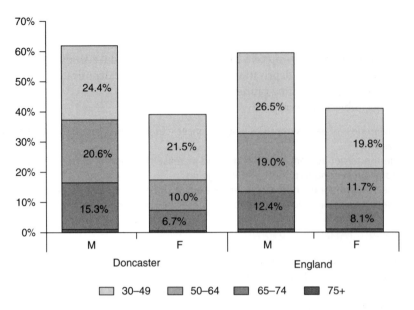

Figure 11.1   Early-Detection graph

Source: © Sixteen Hands.

- ○ PersonicxGeo[5]
- ○ P2: People and Places[6]
- ○ Output Area Classification[7]

These classifications were explored at group, type and sub-type level, in an attempt to identify distinct target groups. Of all the classifications, PersonicxGeo appeared to provide the most accurate system for locating our target with the largest percentage of lung-cancer sufferers, aged over 50, from deprived areas falling into a single grouping – GR5 (Retired – Low Income). In addition, P2: People and Places indicated a strong bias towards 'Weathered Communities'. However, the use of geo-demographics did not, in this instance, provide a clear cut enhancement to the core target audience.

---

[5] PersonicxGeo is a demographic segmentation tool that uses 2001 Census data, Target Group Index data and geography to classify people by where they live into discrete segments. Its initial segmentation uses 5 × 4 categories.

[6] P2: People and Places is a demographic segmentation tool that uses 2001 Census data, Target Group Index data and geography to classify people by where they live into discrete segments. Its initial segmentation uses 14 trees. Further information from Beacon Dodsworth.

[7] Output Area Classification distils key results from the Census for the whole of the UK to indicate the character of local areas. It profiles populations, structures other data, and helps target resources. http://areaclassification.org.uk/2009/05/08/oac-in-summary-overview-of-geode-mographic-segmentation-by-apho/.

SCOPING RESEARCH

Local research included an audit and qualitative interviews with patients to understand the issue in more detail.

AUDIT

An audit of chest X-ray use in the local hospital (Doncaster Royal Infirmary (DRI)) showed that individuals diagnosed with lung cancer had not had chest X-rays for a substantial period of time before diagnosis – 65 per cent of patients had not had a chest X-ray in the six to ten years prior to diagnosis. This may be evidence that people presented late to respiratory physicians (Rogers, 2006).

QUALITATIVE RESEARCH

Sheffield Hallam University conducted qualitative research with lung-cancer survivors. This highlighted several perceived and actual barriers people experienced in their cancer journeys (Tod, 2008). Reasons for the delay in diagnosing lung cancer from a patient perspective included:

- Nature of symptoms experienced
- Mismatch between expectation and experience of symptoms
- Lack of awareness of symptoms
- Initial response to the symptoms.

ACTIONABLE INSIGHTS

Research revealed a key insight: that there was no consistent response to potential lung-cancer symptoms, either by the people experiencing symptoms, or by the primary-care teams who should have acted on potential risk cases.

Findings were grouped into primary, audience and service insights.

PRIMARY INSIGHTS

- The fundamental issue that needs to be addressed is generalised lack of awareness about lung-cancer symptoms.
- The second key issue is the lack of understanding about the benefits of early diagnosis and how this improves prognosis.

AUDIENCE INSIGHTS

- The challenge of raising awareness relates to a broader audience than just the 'at risk' group. The role of the community and family in our priority neighbourhoods suggests that broader awareness raising could provide leverage to encourage other family members to present earlier at GPs.
- There is considerable fatalism and fear around lung cancer, as it is not a disease associated with positive outcomes or linked to positive role models.
- Lung-cancer messages are often subsumed by 'stop-smoking' messages, or misconstrued as being 'stop-smoking' messages. Smokers are adept at 'screening out' stop-smoking advertising.

○ At-risk groups perceive social and educational differentials between themselves and health-care professionals, therefore feel unable to challenge professionals if they do not receive chest X-rays or other appropriate medical responses.
○ Older males tend to be stoical about their health and reticent about presenting at GPs.

SERVICE INSIGHTS

○ To avoid 'bottlenecks' in capacity, radiology departments needed to anticipate an uplift in 'demand' for chest X-rays, and GPs needed to be informed of this additional capacity to reduce their concerns about overloading radiologists with new referrals.
○ GPs also need to be prepared for a potential increase in case load due to the awareness driving campaign.

 MARKETING MIX

The marketing mix incorporated two complementary approaches:

○ Customer 'Push': a public awareness campaign to raise awareness of the symptoms of lung cancer and the benefits of early detection.
○ Service 'Pull': preparing healthcare professionals for the initiative by sharing insights, providing training and supporting capacity management in GP surgeries.

CUSTOMER 'PUSH'

The key message for the intervention was: If you have a persistent cough that lasts for over three weeks, ask your GP about a chest X-ray. Acting quickly is critical. (See Figure 11.2.)

www.3weekcough.org   WE'RE WAITING, YOU SHOULDN'T

Figure 11.2   Early detection of lung cancer, marketing collateral

Source: © Sixteen Hands.

The creative briefing was based on scoping insights, and included:

- Tonally, communications should be clear and encouraging, to address fatalistic beliefs that lung cancer inevitably leads to death. They should make minimal specific reference to cancer (which can inhibit action), but carry enough gravitas to compel people to put pressure on GPs to take action.
- Messages should provide reassurance that early detection can be easily achieved via a simple X-ray referral, and that getting symptoms checked can eliminate worry or enable appropriate early referral.
- Some communications should be targeted at family/friends of people with potential symptoms, emphasising that they can help their loved ones by encouraging them to ask for a chest X-ray.
- Smoking references should be avoided, as they are often screened out by smokers, whilst not smoking (or being an ex- or passive smoker), does not mean you are not at risk from lung cancer.

As a result of this briefing, the following customer 'push' interventions were developed:

CREATIVE-LED COMMUNICATION CAMPAIGNS, TARGETED AT SIX COMMUNITIES

- Outdoor advertising; buses (inside, outside and bus stops); fliers/posters; pharmacy bags in target communities.
- Door drops (leaflets) in target communities.
- Media advertising and PR (print, radio and television), alerting people to the campaign and focusing on stories of lung-cancer survival, to counter the belief that lung cancer is always incurable.

FACE-TO-FACE EVENTS

- Brief intervention training for 'health' workers (e.g. health trainers, community pharmacist staff, community-development workers and cancer-information workers), 'tasking' them to have conversations about a three-week cough with targeted groups and in targeted localities.
- Brief intervention training for community 'influencers' (e.g. community leaders and 'champions' or volunteers), to have informed conversations with people about the dangers of a three-week cough and advise them how to act. These 'influencers' were already known to local community workers, or were identified through stakeholder analysis.
- 'Piggy-backing' on existing activity including fêtes, open days and sports activity.

CO-CREATION INITIATIVES

- Facilitating community organisations or volunteers to develop their own approaches to spreading the message.

ENABLING TOOLS

- To address the perceived social gap between the target audience and their healthcare professionals (see 'Actionable Insights' p. 145), and encourage the audience to request a chest X-ray from their GP, wanted to develop tools or enablers to be used by patients as a shortcut when expressing their concerns to GPs. The team piloted credit-card-style leaflets encouraging those concerned to speak to their GPs, as well as trialling prescription-style pads requesting chest X-rays. However, there was little take-up of the prescription pads.

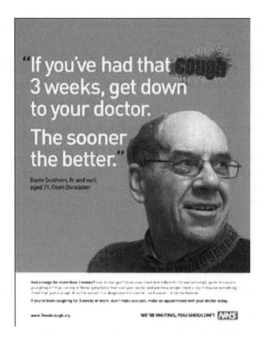

Figure 11.3   Early detection of lung cancer, marketing collateral the primary care trust

Source: © Sixteen Hands

SERVICE 'PULL'

Service 'pull' strategies included:

TIERED APPROACH TO PRIMARY CARE, TARGETED AT 11 GP PRACTICES SERVING THE PROJECT TEAM'S SIX COMMUNITIES

- Practice visits to introduce the initiative.
- Practice training, including:
  - o Raising awareness of lung cancer and symptoms
  - o Reminding about the benefits of early diagnosis
  - o Reminding about best-practice guidance from the National Institute of Clinical Excellence (NICE)[8] on referral with suspected cancer
  - o Delivering Continuing Medical Education (CME) by the secondary-care lung-cancer team to GPs, to highlight the need to review practice in light of NICE referral criteria.
- Brief intervention training with frontline health/social care professionals (e.g. GPs, nurses, pharmacists, social care, reception staff), to respond appropriately if someone presents with a persistent cough.

---

[8] NICE is an independent UK organisation responsible for providing national guidance on promoting good health and preventing and treating ill health. www.nice.org.uk/.

SECONDARY CARE

- Ensure sufficient X-ray and care pathway capacity.
- Review and streamline suspected lung cancer care pathways, including systems for rapid review of abnormal chest X-rays by consultants, as opposed to sending abnormal chest X-ray results back to GPs and asking them to refer under the two-week wait procedure.

 STAKEHOLDER ENGAGEMENT

Stakeholders were identified and grouped into three categories:

- Those who may benefit from the intervention
- Those who would be involved in the delivery of the intervention
- Those who had a role in the governance or authorising of the intervention.

The interests of these three stakeholder categories were brought together in the project steering group.

Those who may benefit from the intervention included primary and secondary audiences, and lung-cancer survivors. Survivors from lung cancer were identified and interviewed in the qualitative research and the barriers that they identified provided the basis for the insight. Representatives from the primary audience were involved in concept testing the creative messages. Survivors of lung cancer volunteered to champion the initiative and provided media interviews. The PCT communication and public-health members of the steering group took responsibility for engaging with these stakeholders.

Those who would be involved in the delivery of the initiative included health and social care staff across primary and secondary care. General Practitioners and their practices were identified that related to the target communities. These practices were visited to raise awareness of the programme, and brief intervention training was given to both GPs and practice staff. Other health staff working in the community were identified and offered training, e.g. community pharmacists. Community influencers were also identified and made aware of the intervention and offered training. The role of secondary care, diagnostic, assessment and treatment services, including chest physicians, specialist nurse and radiology, was identified. The GP and chest physician on the steering group took responsibility for engaging with primary- and secondary-care colleagues.

Those who had a role in governance or authorising the project were identified. All project documents and ultimately the project sign off were taken through the local cancer partnership. The project lead was responsible for identifying other organisational stakeholders and keeping them informed on progress, e.g. the Director of Public Health and Chief Executive.

BARRIERS

There were a number of barriers to implementing this intervention, including the novelty of the approach, primary care buy-in, lack of expertise in social marketing and securing sufficient resource.

Despite the importance of early diagnosis in lung cancer there are relatively few evidence-based interventions available. Although there is substantial evidence for social marketing, we were not aware of its use in lung cancer in particular. NHS

Doncaster was lucky to be involved in the Yorkshire and the Humber SHA social marketing collaborative[9] and, through this, external social marketing expertise was obtained. The resource for the intervention was secured through the social marketing collaborative and through NHS Doncaster's health inequalities programme, with the aid of a robust business case.

The biggest challenge was ensuring that primary care could see that they had a part to play. This was approached through a small feasibility intervention in 2007, and the subsequent championing of this piece of work by both primary and secondary care clinicians. This process of starting with a feasibility intervention helped to break down barriers and to dispel myths about the potential impact on primary care.

MONITORING AND EVALUATION

The structure of the evaluation was based around the key message:

> If you have a persistent cough that lasts for over three weeks ask your GP about a chest X-ray. Acting quickly is critical.

From this statement, an assessment framework was developed, to be broken down into three key measures and three distinct areas:

1 Reach
2 Changing attitudes
3 Response.

KEY MEASURE 1: LIKELIHOOD OF VISITING GP IF HAD A COUGH FOR 3+ WEEKS, PRE AND POST
Related measures:

- Likelihood of making partner/other family member visit GP if had cough for 3+ weeks – pre and post.
- Awareness of lung cancer symptoms – pre and post.
- Comparison of above measures across sampling communities.
- Awareness/recall of different elements of campaign.

This was measured by telephone interviews pre and post the intervention. 100 interviews were conducted in each of the target communities and 200 interviews with a control community in Doncaster. The second sample was matched to the first using demographic variables to maximise the accuracy of the pre/post stage comparisons. Interviews were conducted with the target audience, C2DE[10] who are either: 50+ or; smokers or; people

---

[9] The Yorkshire and the Humber SHA social marketing collaborative was a regional initiative to test the application of social marketing in a number of health care settings including work on Hospital Acquired Infections through to early diagnosis and prevention. The goal was to test approaches in one locality and then be able to systematically apply the intervention to a wider population, up to 5.4 million people.

[10] C2DE is one way of describing the lowest three social and economic groups in society from the A, B, C1, C2, D, E classification.

who have worked/work in heavy industry – both men and women with a slight bias towards men as they are more prevalent in the target audience were interviewed.

KEY MEASURE 2: NUMBER OF CHEST X-RAYS BEING CARRIED OUT, PRE AND POST

This was captured using the records form the radiology department of the local acute hospital. Chest X-ray referral numbers were obtained by GP practices both before and after the intervention.

KEY MEASURE 3: STAGE OF DIAGNOSIS OF LUNG CANCER, PRE AND POST

Related measures:

○ Number of lung cancers diagnosed – pre and post.

This was obtained both before and after the intervention from the LUCADA (lung cancer database) – England's national clinical audit tool.

REACH

This involved measuring the success of the targeting, the coverage of the campaign area and public awareness of the campaign. Measured through:

○ Amount of coverage in target media.
○ Numbers of leaflets, prescriptions, credit cards, etc. being taken from access points indicating which material from menu of campaign materials was most successful.
○ Response to specific media activities (e.g. phone-ins, micro-site).
○ Awareness and penetration of campaign across target communities (from survey in pilot areas).

CHANGING ATTITUDES

This involved measuring the effectiveness of the campaign in increasing likelihood of the target group presenting at GP if they have had a cough for three weeks or more, and also likelihood of proactively asking for a chest X-ray. Measured through:

○ Changes between pre-campaign (benchmarking) survey and post-campaign survey of target.

RESPONSE

This focused on ascertaining how effective the campaign was at getting the target patients showing symptoms of lung cancer to visit their GP and visit and ask for an X-ray. Measured through:

○ Uptake of X-ray from pilot area referrals compared to historic figures and similar non-pilot areas.
○ Numbers presenting at GPs with concerns about persistent coughs/requesting X-ray compared to historic figures and similar non-pilot areas.
○ Feedback from trained practitioners regarding uptake of campaign information and behaviour change of patients/contacts.

FINDINGS

The findings are reflected in three areas:

- Public attitudes
- Chest X-ray referrals
- Lung cancer diagnoses and stage.

Prior to the programme, 93 per cent of people said they would visit the GP if they had a 'bad' cough. Following the intervention this increased to 97 per cent. In addition, whereas 64 per cent of people said they would ask for an X-ray when visiting the GP with a 'bad' cough, this increased to 76 per cent following the intervention. There was no significant difference between men and women.

Overall there was no significant change in the length of time people would leave before visiting their GP if they had a 'bad' cough. The percentage of people who would encourage a friend or relative to see their GP if they had a bad cough increased from 90 per cent to 98 per cent at three weeks. However, people were still more likely to recommend a friend or relative to go to the GP with the same symptom compared to their own action. Smokers and ex-smokers responded better to the campaign than those who had never smoked.

Chest X-ray referrals were reviewed in two ways. First, a comparison with the same six weeks of the previous year, which showed an increase of 40 per cent across Doncaster. This was reflected in a 31 per cent increase in non-targeted practices and 80 per cent increase in targeted practices. Comparing the six weeks before and during the campaign overall, there was an increase of 13 per cent in chest X-ray referrals. This was split into a 9 per cent increase in non-targeted practices and a 27 per cent increase in targeted practices

The number of lung cancers identified increased in April 2008 as a result of the intervention. In April 2008, 54 cases were identified compared to 32 in April 2007. This increase was not sustained in future months. Before the intervention 11 per cent of new diagnoses of lung cancer were early (stage 1 or 2). Following the intervention this number increased to 19 per cent. This is a significant difference chi-square $p < 0.02$.

The initial business case for the intervention proposed that moving the percentage of cases diagnosed with early (Stage I and II) from 10 per cent to 20 per cent could save £100,000. However, this would require all those diagnosed earlier to have undergone curative surgery. Although the intervention budget was greater than this possible saving, future interventions are likely to be less expensive. (See Figure 11.3.)

Figure 11.4   Early detection of lung cancer, marketing collateral

Source: © Sixteen Hands.

LESSONS LEARNT

There were three things that worked particularly well:

- Planning
- Insight
- Integration.

Using a robust planning framework, in this case social marketing, allowed the team to maintain focus and discipline. The development and ownership of the key insights was crucial in providing both inspiration and also a touchstone for the project team. The integrated approach of customer push and consumer pull ensured that raised awareness translated into maximum impact by having health services primed to respond.

However, there were some areas where things may have been done differently. The steering group did not include a member of the primary target audience and this should be remedied in future to ensure decision-making with target audience in mind at all times. There was an underestimation of the amount of time required to visit and train all the relevant GP practices, there was also an underestimation of the time required and the amount of internal communication that was required. Finally, although the evaluation was well thought through, obtaining some of the information was more labour intensive than had been imagined. Initially information from primary care was to be used but this proved too difficult to do.

CHAPTER RECAP

In this chapter we have explored the joint role of service 'pull' and customer 'push' within the social marketing methods mix. We have seen how a strong focus on service readiness is necessary if successful behaviour change is to be achieved. No matter what the social marketing intervention is, behaviour change should never be impeded by the inability of the given system to respond to increased demand.

In the next chapter we will consider how programme planners can work with and build upon existing local services, to create a locally embedded, service-focused programme of support.

SELF-REVIEW QUESTIONS

1 In this chapter you have seen the importance of preparing frontline services for increased demand. The project team in this instance conducted an audit of X-ray activity to understand existing capacity, and then provided training and support to frontline

(Continued)

(Continued)

staff to ensure patients presenting with suspected cancer symptoms were handled optimally. Select a social marketing challenge of your choosing, and identify three ways in which a service 'pull' element might be built into the marketing mix.

2 If you were designing a social marketing programme to increase recycling rates amongst a local community, what 'pull' elements might you build into your intervention mix to ensure the behaviour change was easily achievable?

3 This case study shows how a detailed process of segmentation underpinned targeting of interventions. In this instance, males aged over 50 from socio-economic groups C2, D and E were prioritised. How might the programme have been different, both in terms of 'push' and 'pull' characteristics, if the selected target audience had been females, aged over 25, from areas of low deprivation, and the target behaviour had been attendance for cervical screening?

REFERENCES

Biesalski, H. K., Bueno de Mesquita, B., Chesson, A., et al. (1998). European Consensus Statement on Lung Cancer: Risk factors and prevention. Lung Cancer Panel'. *CA Cancer J Clin* (Smoking is the major risk factor, accounting for about 90 per cent of lung cancer incidence) 48(3): 167–76; discussion 164–6. doi:10.3322/canjclin.48.3.167. PMID 9594919. Available online at: http://caonline.amcancersoc.org/cgi/pmidlookup?view=long&pmid=9594919.

Buccheri, G. and Ferrigno, D. (2004). Lung cancer: Clinical presentation and specialist referral time. *Eur Respir J*, 24: 898–904.

Cancer Research UK. Lung cancer survival statistics. Available online at: http://info.cancerresearchuk.org/cancerstats/types/lung/survival/?a=5441#source5. Accessed April 2010.

Carney, D. N. and Hansen, H. H. (2000). Non-small-cell lung cancer – stalemate or progress? *N Engl J Med*, 343(17): 1261–2.

GLOBOCAN. (2005). *Cancer Incidence, Mortality and Prevalence Worldwide* (2002 estimates). Available online at: http://globocan.iarc.fr/.

NCHOD (National Centre for Health Outcomes Development). Mortality from lung cancer. Available online at: www.nchod.nhs.uk/,

National Institute for Health and Clinical Excellence. CG24 lung cancer: Full guideline. www.nice.org.uk/guidance/CG24. Accessed April 2010.

NICE, National Institute for Health and Clinical Excellence. CG27 referral for suspected cancer: NICE guideline. Available online at: www.nice.org.uk/guidance/CG27. Accessed April 2010.

Quinn, M., Babb, P., Brock, A., Kirby, L. and Jones J. (2001). Cancer trends in England & Wales, 1950–1999. Studies on Medical and Population Subjects No. 66. London: The Stationery Office.

Rogers, T. K. (2006). Lung cancer diagnosis. *Lung Cancer in Practice*, 3(1): 8–9.

Souhami, R. and Tobias, J. (2003). *Cancer and Its Management*, 4th edn. Oxford: Blackwell.

Tod, A., Craven, J. and Allmark, P. (2008). Diagnostic delay in lung cancer: A qualitative study. *Journal of Advanced Nursing*, 61(3): 336–43.

UK Office for National Statistics. (2005). Cancer statistics registrations: Registrations of cancer diagnosed in 2002, England. Series MB1 No. 33. London: National Statistics.

UK National Audit Office. (2004). Tackling cancer in England: Saving more lives. Report by the comptroller and auditor general. London: Stationery Office.

Yorkshire and Humber Public Health Observatory, www.yhpho.org.uk/.

12 WORKING WITH LOCAL SERVICES

VIGNETTE: 'LOVE YOUR MOUTH'

KEY WORD: USER-FRIENDLY SERVICES

Mouth cancer kills one person every five hours in the UK. Survival rates are low due to late presentation of symptoms. 'Love Your Mouth' was a pilot initiative to promote early detection of oral cancer in the North East of England. The aims of the intervention was to create a user-friendly service where people at risk from oral cancer could have their mouth examined by a competent clinician.

'Love Your Mouth' developed a voucher system, which enabled holders to receive a free soft-tissue mouth check at a participating dental practice. Two-thousand vouchers were printed and distributed in booklet form to pharmacies, smoking-cessation services, health trainers, NHS walk-in centres and medical practices.

The pilot had promising results:

- 205 'assessment of risk' vouchers distributed to at-risk individuals
- 50 dental appointments attended for soft tissues mouth checks
- 5 voucher holders referred to specialist oral surgeons by the dentists
- 1 person kept under review as possible cancer sufferer.

This case study is available in full on ShowCase, at www.thensmc.com

This vignette reveals the importance of working with existing local services to meet the target audience's needs, as opposed to building a new service from scratch, which is costly and time-consuming.

ABOUT THIS CHAPTER

As we discussed in Chapter 1, engaging stakeholders and partners is an important aspect of the social marketing process. In this chapter, you will learn:

- The benefits and difficulties of co-production.
- How to work in partnership with existing public-body organisations.

CASE STUDY: WORKLESSNESS COLLABORATIVE PROGRAMME: A COMMUNITY-LED APPROACH TO TACKLE ECONOMIC INACTIVITY BY FOCUSING ON CHILD POVERTY

Adrian Smith and Linda Henry, Unique Improvements

PROJECT OVERVIEW

The Worklessness[1] Collaborative Programme aims to reduce overall levels of worklessness in target communities in north-east Lincolnshire, England. The programme centres on the development of community teams of local residents and service providers to:

- Inspire individuals to achieve personal changes
- Enable them to access appropriate work
- Reduce dependence on benefits and increase overall profitability in two target areas – South ward and East Marsh ward.

The programme is funded through a national Working Neighbourhoods Fund,[2] managed locally by North East Lincolnshire Council and delivered as part of its Change Programme,[3] a framework of 22 organisations brought together to tackle worklessness.

North-east Lincolnshire is a small coastal area near Yorkshire and Humber on the edge of the north-east of England. It has a population of 158,200 and is an area of great contrast, combining urban areas with a popular seaside resort and a number of smaller rural settlements. Although significant industry employment still exists, the area has suffered from a decline in manufacturing and fishing activity. Worklessness rates have remained relatively

---

[1] There are several definitions of worklessness. For the purposes of consistency, at the time of this project, people who are claiming Working Age Client Group Benefits (WACG) are considered workless. Those benefits are: Job Seekers Allowance, Incapacity Benefit, Lone Parents Benefit, Carers Benefits, People with Disability, the bereaved and others on income-related benefits

[2] The Working Neighbourhoods Fund totalled £1.5 billion and provides resources 2009–11 to local authorities to tackle worklessness and low levels of skills and enterprise in their most deprived areas. The funding is designed to enable maximum flexibility to design local programmes to meet local needs.

[3] www.nelincs.gov.uk/community-people-and-living/community-investment/framework-change/.

constant, continuing to exceed national and regional rates overall and significantly in its most deprived communities. Overall worklessness levels stand at 17.5 per cent of the population compared to 13.2 per cent in England as a whole.[4]

The pilot commenced in April 2009, and was completed in September 2010. The teams involved continue to develop local interventions and have spread their involvement into additional community-change agent activity. The learning from the pilot has been incorporated to provide posts to support community involvement across future work.

PROJECT RATIONALE

The Worklessness Collaborative is an innovative programme funded through the Working Neighbourhoods Fund, managed locally by North East Lincolnshire Council, to address the levels of unemployment in two deprived areas of Grimsby.

The programme aims to reduce overall levels of worklessness in target communities in north-east Lincolnshire by focusing on reducing child poverty and engaging target audiences in common activity with services. Locally, there are stubborn high levels of worklessness and child poverty in target wards. Evidence in the field of reducing worklessness suggests that activity is more likely to succeed if it adopts co-production approaches. Co-production involves engaging those who are hardest to reach in the design and delivery of interventions; and matches personalised approaches to the needs of different audiences (Meadows, 2006).

North East Lincolnshire Council has a history of innovation and success on enterprise initiatives and this pilot was designed to complement the existing provision and dovetail with the newly established Change Programme. The collaborative builds on the highly successful collaboratives already in existence within the area, including the award-winning Early Presentation of Cancer Symptoms Collaborative.[5]

The project engages groups of local residents and services who have an interest in improving employability within their geographical area. Teams, consisting both of residents and service providers, have been established for two areas – South and East Marsh – which have the highest levels of deprivation and the highest levels of claimants in receipt of incapacity benefit and Job Seeker Allowance. In addition, these two wards have the highest levels of child poverty, with north-east Lincolnshire average being 25 per cent; the two participating wards have 44 and 48 per cent registered child poverty (UK Office of National Statistics, 2010).

 AIMS AND OBJECTIVES

The overall aim of the project was to reduce child poverty in South and East Marsh wards by increasing profitability in these areas. It was proposed that this could be achieved by increasing benefit uptake where appropriate, increasing economic activity and pre-work readiness. Early insight work identified over 200 separate organisations providing support

---

[4] Worklessness in England stood at 4,202,170 individuals as measured by the DWP Working Age Client Group in August 2009, equating to 13.2 per cent of the working age population. Source: UK Office for National Statistics and Department of Work and Pensions

[5] Details of the project can be found at www.thensmc.com.

and advice for unemployed people. However, many people within the participating communities were not accessing this support. Programme aims were therefore to:

- Raise awareness of what was currently available – not to create more provision.
- Help people to access this support.
- Increase the number of people accessing help.

Other specific objectives for the programme included:

- To increase community engagement/interaction with the programme by at least 1,100 people.
- To increase the number in regular volunteering roles by at least five people.
- To increase the availability of new jobs to achieve a target of three full-time job placements.
- To increase publicity for the programme (by utilising media opportunities in a proactive manner), by at least 12 media placements in one year.
- To Increase utilisation of other framework programmes by 15 referrals.

IDENTIFYING TARGET AUDIENCES

The project is based within two distinct localities and ward populations. These localities were selected due to high levels of worklessness (work-based benefit claimants) but also because of high levels of deprivation (low educational attainment, high levels of ill health and so on). The data suggested initial segmentation based on economic activity – focusing on reducing people claiming Incapacity Benefit (data suggests a focus on people with mental ill health) and Lone Parent Benefits. Early segmentation into communities of interest highlighted lone parents (largely women although men were also considered).

Acknowledging this, there was additional segmentation according to readiness and motivation to change, and the point on the pathway to work a person may be at:

- Initial engagement (sometimes call pre-engagement)
- Thinking about work in the future
- Actively looking for work
- Working (and staying in work).

Primary audiences included economically inactive local people within East Marsh and South wards, with a specific focus on carers (parents, grandparents and others) and lone parents. These were categorised as follows:

- Out of work but keen to re-engage: requires some assistance with skills/application process.
- Not working but potentially keen to re-engage: barriers include childcare, numeracy skills.
- Out of work and lacking motivation: requires support with skills building, and help to overcome barriers.
- Out of work for some time: has significant support needs and possible health difficulties.

Secondary audiences included:

- Local service providers across the Change Programme (referenced earlier) delivering interventions.
- Local service providers with indirect influence on supporting our target primary audiences, including NHS organisations, local authority, voluntary sector and community organisations.
- Children of parents in the primary audience group.

SCOPING RESEARCH

The scoping stage of the project comprised mapping of local community networks, projects and services, community desk-based research and primary research with the target audience and other stakeholders. During the scoping phase, a mixture of the following data was used to build a picture of the problem and the target audiences' lives, attitudes and current behaviours:

- A desk-based review of best practice, policy and case studies.[6]
- Review of local data, including benefit recipients.[7]
- Stakeholder mapping, including community assets mapping.

In addition to the scoping work detailed above, community teams were supported to develop research skills so that they could carry out interviews with their peers and other local people from across their networks.

Findings from the scoping research were then categorised into four main themes:

1 Services
2 Barriers
3 Social norms
4 Social advertising.

SERVICES

Research suggested that the development and delivery of local services should take place within existing community hubs such as Sure Start Centres[8] and local community buildings. However, services would only be valued by the target audience if they were offered virtually (i.e. delivered locally but with no physical base). Examples offered by audiences included

---

[6] Supported by Spirals Consulting, www.spiralconsulting.com.

[7] For the purposes of our programme we mean Working Age Client Group Benefits described in fn. 1. These paid through social security payments from central government

[8] Sure Start is the UK government's programme to deliver the best start in life for every child by bringing together early education, childcare, health and family support. By 2010, approximately 3,500 centres provide a hub for a range of services for children and families

personalised web based services or telephone services. In terms of how these services should be delivered, the research suggested that people would value:

○ A use of the talents and resources of local people.
○ Flexible points of access, which allowed participation in non-threatening ways at convenient times.
○ Distance from official bureaucracy and social security services, so that people would not feel 'at risk' when accessing services. The close working relationship between social security and support services often caused users to fear changes to their benefits as a result of accessing support.
○ Services using peer-to-peer approaches were valued and trusted.
○ Services providing prompt and clear feedback to users.
○ Services and campaigns that support people to explore what is on offer and signpost into other relevant support.

Overall, given the variety of audiences and possible behaviours that comprise job seeking, one size did not fit all and there was a strong desire for flexible and tailored services amongst the target audiences.

BARRIERS

There was a mixed view of the value to existing services and some significant barriers were identified.

○ Services could not respond quickly or flexibly to the individual context of people's circumstances. This was the most significant and was mentioned most often.
○ Inappropriateness, i.e. there is nothing from the range of services on offer that suited people's individual needs.
○ Poor customer service was articulated as being 'lecturing' or 'judgemental' and it was commonly reported that service staff did not display friendly or respectful behaviour. Negative experience of service staff included being unhelpful or condescending.
○ Experiences of service staff were needn't be experienced first hand to affect service use. 'Perception' of the likely response to the claimant by service staff was enough to prevent service users from accessing services. Sometimes the perception was not gained personally but instead through stories and urban myths from within the communities. (Conversely, a positive story from an existing service user was enough to influence use of a service).
○ If general motivation and confidence were low then the likelihood of audiences accessing services was low, no matter how important the service was or how local.

SOCIAL NORMS

The role of social norms includes the influence (both implicit and explicit) of established and approved ways of doing things most commonly, this is viewed as what is 'acceptable' or 'not acceptable' by peers or people invested with authority. Insight highlighted a significant framing made by reference to local geography, although influence also extended across interest groups (such as lone parents or migrants). These were described in both supportive and negative ways. Examples included opinions towards migrants (taking 'our' jobs).

Peer groups were commonly cited as important places for support and opinion and exerted a strong pull. They wielded considerable influence and opportunities for engaging target audiences.

In relation to job seeking and associated behaviours, the insight suggested there was significant opportunity to reframe local norms to influence attitudes and behaviours of target audiences. It is therefore perhaps unsurprising that children and their needs carried significant influence with parent target audiences. Parents and lone parents reported deferring serious job-hunting until children reached at least five years old, with school age being the significant transition point. The view almost universally held was that it was better for a mother to be at home/close at hand during these formative years. Where there was a rare divergence from that opinion, it was strongly challenged by peers in the group discussions.

Whilst childcare was valued, it was regarded as a second-best option and often unaffordable. Insight suggested that the importance which audiences ascribed to 'putting children first' represented a significant barrier to job seeking behaviours.

SOCIAL ADVERTISING

Target audiences were able to list a range of existing services, but with varying degrees of accuracy. It was therefore evident that work to increase awareness of offers already in place might be useful. Any brand model would need to take into account the plethora of existing services and brands. Research showed that any brand should communicate flexibility, choice, be trusted and be seen as local. All target audiences reported that the message strategy should be reassuring and supportive and focused on the messages of being 'here to help' and 'available if needed'. Drawing on the social-norm insight, there was also scope for motivating people and challenging misinformation. It was concluded that social advertising approaches should reinforce activity which supports people to end negative and habitual behaviour and challenge social norms such as 'there are no jobs out there' and 'I can't do that'. Messages should promote a sense of immediacy and build beliefs that 'this is possible' and 'I can make a change'.

Target audiences were clear that campaigns should use channels such as personal and community networks and make use of service hubs (both online and physical services) as well as traditional media channels.

ACTIONABLE INSIGHTS

The scoping stage highlighted a number of actionable insights, which were used to shape interventions across the methods mix. We summarise some of the findings below.

- Worklessness: The target audience's view of worklessness typically came with few positives (the only one being that it allowed more time with young children). However, what people felt about being out of work was sometimes exposed as being different from actual behaviours, and knowledge of future job trends was low.
- Responsibilities: Across audiences there was little evidence of the 'welfare dependency culture' that is sometimes ascribed to similar communities. That is not to say it does not exist, but it was believed that the responsibility for job seeking and job preparedness should be shared

by individuals and the government (including the local council). The evidence from insight and from the wider programme activity is that there are a significant number of people who were prepared to take an active and positive part in job-seeking activity. Another example was the willingness of audiences to explore self-employment opportunities. This was mitigated by a lack of trust in the local self-employment organisations whose purpose was to support steps into enterprise.

○ Job Centre Plus[9]: Despite being a service that almost every unemployed person of working age should access regularly, few positive experiences of Job Centre Plus were noted. Audiences (particularly women and mothers) described the physical building as an unpleasant place to visit and they found the groups of people hanging around outside the building intimidating. Once inside, because they regularly saw different advisors, they described poor customer care and low understanding of personal needs. Beliefs included that information was skewed, incorrect and given to encourage people into work at any cost.

○ Attitudes towards study: Supporting progress in study, preparation for study, and gaining new skills and confidence are goals of the Worklessness Programme. The insight highlighted positive attitudes towards study but differences between audiences. For example, the closer to school age respondents were, the more negative were their attitudes. The location of study also influenced attitude and motivation – local, flexible opportunities were preferred to more traditional learning providers. Locally, for example, Grimsby College was viewed by older participants as being 'for young people'.

○ Childcare: for parents and carers, childcare remained a persistent issue, and in this instance availability of suitable childcare facilities for learners was important.

○ Volunteering: People were positive about volunteering opportunities if they felt the activity to be rewarding and productive. Clear links to job preparedness increased volunteer motivation, and value increased if concrete outcomes such as certificates, references or letters outlining skills were available.

○ Help seeking and advice: Many of the audiences exhibited a general distrust of 'official' sources of information, unless they had had a specific positive experience of them. This was especially true of those parents who had been out of work for some time, and Job Agencies in particular elicited low opinions. The influence of peers was strong and has been noted above – often people would go to friends and family in the first instance and then validate elsewhere, perhaps with official services.

○ Time and effort: The main perceived 'costs' were non-monetary, namely time and effort. There was a cost in regard to the perceived time and effort involved in job searching. This was related to the type of jobs available, the amount of pay and the compulsion placed on job seeking by the Job Centre. As an attempt to respond to this, the total range of job benefits were highlighted, including being a positive role model for children, developing skills and gaining socialising opportunities. However, pay was described as the single biggest factor. Transport (distance to travel) was not significant if the employment was within the area.

IMPLEMENTATION OF INSIGHTS

These insights led to the development of a creative concept called 'First Things First', which appealed to parents and carers by drawing on their emotional and physical relationships with children.

---

[9] Jobcentre Plus is a public-sector service and is part of the Department for Work and Pensions. It provides services that support people from welfare into work, and helps employers to fill their vacancies.

A range of interventions were developed from the insight, including social advertising, supporting new worker roles and community mobilisation. A community-led social marketing approach was adopted (Smith and Henry, 2009), which built in co-production activity and engaged communities within the design, development and delivery of the programme.

A series of audience-specific messages were developed. For example, the messages addressed the difficulty audiences feared balancing work and caring responsibilities, some acknowledged and used the transition points of reaching school age to motivating parents into preparing for work. Others implicitly drew on parents as role models. The exact messages and look of each were pre-tested across target audiences. Illustration was used to reinforce look and feel of the resource and the child-focused feel was maintained by using fridge magnets, postcards, stickers and flash cards.

 ## STAKEHOLDER ENGAGEMENT

The programme strives to create successful conditions for partnership working. Recognising the influence of different providers across local networks and organisations, considerable effort was placed on engaging stakeholders. At the commencement of the programme, an 'Experts on the Ground' event brought interested people together. The event started scoping activity, generated ownership, identified networks and raised awareness of the programme locally. People were mobilised into two community teams, based around priority neighbourhood areas. Teams were put together to comprise at least 50 per cent local people, supported by a range of professionals who contributed their service expertise.

Local learning workshops brought together local people and a range of service providers services at three-day residential events, where they were shown best practice from across the country. In between learning events, stakeholders were supported to understand local needs, test interventions, celebrate success, engage peers and so on.

A multi-agency Steering Group meets bi-monthly to support teams. Representatives take challenges back to their own organisation to support implementation and system change. A longer-term focus is maintained by identifying opportunities to develop skills and confidence between community and staff groups.

BARRIERS

A competition analysis was conducted to identify the main barriers to implementation and impact. The main barriers identified included:

- Child dependence: Children provided a significant draw away from work, learning, volunteering and work preparedness. With key target groups, this was one of the most significant sources of competition.
- Peers: Peers were identified as a significant influence on behaviours, in terms of validating behaviours or offering information and advice. The research showed that it peers often wielded a negative influence on job-seeking behaviours.
- The wider economic downturn: Given the worsening economic context, our programme was competing with a range of information being delivered through national and local media. This was often pessimistic and largely negative. The influence on audiences was to reinforce existing fatalistic attitudes, compound low self-esteem and leave people thinking 'what's the point?'

○ Immigration: There were significant negative attitudes towards immigrants, in particular communities from former Eastern Europe, who were seen to be taking local jobs.
○ Financial disincentives: Even when similar amounts of financial benefit were on offer, the overall package had to be significantly greater to mobilise people.
○ Lack of trust in official services: Specifically Job Centre Plus.
○ Health and well-being: Physical, and specifically mental health, was a significant influence on behaviour and perceptions of ability to influence change. Although we did not record it, there was a high proportion of respondents with physical ill health and disabilities. Many people spoke about the negative effect unemployment can have on mental health. This was often described as propagating low self-esteem, pessimism and stress.

MARKETING MIX

The marketing mix included a multi-factorial range of interventions, developed in an attempt to overcome the 'price' and other barriers identified during the scoping phase.

PRODUCT

The core product (i.e. benefit promised) was to reduce child poverty by increasing profitability in the participating areas. This is difficult to measure in the short term, as the project was only in existence for 12 months at time of writing.

The actual product (i.e. desired behaviour) was to support and encourage people to access the services which were currently being provided and to track them through the system of support to employment.

The augmented product (tangible object/service) included:

○ Positioning of new 'Key Worker Posts' within community teams. These people would provide support to the community teams and also act as an entry point for the unemployed and unengaged; providing support, information, giving the participant direction and purpose, and putting together a plan of action that moves the participant towards employment and beyond. The workers support individuals during their initial employment and will monitor the individual's journey to gainful activity
○ Referral and signposting into services through community events and peer-to-peer interaction across community networks to engage out-of-work people and refer them into services
○ Providing new volunteering opportunities and promotion of existing opportunities.
○ Implicit and explicit rewards for the community team members including:
  o Acquisition of new skills such as training for community members around research skills.
  o Development of confidence and perceptions of ability to influence change within communities.
  o Participation within residential learning events.

COST/EXCHANGE

In addition to time and effort costs, the following costs were addressed by the programme:

○ Many parents deferred job seeking (postponing potential enjoyment, learning and voluntary opportunities) for the sake of their children. The response was to minimise the perceived loss of time with children, and maximise outcomes of employment for parent and children.

○ Costs were also viewed in terms of the range of benefit and support packages (largely financial, such as housing benefit and council-tax rebate) that would be withdrawn on return to work. Even when Benefit Advisers demonstrated that people would be financially better off in employment, there was a reluctance to believe them. By linking the target group up with a range of sources of financial advice, it was possible to direct people to a range of support services.

○ Costs in terms of social standing – both positive and negative. Most friends and peer groups exerted an implicit influence on people, and sanctions were put in place if they did not comply. Sanctions included challenge to behaviour and negative comments which were all observed during group discussions. The Worklessness Programme engaged people and used implicit and explicit reward mechanisms to support their involvement in the scheme. By engaging local people in the delivery of messages to peers the programme sought to draw on the influence peers can exert.

PLACE

In order to avoid costly duplication, the project focused on engaging with existing services and supporting people to access those services. Local networks, focusing on where parents and carers engage, were also used. These included, primary schools, children's centres, local shops and supermarkets, post offices (where receipt of benefit takes place) and Job Centre Plus. In addition to local networks, community-service networks were also used, such as local car-boot sales, community centres and social clubs.

Innovative settings were also targeted. For example, by identifying 400 families who were out of work but used the local children's centre, a coach trip was organised as a means of recruiting and engaging those families on the coach. A healthy burger van is being planned by one parent as a means of engaging people outside of the job centre.

Finally, personal networks were utilised in the form of peer-to-peer engagement. Local relationships have acted as 'passports' and identified a range of networks to use, many of which are closed to professionals. Community members get into relationship marketing approaches and have been successful at using interpersonal channels.

PROMOTION

A social advertising campaign, 'How 2', which drew on key messages around preparedness for work, was developed, targeting different audience segments (such as mothers with children approaching school age or people believing they have no time to volunteer/learn new skills). The objective of this campaign was to:

> Get parents to make a step towards working – this might be training, careers advice, or job seeking action.

The proposition was not 'get a job'. It is wider than this, in acknowledgement of the multiple steps people sometimes must take before they 'get a job'. The proposition was 'Plan for your child's future by getting ready for work now' (see Figures 12.1 and 12.2).

Figure 12.1 Social advertising campaign

Figure 12.2 'First Things First' posters

MONITORING AND EVALUATION

A variation of the Total Process Planning framework (see Chapter 3) (National Social Marketing Centre, 2009) was used to approach the overall project in sequential and together with the PDSA (the Plan Do See Act approach developed by Deming, 1993). In addition, small change cycles were used at each individual stage of planning and intervention to understand the impact and effectiveness of their intervention. Using the PDSA methodology offers a very simple and straightforward approach to testing out interventions.

FINDINGS

The approach used to achieve the outcome of improved economic activity has been to raise awareness of the services already in place to assist the unemployed back into work and to 'nudge' them to use these services. Initial targets have predominantly been achieved or surpassed (see Table 12.1).

Table 12.1   Evaluation data

Indicator Description	Annual Target	Target to Sept 2010	Actual Sept 2010
Increasing engagement/ interaction with the programme	1100	1100	1140
Increasing the availability of new jobs (the number of people getting a new job)	3	3	2
Demonstrating partnership working by working with other agencies to develop new employment opportunities (the number of agencies worked with who then provided new employment opportunities)	3	3	11
Increasing referral to the key workers programme	4	4	20
Increasing utilisation of other framework programmes (number of people accessing other framework programmes as a result of engagement with this programme)	15	15	435
Increasing confidence in individuals to access what is already in existence for them (measured by self reported case studies)	5	5	5
Increasing the number in regular volunteering roles	5	5	21
Increasing publicity for the programme by utilising media opportunities in a proactive manner	12	12	29

Specific work around return on investment is taking place now to demonstrate the contribution of the programme.

 ## LESSONS LEARNT

The key lessons learnt were:

1 Increases in levels of confidence have been difficult to measure: Originally the programme planned to develop its own confidence measuring tool but this plan was discarded to enable consistency within the Change Programme by adopting the Rickter Tool.[10] However, the training has still not been organised within the Change Programme, preventing our teams from accessing it and recording confidence. The teams decided to demonstrate confidence by recording case studies and testimonials.
2 Difficulty of engaging with Job Centre Plus: Despite a lot of effort, the inclusion of key services within the programme has been difficult and this may relate to their ability to agree involvement at a local level, or conflicting priorities. Typically, strategic involvement is at a level too high to properly allow local services to get involved. An understanding of this arrangement may have helped engage more local managers who might have been better levers for change.
3 Managing complexity: There are significant advantages of adopting co-production approaches within social marketing projects but it also brings added complexity and project management demands, which stakeholders need to plan for. Specific and dedicated project management is essential, as is an organisational culture that can respond quickly and flexibly to meet community member's needs. Examples include practical considerations, such as meeting at times and places to suit community members, and adopting values that champion communities as assets and equal partners.
4 Developing stakeholder and partner assets: The number and variety of local stakeholders provided specific challenge and this was compounded by the great variety in confidence, skill and value given to engaging communities. The importance of developing a clear stakeholder and partner development and management plan is an important tactic when working to develop effective coalitions.

CHAPTER RECAP

This chapter has shown that utilising and improving existing services is far more cost effective than developing new services. However, when dealing with established services, barriers exist. As with your target audience, you also have to understand your partners' priorities and make sure you offer them an exchange that they value, or be able to show how your work helps to meet their current priorities.

In the next chapter we will learn how strong 'messaging' can be used to shift social norms and attitudes.

---

[10] The Rickter Scale© is produced by the Rickter Company Ltd and is a board used to first chart a baseline of where a person currently is, then at the end of an intervention, so that you can record changes and improvements in knowledge and confidence.

SELF-REVIEW QUESTIONS

1 The overall aim of this project was to reduce child poverty by increasing profitability in the participating areas. In the lessons learnt, the project team described their difficulties in measuring their impact in this area. What measures would you use to evaluate your impact with this or a similar project?
2 A barrier was 'Lack of trust in official services'. What interventions would you develop to try and specifically reduce or remove this barrier?
3 In addition to service redesign, social advertising was used. Based on the insights and barriers discussed in this chapter, what key messages would you develop and why?

REFERENCES

Deming, W. E. (1993). *The New Economics for Industry, Government, Education*. Cambridge, MA: MIT Press.

Longlands, S., Jackson M., Brown, G. and Smith J. (2009). Making it work: Analysing different ways of tackling worklessness. Mancheester: Centre for Local Economic Strategies.

Meadows, P. (2006). What works with tackling worklessness. London: London Development Agency.

National Social Marketing Centre. (2009). *Social Marketing – Big Pocket Guide*. Available online at: www.thensmc.com/component/remository/NSMC-Publications/Social-Marketing-Big-Pocket-guide/. Accessed August 2010.

Ritchie, H., Casebourne, J. and Rick J. (2005). Understanding workless people and communities: A literature review. London: HMSO.

Smith, A. and Henry, L. (2009). Setting the guinea pigs free: Towards a new model of community led social marketing. *Public Health* 123, Suppl. 1: 1–5.

UK Office of National Statistics. www.nomisweb.co.uk. Accessed December 2010.

13 BUILDING STRONG COMMUNICATIONS INTO THE MARKETING MIX

VIGNETTE: 'SAVE THE CRABS – THEN EAT 'EM'

KEY WORD: REFRAMING THE ISSUE

To reduce nutrient pollution flowing into the Chesapeake Bay, USA, this media-based programme convinced area residents to fertilise their lawns in the autumn rather than spring, in order to minimise pollution impact on a regional icon – the Blue Crab.

The programme was run by the Academy for Educational Development, and framed not as an environmental appeal, but as an appeal to the target audience's stomachs – as a way to ensure the continued availability of Chesapeake Bay seafood. This helped to tune in audiences who may otherwise have tuned out, and was sufficiently newsworthy to gain significant media coverage.

The programme resulted in statistically significant reductions in spring-time lawn fertilisation, and widespread programme recall.

This case study is available in full at: www.thensmc.com.

This vignette makes the point that strong communications can be a crucial component of the marketing mix, and that reframing a traditional message can be a powerful tool for gaining target audience and media buy-in.

ABOUT THIS CHAPTER

As we discussed in Chapter 1, a combination of an appropriate range of methods is one of social marketing's key principles. On its own, promotion, or 'communication', is not enough to change behaviours. However, it is an important part of the mix and in some instances it is based on robust research, and creatively produced and delivered it can have dramatic effects.

In this chapter you will learn:

- How strong 'messaging' can be used to shift social norms and attitudes.
- How a social marketing planning team successfully reframed the issue of domestic violence to focus not on naming and blaming perpetrators, but on offering the hope of a better future.
- How a project team worked in partnership with journalists and the media to reduce media misreporting of domestic violence 'myths', and to ensure reframing of the message occurred via local and national press.

CASE STUDY: PROGRAMME FOR ACTION ON FAMILY VIOLENCE 'IT'S NOT OK'

Tracey Bridges, Senate Communications, New Zealand

This case study appears in full on the National Social Marketing Centre's ShowCase resource (www.thensmc.com), and further information is available on the 'It's Not OK' website at www.areyouok.org.nz.

PROJECT OVERVIEW

The Programme for Action on Family Violence is an initiative of the New Zealand Taskforce for Action on Violence within Families, which is made up of 17 government and non-government organisations.

The 'Family Violence: It's Not OK' social marketing programme is led by the New Zealand Ministry of Social Development and the Families Commission, with a mass-media programme designed to provide an umbrella for communication and marketing activities run by organisations throughout New Zealand.

This work has a budget of NZ$14 million over four years.

PROJECT RATIONALE

At the time the programme was initiated, an average of 14 women, 10 children and six men died each year as a result of family violence, with many more being hurt, physically, mentally or emotionally (NZFVCH, 2007).

The economic cost of family violence is estimated at between NZ$1.2 and NZ$5.3 billion each year (Snively, 1994).

In 2005, the New Zealand government established a Taskforce for Action on Violence within Families, to address this problem in a systematic way. The Taskforce's vision is that 'all families and whanau [extended family] have healthy, respectful, stable relationships, free from violence'. The Taskforce's work programme includes:

- Encouraging leadership to end family violence and promote stable families.
- Working with communities to change attitudes and behaviours towards violence.

○ Seeking a highly responsive justice sector to ensure the safety of victims and observers and hold perpetrators accountable.
○ Ensuring service providers have the capability and capacity to meet demand for services.

The Programme for Action on Family Violence is one of the Taskforce's initiatives.

 AIMS AND OBJECTIVES

The programme aimed to mobilise New Zealanders to change the way they think and act about family violence, as part of a broader programme of policies and initiatives. The long-term behavioural goals are to:

○ Reduce the incidence of family violence in New Zealand.
○ Increase the number of New Zealanders prepared to talk about family violence.
○ Increase the number of New Zealanders prepared to offer help in family violence situations.
○ Increase the number of New Zealanders prepared to seek help.
○ Reduce the media's reporting of family violence myths.

IDENTIFYING TARGET AUDIENCES

Family violence is a complex social issue, covering child maltreatment, abuse of elders and intimate partner violence, as well as many degrees of physical and emotional abuse.

This programme began with the hypothesis that the problem that should be targeted initially was 'male perpetrated intimate partner violence', on the basis that this was the most prevalent form of violence, the form that was associated with the most serious physical harm, and that it was often accompanied by other forms of violence (such as child maltreatment).

From this hypothesis, the project team expected that the primary target audiences might be the perpetrators of intimate partner violence and their influencers, as well as those affected by or aware of it. The project began with formative research to better understand these audiences, their perspectives, the likelihood of change and their openness to mass media messages. The team expected that this research would identify a defined audience segment, to guide them in targeting behavioural messages and channels. However, against expectations, the research identified that a more general population shift in attitudes to domestic violence was needed. Thus, instead of a narrow audience focus, the programme would need to engage a wider audience to contribute to a supportive social norm and create a context for later, more segment-specific, interventions.

So the target audience for Phase 1 of the programme was the whole New Zealand population. This provided a strong and consistent foundation for Phase 2 of the programme, which specifically addressed male perpetrators of intimate partner violence, with their influencers as a secondary audience.

Phase 3 was designed to target people who are able to offer help (primarily families and friends), as well as those who might ask for or accept help (perpetrators and victims).

Clearly underpinning all of this activity is the support sector that works in the area of family violence, such as police, social care and family welfare. This sector is not a direct target audience in itself, but was a critical audience for programme communications, and without its support and engagement the programme would not have succeeded.

SCOPING RESEARCH

LITERATURE REVIEW

The first stage of research consisted of a literature review, which searched out studies from other agencies and jurisdictions into family-violence-related interventions and media programmes. This review identified factors contributing to the success of previous international and local social marketing programmes (Davies, 2003; Gravitas, 2006).

QUALITATIVE RESEARCH

The next stage consisted of qualitative audience research, made up of interviews and focus groups with male perpetrators of intimate partner violence, their partners and others around them. This research identified:

- Divergent opinions about what is considered to be 'right' or 'wrong'; whose fault domestic violence is; how and why violence happens; and how it might be stopped. It revealed that men who perpetrate violence minimise, justify or disassociate themselves from this violence; and that people around them do the same. It also revealed that taking a polarised approach to domestic violence would mean the complexity of the issue would be overlooked as people would simply choose 'sides'.
- Way of life: violence is a way of life for many people, and many do not know any other response when they are under pressure or not getting what they want. This meant that if the programme was going to ask them to give up that behaviour, it would have to offer a real alternative.
- Lack of a common language: this phase of research also identified that there was no common definition of family violence and no agreed way to talk about it.

UNDERSTANDING THE ISSUE OF HELP

As the programme developed, the focus turned to the issue of giving and receiving help. Evaluation of the early phases showed that the programme had increased the personal relevance of family violence and increased people's propensity to act, but people were still unsure about the actions they could take.

The next phase of research focused around the issue of giving and receiving help. This research showed that:

- Victims and perpetrators want to access support from those around them.
- Informal support networks play a highly influential role.
- Many people are motivated to help but are offering help in ineffective ways.
- Every person who had made positive changes had someone on their side who believed in them and supported them.
- The help of just one person was often enough to make the difference.
- One person 'making a stand' against violence can act as a catalyst for change and attract others to join them.
- Displeasure and challenges from a number of family members can influence a positive change in perpetrators' behaviour. (Metzger, 2010)

ACTIONABLE INSIGHTS

One of the programme's most important insights came through from the key informant interviews, audience research and discussions with Taskforce members. In the words of one informant:

> We're not just talking about shitty men. [Sometimes], we're talking about good men with shitty behaviour.

This insight helped the project team to understand that the programme could begin by focusing on people who wanted, or were prepared, to change their behaviour. It also showed that if the programme was to succeed, it would be important to present a hopeful message that change was possible. Simply shaming and blaming perpetrators and victims would not lead to success.

Based on this insight, the programme was developed around the key concept of balancing 'light and dark'.

Family violence is a dark issue, and needs to be taken seriously, without risk of downplaying the harm it causes. But the literature review (Davies, 2003) confirmed that enacting violence causes people to distance themselves from the issue, and to take a defensive stance. This campaign needed to have a hopeful and positive side that helped people see themselves in the issue and see that change was possible.

The next insight was that a language was needed for talking about family violence, so people felt confident and empowered to talk to each other. The project team wanted a phrase that was already part of the vernacular, easy to use and unequivocal, but not too 'preachy'. The phrase needed to balance the light and dark sides of this issue.

The selected phrase and guiding principles for the programme were:

> Family violence, it's not OK. But it is OK to ask for help.

See Figure 13.1. The working components of this are:

- 'It's Not OK' as a catch phrase for the issue and the programme.
- 'Are you OK?', which is the website URL, and has also become a question people can use when they are offering help to others.
- 'It is OK to ask for help', which is a behaviour message around the programme's core product: help.

Figure 13.1 The programme image

Source: The Campaign for Action on Family Violence: www.areyouok.org.nz

Another important insight was that, at least initially, the programme would not reach perpetrators and their partners if it did not also reach the people around them. A change in attitude first needed to be achieved at a population level, so that future executions of the campaign would have a consistent context within which to resonate.

COMPETITION

Competition was considered from several different angles. The programme was competing with:

- A social norm that supports and normalises violence.
- Ingrained personal mechanisms for dealing with anger and frustration.
- News stories that perpetuated myths about family violence.
- Other government programmes competing for public attention and for individual behaviour change.

An understanding of these competitive factors influenced how the programme was developed, the messages that were selected, the channels that were used to promote it and the partners that were chosen to help deliver change.

 MARKETING MIX

PRODUCT

The core product for this programme is a reduction in domestic violence, achieved by shifting social norms and providing easier access to 'help'. The key purpose of the programme was to encourage people to get help, ask for help, offer help and accept help. The major benefit of the product is a better life.

PRICE, COST AND EXCHANGE

The product has a surprisingly high price. Research demonstrated that it is not only difficult to ask for help, it's also difficult to offer it, and in many cases to accept it. Asking for, and accepting, help is made difficult by social expectations that we should be able to cope without help; reluctance to betray or let down family members; fear of consequences (loss of family; loss of social standing; loss of friendships; greater harm); a sense that your circumstance is normal; not knowing who will help or where to get help; not believing you deserve help; fear that the help will come with too many 'strings' – and much more.

Offering help is made difficult by uncertainty or doubt that there really is something wrong; a New Zealand culture of 'minding your own business'; a lack of confidence that it's your 'place' to help; lack of knowledge about how to help; fear that trying to help could make matters worse; lack of confidence in your ability to help; fear of being rejected or losing the relationship.

'It's Not OK' aims to bring the price of help down, and encourage people to seek, offer or accept help.

PROMOTION AND PLACE

The programme was promoted through a variety of channels and had a clear and consistent tone:

1 Positive messaging: Although one group of messages paints a clear picture about what's not OK ('It's not OK to teach your kids that violence is the way to get what you want; it's not OK to blame the drink; it's not OK to punch a hole in the wall to show your wife who's boss…'), the programme always concludes with a clear and positive message about what is OK ('It is OK to ask for help'). The programme also uses stories of positive change to demonstrate the benefits of asking for help (four men, not actors, telling their personal stories, showing that the reward for getting help is a better life).
2 News media advocacy: Used extensively, promoting the product through the news media, and working closely with the news media to change the way they report family violence. The aim was to change the reporting and perpetuation of myths around family violence and therefore increase the cost of the competitive product (continuing to be violent).
3 Website and freephone number: Used to ensure help and support was easily available for those who were ready to act. The freephone telephone helpline was available seven days a week. The programme also promoted other helplines and services, including local crisis and support services.
4 A community Action Fund: For groups to create projects in their local communities and create a greater reach for the promotion materials.
5 Influencing popular culture: The project team worked on getting programme messages into popular television programmes, via story lines.
6 Mass media: There was an integrated mass-media strategy promoting the programme messages through television advertising, radio advertising for specific targeted audience groups (Maori and Pacific Island) and billboards.
7 Partnerships: The programme worked with local government, businesses, sports teams, churches, youth organisations and many others to expand its influence and reach, by organising community events and mobilising local networks.
8 Printed collateral: Support materials were produced and distributed to all partners to use in their communities, including posters, bumper stickers, balloons and other items.

 ## STAKEHOLDER ENGAGEMENT

Stakeholder engagement was positioned at the heart of the programme. Family violence is a problem that central government cannot solve on its own, and that is unlikely to respond to a traditional command-and-control approach. In response to this, the project team chose to embrace complexity, creating a strong sense of purpose and a core 'idea' to guide communications, but then opening the door to partners and collaborators to help shape it, create ideas, and let it unfold.

The project leaders invested a significant amount of energy in liaising with all the different parties involved in the management or governance of the project, to ensure they were informed of the programme's progress, and continued to support it. It was clear from the start that this project provided an opportunity to tap into a community movement, to engage the energy of the many people already working on the issue, and to bring together their 'many voices'. The project team were also aware that if they did not gain that support and develop a programme that made sense to, and was useful to these stakeholders, the initiative risked alienating people who were working hard on this issue, and undermining them in their work.

In the early stages of the programme, the stakeholder-engagement strategy was to reach as many stakeholders as possible. The project team took a rough cut of the advertising concept and strap-line to numerous meetings, to show stakeholders what the planned programme looked like and allow them an opportunity to influence it. It was important to understand if the proposals resonated with the community and stakeholders; to assess if there were issues to be aware of; and to give people a chance to start thinking about how they could work alongside the project.

A key part of the programme was the Community Action Fund. The fund accounted for around a third of the project's funding, and enabled groups around New Zealand to develop their own ways to tap into the programme aims, imagery and messaging, and take the programme into their own communities. (See Figure 13.2.)

MONITORING AND EVALUATION

The evolution of the programme was informed by a range of measures:

- Face-to-face survey of 2,444 people to test overall attitudes and beliefs relating to family violence, and awareness of the programme (McLaren, 2008).
- Community study (CSRE, 2010) to review programme impact in four communities. The study included one-on-one interviews, telephone interviews and group interviews. Respondents included members of the public, service providers and service users from communities chosen to represent different aspects of New Zealand society, including ethnicity, socio-economic and level of social services.
- Three tracking surveys (McLaren, 2010) measuring mass-media reach and retention, in December 2001, April 2008 and September 2008. In total, 2,695 people aged 18–49 were surveyed by telephone.
- Regular media audits, identifying progress of the news-media advocacy project and identifying areas for future focus (NZ Ministry of Social Development, 2010).
- An independent review (Point Research, 2010) into the insights and lessons learnt from the 'It's Not OK' programme.

The programme also gathers direct feedback from partners and the community.

Figure 13.2 'It's Not Ok' marketing collateral

Source: The Campaign for Action on Family Violence: www.areyouok.org.nz

FINDINGS

The programme team acknowledge that benchmarking could have been stronger, and have worked hard to improve evaluation processes as the programme has evolved. However, there are still some strong results to demonstrate that 'It's Not OK' is having impact:

CREATING A COMMON LANGUAGE

'It's Not OK' has become a phrase that people associate with family violence in New Zealand and that they use to describe the behaviour of others or themselves, and to prompt action. Asking 'Are you OK?' has become a coded way to safely raise the issue of family violence (community feedback, anecdotal).

ACCESS TO SUPPORT SERVICES

As a result of the programme, individuals, particularly men, are seeking help to change their behaviours, and direct feedback from frontline workers shows that people are citing the programme as the reason they have sought help:

> Joe came to us as a result of ringing the 0800 number he saw on television. He said 'I felt it was me up there on the screen … It's not OK, what I do to Maria and the kids … The ad said "It's OK, we can help you", so I wrote the number down.' (Relationship Services)

> These guys are coming along to our programmes of their own volition, rather than being shown along by the courts. One said 'I saw those "It's Not OK" ads and I was thinking about it … I don't want my kids to be scared of me, so here I am.' (Preventing Violence in the Home)

> It is striking how much attention and conversation the campaign is creating. Referrals are almost universally up, with clients mentioning the advertisements as a reason they have decided to seek help. We have also heard many stories indicating that the campaign is producing increased levels of intervention when people witness inappropriate or unsafe interactions. (Jigsaw Family Services)

MEDIA COVERAGE

Annual media audits have found that the campaign's media-advocacy programme has brought about a measurable change in the way family violence is covered by the New Zealand press (NZ Ministry of Social Development, 2010). Evaluation found that, compared to pre-campaign, news stories about family violence now:

- Contain fewer myths about violence than before the campaign began
- Contain comment from more experts
- Contain information about where help and information can be found.

COMMUNITY MOBILISATION

The Community Study, undertaken in four communities in 2008, found that 'It's Not OK' legitimises local family violence initiatives, gives community groups confidence to carry out their own local campaigns and has contributed to increased membership of groups involved in family violence (all communities reported increased collaboration amongst community groups and increased demand on services) (CSRE, 2010). The study also showed that 'It's Not OK' has given people permission to intervene in family violence; increased willingness to offer help and support; and raised awareness of ways to get help (25 per cent of respondents said they had done something to stop family violence, and 50 per cent of those said that the campaign had contributed to their decision to act) (CSRE, 2010).

AWARENESS AND BEHAVIOUR CHANGE

The mass-media tracking survey in September 2008 found that 95 per cent of respondents recalled seeing at least one of the campaign advertisements (Fleur, 2010). Of those:

- 68 per cent agreed that the campaign helped them to understand more about behaviours that should not be tolerated.
- 88 per cent agreed that the campaign made them see that change is possible.
- 57 per cent agreed that the advertisements made them feel that they could help to influence someone to change their violent behaviour. This feeling was particularly strong for Pacific peoples.
- 68 per cent had discussed the campaign with someone else.
- 22 per cent reported taking at least one action as a result of seeing the campaign. Actions included talking to friends and family about violence they were worried about (14 per cent), obtaining information about family violence (8 per cent) and contacting an organisation or professional to talk about violence they were worried about (5 per cent).

LESSONS LEARNT

Although developing strong relationships was a big part of the programme's success, the team acknowledges that it could have worked with stakeholders better. In hindsight, the project team might have moved more quickly to form relationships. If a strength was being open and involving others, then in hindsight a lesson is to do that even more: more openly, more quickly, more confidently.

In terms of what has made this programme strong, the most powerful lessons include:

- Letting go and involving others: Being able to share ownership and control of the programme – creating a clear intention and a solid core and then opening the programme up for others to use and build and extend however they chose to.
- Authenticity and redemption: The stories of positive change from men who have been violent, sometimes terribly so, have been enormously powerful. They have contributed to this programme being about much more than just awareness – fundamentally about change. Similarly, the focus on the possibility of redemption – rather than just blaming and shaming people who have been violent – has allowed 'It's Not OK' to engage many people and contributed to a sense of hope.
- Tapping into a movement: There is a movement of New Zealanders who want to put a stop to violence in our community. The team made it their mission to tap into, and add strength to, that movement. That has gave the project more momentum than if it had tried to create something new that was driven solely from central government.

Finally: always remember that it is OK to ask for help. If you want to know more, visit www.areyouok.org.nz.

CHAPTER RECAP

In this chapter we have explored the role of communications within the social marketing methods mix. We have seen how appropriate and emotive 'messaging' can be used to shift social norms and attitudes, and how working closely with the media and community groups can be an important tool when ensuring appropriate portrayal of the issue you are seeking to change.

In the next chapter we will consider the role of enforcement in the marketing mix, and learn how a strong engagement from police and licensing authorities helped to generate strong project outcomes for reducing alcohol-related harm.

SELF-REVIEW QUESTIONS

1 In this chapter you have seen the importance of reframing a traditionally divisive issue, to generate a sense of positive hope for the future. In your opinion, what are the relevant benefits of a shock tactics, or scaremongering approach, versus a more positive portrayal of alternative possibilities?

2 'It's Not OK' illustrates how projects sometimes have to generate a whole-population level of awareness before more targeted interventions can be developed. What might have been the risks to this programme if it had only focused on interventions with the perpetrators and victims of domestic abuse?

3 The role of the media was at the centre of this programme, as project leads were aware that domestic abuse was commonly misrepresented by the media. Consider how the media might be involved in other social marketing programmes, and list five ways in which they could be engaged to support a behaviour change of your choosing.

REFERENCES

CSRE (Centre for Social Research and Evaluation). (2010). *Community Study Summary Report, the Programme for Action on Family Violence.* Wellington, NZ: CSRE.

Davies, E., Hammerton, H., Hassall, I., Fortune, C. A. and Moeller, I. (2003). How can the literature inform implementation of Action Area 13 of TeRito: Public education and awareness. Wellington, NZ: Ministry of Health and Ministry of Social Development.

Gravitas Research and Strategy Limited. (2006). Reducing family violence: Social marketing programme formative research. Wellington, NZ: GRSL.

McLaren, Fleur. (2008). Attitudes, values and beliefs about violence within families. Wellington, NZ: Centre for Social Research and Evaluation.

McLaren, Fleur. (2010). Programme for Action on Family Violence: Reach and retention of the 'It's Not OK' television advertisements. Wellington, NZ: Centre for Social Research and Evaluation.

Metzger, N. and Woodley, A. (2010). Report on giving, receiving and seeking help: The Programme for Action on Family Violence. Wellington, NZ: Ministry of Social Development.

New Zealand Ministry of Social Development. (2010). Media advocacy project review. Wellington, NZ: MSD.

NZFVC (New Zealand Family Violence Clearinghouse). (2007). Fact sheet – Family violence statistics. Christchurch, NZ: NZFVC.

Point Research. (2010). An innovative approach to changing social attitudes around family violence in New Zealand: Key ideas, insights, and lessons learnt. Wellington, NZ: Point Research.

Snively, S. (1994). The New Zealand economic cost of family violence. *Social Policy Journal of New Zealand*, 4. Available online at: www.msd.govt.nz/about-msd-and-our-work/publications-resources/journals-and-magazines/social-policy-journal/spj04/04-the-new-zealand-economic-cost-of-family-violence.html

14 USING ENFORCEMENT IN THE METHODS MIX

VIGNETTE: 'DON'T MESS WITH TEXAS'

KEY WORD: ENFORCEMENT

Back in 1985, the US state of Texas had a big problem with litter. To battle this large and expensive roadside mess, the Texas Highway Commission launched an extensive public education campaign, 'Don't Mess With Texas', which has been running ever since and help-ing to keep litter off the roads. As well as awareness raising and practical litter-tackling programmes, such as Campus Cleanups and 'Trash Off' (the state's largest single-day road-side clean-up), 'Don't Mess With Texas' also builds enforcement into its intervention mix.

'Report A Litterer' is a sub-programme of 'Don't Mess With Texas', which encourages people who witness road littering to report the perpetrator via a dedicated website forum. Wit-nesses report the date, time and location of the incident, along with the litterer's car-number plate, make and description. This information is then cross-referenced with the Texas Department of Transportation's registration database, and when an exact match is located, a 'Don't Mess With Texas' litter bag and warning letter are sent to the perpetrator's home.

The programme has generated high recall rates, and reductions in roadside littering.

This vignette makes the point that a 'control' element can be built into social marketing programmes, whereby 'forbidden' behaviours can be punished or discouraged via appro-priate enforcement techniques.

For full information, see: www.dontmesswithtexas.org.

ABOUT THIS CHAPTER

As we discussed in Chapter 1, successful social marketing interventions typically employ a combination of different intervention typologies, covering product, price, place and pro-motion, to support and sustain behaviour change.

In this chapter, we will explore how a strong focus on enforcement (the 'Control' ele-ment of the de-CIDES model set out in Chapter 1) can be an essential component of the intervention mix. We will see how police regulation and enforcement of licensing laws ensured that a promoted behaviour (reduced alcohol consumption) was underpinned by legislative authority, in a supportive and positive way. You will also explore how a strong partnership approach ensures that enforcement activity is truly integrated within the wider intervention mix.

CASE STUDY: 'KEEP IT SAFE': MINIMISING ALCOHOL-RELATED HARM THROUGH STREET INTERVENTIONS

Ros Jervis, Wolverhampton City Primary Care Trust; Michelle Smith, Wolverhampton City Primary Care Trust (PCT)

PROJECT OVERVIEW

'Keep It Safe' is a programme of activity, commissioned by Wolverhampton City Primary Care Trust (PCT), in the UK, which took place in Wolverhampton's city centre, as well as in two outlying town centres (Bilston and Wednesfield), in the West Midlands. Wolverhampton is one of the most densely populated places in the United Kingdom, with nearly 9,000 residents per square mile, and the city is ranked 28th most deprived out of 354 local authorities in England.

'Keep It Safe' was designed to support a multi-agency approach to tackling the harmful impacts of alcohol misuse. The intervention was delivered in two phases. Phase 1 ran on Thursdays, Fridays and Saturdays, for a total of 13 days. It started on 5 December 2008 and encompassed Christmas and the New Year celebrations. Phase 2 ran on Fridays and Saturdays, from 9 January to 21 March 2009. During the intervention period, activities ran from 20.00 to 04.00 in Wolverhampton city centre, and from 17.00 to 01.00 in Bilston and Wednesfield town centres.

The programme was led by the PCT, with significant input from multi-agency partners. It offered a practical response to the dangers of alcohol misuse, including increased police presence; voluntary 'street pastors'; temporary 'safe havens' for revellers; a temporary medical centre to alleviate pressure on the accident and emergency (A&E) department; and work to reduce use of unlicensed taxi cabs.

PROJECT RATIONALE

Reducing the impact of alcohol abuse is one of 11 goals set by Wolverhampton City PCT, in order to reduce gaps in mortality rates by tackling cardiovascular diseases and alcohol-related deaths (Wolverhampton City PCT, 2008).

Alcohol abuse accounts for 11 per cent of the gap in life expectancy in Wolverhampton. The city has over twice the national rate of alcohol abuse (Jervis, 2009), and is a national outlier for deaths from liver disease. Its effects are also seen on teenage pregnancy and levels of crime and disorder in the city: 70 per cent of A&E attendances between midnight and 05.00 on weekend nights are related to alcohol, and Wolverhampton is no exception with its busiest periods during these hours (UK Cabinet Office, 2004).

The misuse of alcohol also affects the safety of the public, and can make the city centre a dangerous place to visit.

Using an 'Alcohol Needs Assessment Research Project Modelling Tool' (2004) the PCT calculated that, at the time of programme inception, Wolverhampton had over 40,000 'hazardous' and 'harmful' drinkers (aged 16–64) and nearly 7,000 dependent drinkers (aged 16–64).[1]

Traditionally, those agencies involved in tackling alcohol-related harm have focused resources only on areas of harm that are directly relevant to them. 'Keep It Safe' replaces this disjointed approach with a multi-agency response to alcohol management, based on the premise that partnership will be required to tackle the multi-faceted issues relating to alcohol.

 ## AIMS AND OBJECTIVES

'Keep It Safe' aimed to reduce the number of alcohol-related violent assaults, alcohol-related A&E attendances and alcohol-related ambulance call-outs.

Its core objective was to keep revellers safe during busy Christmas and New Year celebrations by promoting and enabling safe behaviours around sensible drinking and getting home safely.

Secondary objectives included:

- Gathering local intelligence in relation to problematic licensed premises.
- Collecting evidence for the pursuance of license premises reviews, by premises known to be problematic by regulatory and enforcement agencies.
- Respond to domestic violence incidents more effectively.
- Increase awareness among young people of the harms that can be caused by alcohol.

 ## IDENTIFYING TARGET AUDIENCES

Intervention activities were not age-restrictive, but the programme's main target audience was 18–25-year-olds, who (based on anecdotal feedback and service data from police and medical staff) are at higher risk of drinking in excess of recommended levels, and thus of higher incidence of unprotected sex, street violence and acute intoxication.

SCOPING RESEARCH AND INSIGHTS

Extensive scoping research was undertaken, including:

EVIDENCE REVIEW

Extensive desk research was undertaken, including a review of evidence and best practice from other sites. The following interventions were reviewed and influenced the development of 'Keep It Safe':

- 'Street pastors', who were found to significantly reduce crime incidence during pilot trials in two London wards (95 per cent reduction in Peckham, and 74 per cent reduction in Camberwell) (Ascension Trust, 2007).

---

[1] In the UK, a 'hazardous' drinker is defined as somebody who drinks over the recommended weekly amount (21 units for men and 14 units for women). A 'harmful' drinker is defined as somebody who drinks over the recommended weekly amount and experiences health problems directly relating to alcohol.

◌ Use of temporary medical facilities, and multi-agency crime force to tackle rogue premises, both of which had been successfully implemented in Birmingham.

◌ Implementation of the 'Cardiff Model', which enables anonymised A&E data about time and place of violent assaults to be shared with the police, so that they can send additional officers to violence hotspots (Cardiff Model, 2007).

◌ Liverpool's 'CitySafe' model, which used a range of multi-agency interventions to achieve a 30 per cent increase in the number of people who felt safe in the evening, and 10 per cent reductions in robbery and violent crime (Liverpool, 2009). Based on Liverpool's successes, and similarities between Wolverhampton and Liverpool (both have a large city centre, with busy outlying town-centre areas), Wolverhampton integrated the additional provision of high visibility additional policing into the 'Keep It Safe' design.

YOUTH CONSULTATION

A consultation event with Wolverhampton Youth Council, and a focus group at Wolverhampton College, enabled young people to contribute to the development of Wolverhampton's first alcohol strategy (Wolverhampton Alcohol Strategy, 2008).

Young people aged 18–25 took part in focus groups to explore making Wolverhampton a safer place. When asked what made them feel unsafe they cited lack of street lighting, lack of people around venues in the early hours and congregations of people around the bus depot. When asked what would make them feel safe they mentioned the presence of more police officers. They also liked the idea of having 'safe havens' in areas where they felt most unsafe (e.g. the bus depot), and requested somewhere safe to wait for taxis.

On drinking alcohol, all agreed that drinking with friends was their main activity at weekends, and all agreed that Christmas and New Year offered more opportunities to drink. Most admitted to binge drinking – 'I'll drink a lot when I'm out with friends and then I won't drink at all for two weeks'. Most accepted that drinking to excess made them more vulnerable. Females in particular said they were aware that they needed to keep their wits about them to get home.

PUBLIC SURVEYS

City-centre surveys were conducted with members of the public. These revealed repeated problems getting taxis home at the end of the night. This informed the work around taxi promotion and safety.

 ### STAKEHOLDER INTERVIEWS

Key stakeholders were also interviewed, and their priorities were identified as follows:

◌ Tackling under-age alcohol sales in licensed premises.

◌ The need for a multi-agency licensing strategy, and wider enforcement of premises license reviews, under the Licensing Act (2003).

◌ The need for taxi marshalling.

◌ Reducing alcohol-related domestic violence.

◌ Addressing alcohol-related A&E attendances.

◌ Improving night-time transport out of the city centre.

STAKEHOLDER ENGAGEMENT

Key stakeholders included:

- Local business owners/managers
- Private-hire and hackney-carriage taxi trade
- Patrons of the night-time economy
- Local residents
- Local councillors
- Local press and radio stations.

Project partners and contributors (data) included:

- Wolverhampton City PCT
- Wolverhampton City Council
- West Midlands Police
- West Midlands Ambulance Service
- Wolverhampton City Centre Management Company[2]
- Royal Wolverhampton Hospitals Trust
- West Midlands Fire Service
- The Haven (Women's refuge)
- British Red Cross
- Wolverhampton street pastors.

Whilst stakeholder engagement was not extensive, due to the lack of planning time available to the project team, engagement activities were carried out as follows:

- Local Councillors were engaged with via regular briefing notes.
- The city-centre management team co-ordinated all communication with city-centre businesses and licensed premises.
- Relevant members of the project team engaged with representatives of alcohol-licensed trade at 'PubWatch' meetings to identify key issues facing licensed premises during the festive period.
- Engagement was also carried out with the taxi trade at private-hire and hackney-carriage working groups.
- Weekly meetings and several teleconferences were held between key partners throughout the planning phase and duration of the intervention.

MARKETING MIX

'Keep It Safe' offered a practical response to the dangers of alcohol misuse and consisted of the following interventions, which incorporated four elements of the de-CIDES model set out in Chapter 1.

---

[2] Works with a wide range of partners across the city to encourage continued improvement in the city's environment, safety and investment opportunities.

ENFORCEMENT/CONTROL

In response to stakeholder concerns about irresponsible licensees selling to under-age customers, and to ensure bars were complying with licensing and safety conditions, numerous
multi-agency visits to licensed premises were carried out.

To tackle high levels of 'plying for hire' in the city (i.e. when minicab drivers
accept passengers who have not pre-booked, thereby breaching their taxi-licensing
conditions and resulting in the journey being uninsured), taxi-enforcement officers
patrolled the city centre during the evenings to monitor unlicensed 'plying for hire'
activities.

To provide reassurance and enhanced safety, increased police presence was provided
during the evenings, in Wolverhampton city centre, and in Bilston and Wednesfield
town centres. Specialist police officers were also trained to respond to 999 domestic-
abuse incidents in two designated vehicles – one which patrolled the city centre, and the
other which patrolled Bilston, Wednesfield and outlying areas. This targeted force was
intended to reduce alcohol-fuelled domestic violence, which typically escalated during
the festive period. They also helped to raise awareness of the 24-hour advice helpline for
victims of domestic abuse, by distributing cards with the helpline number to victims.
(See Figure 14.1.)

Figure 14.1   'Keep It Safe' in action

SUPPORT

In addition to the police, voluntary street pastors also patrolled the city centre. Street pastors are an inter-denominational church response to urban problems, who engage with people on the streets to care, listen and help. Wolverhampton's team is one of over 100 in the UK, and is run in partnership with the police, council and other statutory agencies.

'Safe Havens' were also provided for revellers, offering a place to rest, alcohol-free drinks and a free phone call to licensed taxi companies.

A temporary medical centre was erected to alleviate pressure on the city's A&E department. The clinic was staffed by PCT nurses and Emergency Medicine Doctors, and offered on-the-spot medical care in the city centre. In addition, a triage ambulance also patrolled the rest of Wolverhampton. (See Figure 14.2.)

INFORM

An information campaign was run, encouraging young people to enjoy themselves safely and responsibly, and to get home safely. Posters were displayed in pub and club toilets and emphasised the risks of excessive drinking.

It was important that the programme was 'recognised' by the public and that services required by the public were clearly signposted for access. Therefore, a consistent brand style was developed, pre-tested with the target audience (via focus groups and an advertising workshop), and applied to all marketing and communication collateral. The chosen approach was largely pictorial to overcome language barriers and literacy levels, and collateral was distributed widely across the city.

Figure 14.2 'Keep it Safe' safe haven

In addition, free publicity was secured, including regular press releases in local newspapers, particularly when evidence of the programme's impact began to be available via police and A&E statistics.

All of the partners' websites were used to raise awareness and promote the programme, using a clear and consistent message about 'Keep It Safe', with links to the partner organisations for further information if required.

The impact of this marketing approach was to raise the profile of the street-level interventions (e.g. enhanced policing, safe haven and street pastors), giving the public a sense of safety and reassurance, especially once the intervention began to have an impact on crime and accident levels. (See Figure 14.3.)

DESIGN

Promotional and environmental collateral included:

- ○ 50,000 anti-drink tampering devices (spikeys), distributed to city-centre pubs and clubs, to deter the insertion of rohypnol (the date-rape drug) into bottled drinks.
- ○ Specially branded beer mats which reinforced the 'Keep It Safe' message, and displayed taxi-company telephone numbers.
- ○ 'Survival kits', containing advice on sensible drinking and sexual health, a sticking plaster for sore heels, condoms, contact numbers for local taxi firms and information about where the safe havens could be found. These were available from licensed premises and each of the safe havens.
- ○ Flip-flops were given to women leaving nightclubs to reduce the number of sprains and accidents that occur at this time.

BARRIERS

The main barriers to implementation included having a short space of time to plan the project (four weeks in total before the Christmas run-up) and the logistics of bringing together each agency at project meetings. The latter was minimised by holding teleconferences, instead of time consuming face-to-face meetings.

The project director also struggled with juggling full-time work priorities whilst trying to roll this programme out – unfortunately it was too late to recruit additional project

Figure 14.3   'Keep it Safe' branding

officers. However, due to determination, hard work and a drive to make a positive impact on alcohol-related harm, a successful programme was delivered.

MONITORING AND EVALUATION

Quantitative evaluation was based on performance assessment against three primary data sets:

1   Crime data provide by each police occupational command unit: crime data was provided for each of the dates in the intervention that the police were involved. These time/date periods were compared to the equivalent time/date periods for 2007/8. The categories used were violent crime, total crime and serious violent crime.
2   A&E attendance data: A&E data was received as raw attendance data against a series of codes as there is no specific alcohol-related attendance code. This again was time/date-specific and was compared to the equivalent date period from 2007/8. This data was refined by removing all attendance codes that could definitely be excluded as not being related to alcohol in any way. All attendances for those aged over 50 were also removed to eliminate those attendances due to winter pressures and non-alcohol-related attendances.
3   Ambulance call-out data for Wolverhampton: Ambulance call-out data was refined using the same methods as A&E data.

The project team held teleconferences each Monday following the weekends the intervention was in operation. During these teleconferences, each agency would give status updates and feed back any issues experienced. One issue was that it was difficult for agencies to provide regular data during the intervention period due to the complexity and resourcing of the data request.

FINDINGS

A full evaluation of 'Keep It Safe' (Jervis, 2009) demonstrates significant impact from the programme, and strong return on investment. All citations below are from Jervis (2009).

Findings show that Phase 1 (December 2008 until New Year's Eve) had a dramatic impact, with violent crime within the city centre decreasing by 41 per cent when compared with the same period in 2007/8. Across the rest of the city there was a 35 per cent reduction in violent crime and a 60 per cent reduction in serious assaults.

In total there was a 37.2 per cent reduction in violent crime across the whole of Wolverhampton when compared to the same periods in 2007/8.

In terms of A&E attendances, during Phase 1 there was a 7.4 per cent drop, whilst on New Year's Eve a 36 per cent reduction was seen.

Data from West Midlands Ambulance Service comparing the same periods also suggests that alcohol-related call-outs dropped by 13.6 per cent, whilst on New Year's Eve alcohol-related call-outs fell by 28 per cent.

Phase 2 (January to March 2009) was predominantly concentrated on enforcement activities, therefore the reductions were not as evident. However, violent crime still reduced by a total of 12 per cent across Wolverhampton compared to the same periods in 2007/8.

Ambulance call-outs to under-50-year-olds experienced an adverse effect with a 5 per cent increase. However, A&E attendances were down 8.5 per cent during Phase 2.

Combined outcomes from phase 1 and 2 of 'Keep It Safe' show that, on average:

○ Violent crime reduced by 29 per cent
○ Alcohol-related ambulance call-outs dropped by 7 per cent
○ A&E attendances decreased by 8 per cent.

ENFORCEMENT

Enforcement officers carried out a total of 125 visits to licensed premises. Several of these visits resulted in follow-up inspections, warning letters, one prosecution and three reviews of premises' licences for the most severe cases.

In terms of taxi activities, 10 out of 12 drivers were prosecuted for plying for hire.[3] These enforcement activities enforced the 'get home safely' message. Nine drivers received points on their licences and two drivers received a caution and a written warning respectively.

Fire Officers carried out a total of 38 inspections across 24 premises. Of these premises, 23 required further action in the form of enforcement alteration notices and informal notices. Issues picked up were in relation to means of escape and insufficient fire-risk assessments – again it not possible to measure the savings made in terms of public-safety issues being dealt with proactively rather than reactively.

During Phases 1 and 2, 1,200 visits were carried out to licensed premises across the city resulting in one premise licence review, and three irresponsible managers removed from post with one manager receiving a final warning. All premises were monitored using action plan for 12 months following the campaign.

In terms of the Domestic Violence Enforcement Campaign (DVEC), 173 domestic violence incidents were logged to both Occupational Command Units, which resulted in 123 arrests. 'Keep It Safe' funded the DVEC cars to operate during Phase 2, so that calls could go straight through to the police station, from where the DVEC cars were then dispatched.

The 24-hour helpline set up by trained volunteers of the Haven for victims of domestic abuse received three direct referrals, which were recorded by the Haven following DV work from the campaign. Of these referrals, one was provided with temporary refuge accommodation and two were, and continued after the campaign to be, supported in their homes by the Haven's specialist advocacy service.

Whilst the number of referrals received was considerably low it was anticipated that women who received the helpline cards would call at a later stage when it was safe and convenient for them to do so. It is thought the limitation of only having two designated police-response vehicles (one serving each OCU) restricted the opportunity for more cases to be advised of the service.

PROMOTION

The project team designed a questionnaire to assess how successful the PCT had been in publicising 'Keep It Safe' and communicating its key messages to the public. The questionnaire also explored with the public if the merchandise and initiatives chosen were useful and valued.

---

[3] Plying for hire happens when a minicab picks up passengers that have not previously prebooked the taxi, therefore contravening the conditions of their taxi driver's licence and resulting in the journey being uninsured.

Enforcement officers surveyed customers who were waiting in queues to enter pubs and clubs on Saturday nights during Phase 2. A total of 104 questionnaires were completed:

○ When asked if the city centre felt safer during the Christmas period, 21 per cent of revellers said it did; 66 per cent said it didn't; and 13 per cent did not visit the city centre during Christmas.
○ In terms of awareness, 13 per cent said they were aware of the campaign whilst 21 per cent had not heard of it.
○ 39 per cent of those respondents asked had received merchandise and 36 per cent of people said having somewhere safe to wait for a taxi was the most useful thing on a night. 27 per cent thought having taxi numbers was important.

The questionnaire asked what else the campaign could have done to keep people safe, and the overwhelming response was to have more police officers or a greater uniformed presence patrolling the streets of the city centre. Increased availability of taxis was also listed, to enable people to get home more safely and without having to wait in queues where fights are prone to develop.

RETURN ON INVESTMENT
The final spend of the project was £218,786, broken down as follows:

○ British Red Cross mobile triage unit: 2,622
○ Safe havens: £8,704
○ Toilet provision and enhanced street cleansing: £5,626
○ High-visibility police: £84,045
○ Street pastors: £1,800
○ Domestic violence enforcement campaign: £31,683
○ Multi-agency team: £4,680
○ Training: £2,775
○ Trading-standards proxy sales: £7,480
○ Marketing and communications: £55,305.

To calculate return on investment on this budget, simple calculations were undertaken relating to reductions in violent crimes, A&E attendances and ambulance call-outs.

VIOLENT CRIME
The UK Home Office report *The Economic and Social Costs of Crime Against Individuals and Households 2003/4* provided estimated costs for violent crimes. Wolverhampton data for violent crimes following 'Keep It Safe' was compared with data for the equivalent period the previous year, to provide the number and category of violent crimes, in order to generate an estimate of cost savings.

A&E ATTENDANCES
To calculate the impact of a reduction in A&E attendances the figure of £77.00 per attendance was used.

AMBULANCE CALL-OUTS

For ambulance call-out data the figure provided by the West Midlands Ambulance Service for Wolverhampton PCT is £144.00 per call-out.

Based on these cost assumptions, the following savings were estimated (see also Table 14.1): Estimated direct cost savings of £235,382 on a budget of £218,786 suggest that the programme more than paid for itself, even without non-direct costs being included within estimations.

It is thought that advice and guidance relayed through the licensed visits has prevented numerous reviews of premises/prosecutions resulting in savings to the licensing authority in both a time and financial sense (officer time, legal costs, etc.). Unfortunately it is impossible to measure any potential savings made.

Table 14.1   Estimated programme savings

Service	Phase 1	Phase 2	Combined
Ambulance	£9,648	−£720	£8,928
A&E	£12,616	£14,036	£26,652
Police	£125,864	£73,938	£199,802
Total	£148,128	£87,254	£235,382

 LESSONS LEARNT

'Keep It Safe' broke barriers and made great headway in terms of bringing partners from key agencies together to tackle common goals. This approach had never been taken before in Wolverhampton. It was essential to work together and pool resources, as such a complex issue could not have been tackled holistically by agencies working in isolation.

Additional police officers in high visibility clothing, especially those situated at fixed security points worked extremely well in deterring criminal activity and offering the public reassurance.

Communication between partners was extremely well co-ordinated via regular partnership meetings and weekly teleconferences to update on the previous weekend's activities. Businesses and licensed premises were very positive about the campaign and co-operated well.

The dedication and effort of staff from each agency at short notice was a key success factor.

In terms of lessons learned:

- The project was implemented within four weeks, which hindered planning and preparation time, including early engagement.
- The response from taxi companies to picking patrons up from safe havens was less than favourable. Taxi companies were liaised with and there was an understanding that priority would be given to 'Keep It Safe' customers – but this did not happen.
- Due to the short notice of the project, some of the data collected was not fit for purpose and required refinement which in turn entailed additional resources. Future campaigns carried out have addressed this issue and emphasised robust data collection against specific outcome measures.

- ○ Early engagement with A&E and the Ambulance Service may have ensured better cooperation from the outset and may have saved valuable 'chasing' time. Also, engagement with local media may have prevented initial negative press.
- ○ There was a lack of signage and publicity for the campaign. More focus would need to be given in future as awareness of the campaign was not as high as expected.
- ○ The domestic-violence intervention highlighted the need to incorporate domestic violence training across all police officers, as it is thought that widespread training would have helped to develop a better referral mechanism for domestic violence victims to be signposted to support services.

CHAPTER RECAP

This chapter has shown how an intervention mix can incorporate enforcement and regulatory measures, without diverging from social marketing's key priority – the wishes and benefits of the customer.

This programme incorporated consistent and unequivocal regulation and enforcement of premises' licensing, fire regulations and taxi marshalling, as well as increased on-street police presence (as requested by members of the public), and enhanced police response to domestic violence call-outs. Without these enforcement activities, the awareness raising element of 'Keep It Safe' would not, in isolation, have delivered the strong behavioural changes that the combined intervention achieved.

In the next chapter we will learn how evaluation and a strong focus on return on investment underpin England's national response to tackling childhood obesity, and explore the final of our 5Cs – 'Continuation'.

SELF-REVIEW QUESTIONS

1 The role of enforcement was essential to 'Keep It Safe'. In addition to licensed premises visits, and enhanced police response, what additional enforcement activities might have been incorporated into the methods mix, to reduce alcohol-related harm?

2 One of the key insights for this programme was that members of the public felt unsafe on the streets at night, and actively requested increased police presence. However, if you were working on a behaviour-change area, which didn't directly involve public safety (e.g. obesity, recycling), what other enforcement activities might you consider as part of your intervention mix?

3 In this case study, enforcement activity was underpinned by key practical and promotional interventions which also addressed the issue of safety (for example, the safe havens, which provided a safe place to wait for a taxi). Could this programme have delivered behaviour-change impact if the police had worked in isolation and, if so, what might this have looked like?

REFERENCES

Ascension Trust figures, cited in 'Pastors plan to tackle disorder', BBC article, 17 April 2007, available at http://news.bbc.co.uk/1/hi/scotland/tayside_and_central/6559477.stm. Accessed 12 Dec. 2010.

Cardiff Model: Effective NHS Contributions to Violence Prevention, October 2007. Available online at: www.vrg.cf.ac.uk/Files/vrg_violence_prevention.pdf. Accessed Feb. 2011.

Home Office, The economic and social costs of crime against individuals and households, 2003/04. Available online at: http://rds.homeoffice.gov.uk/rds/pdfs05/rdsolr3005.pdf. Accessed Feb. 2011.

Jervis, R. (2009). Wolverhampton 'Keep It Safe': An evaluation report. Available online at: www.wolverhamptonhealth.nhs.uk/Library/Documents/Alcohol_Strategy/Microsoft%20Word%20-%20KIS%20Evaluation%20Report%20FINAL.pdf. Accessed Feb. 2011.

Liverpool Citysafe reports, 2009/10, available online at www.liverpool.gov.uk/policing_and_public_safety/citysafe/index.asp. Accessed 12 Dec. 2010.

UK Cabinet Office, Prime Minister's Strategy Unit. (2004). Alcohol harm reduction strategy for England. London: Cabinet Office.

Wolverhampton Alcohol Strategy 2008–11, Draft analysis of interview data (Kilbride Smith, June 2008).

Wolverhampton City Primary Care Trust, Strategic Plan 2008–14. Available online at: www.wolverhamptonhealth.nhs.uk/Library/Documents/Publications/Strategic%20Plan%202008-13%20Final%20Updated%20Feb2010.pdf. Accessed Feb. 2011.

15 CREATING ACCESS TO THE RIGHT PRODUCTS

VIGNETTE: 'HEALTHY FOOTBALL DADS', NEWCASTLE UNITED FOUNDATION

KEY WORD: APPROPRIATE PRODUCT

West End and Ashington (two deprived wards in the city of Newcastle, UK) suffer high levels of heart disease, cancer and mental illness, and some of the lowest life expectancy levels in the UK. In 2009, Newcastle United Foundation (which is funded by Newcastle United Football Club) employed two new health trainers to use football as a way of engaging dads who wanted to improve their health. Following focus groups to understand customer 'wants and needs', an appealing 'service product' was developed to help dads change their health habits. The service consisted of twice-weekly football/multi-sports sessions, to support dads in programmes to gain football/sports-coaching qualifications, something that they were all highly motivated to achieve. At these same sessions, men also received one-to-one and group support to help them tackle health issues focusing on: physical activity, obesity and weight management, alcohol and smoking. In the first phase of the project, 118 dads took part. All the participants stuck with the programme. 100 per cent of participants registered increased self-esteem; 17 participants expressed interest in taking a football-coaching certificate; 12 quit smoking; and 40 dads lost weight. This project demonstrates that having the right product offered by the right people in the right way results in success.

More information is available at: www.nufc.co.uk/page/Foundation/About.

This vignette demonstrates the value of working with the commercial companies to ensure appropriate products and services are widely available.

ABOUT THIS CHAPTER

As we discussed in Chapter 1, it is important to have clear behavioural goals from the start of a project. However, that can be difficult to achieve, due to the range of areas and stakeholders engaged in a programme. In this chapter you will learn:

- The need to focus on a clear behavioural goal.
- The importance of creating a consistent environment for evaluation and programme improvement to take place.

○ Economies of scale and improvements to services can be gained when local areas working together in partnership.
○ Developing a national platform can help to improve engagement with the private sector.

CASE STUDY: SWEEPING IT UNDER THE CARPET: REDUCING NEW ZEALAND'S HOUSEHOLD RUBBISH

Luke van der Beeke, National Social Marketing Centre

PROJECT OVERVIEW

By 2002, it was estimated that 4 million New Zealanders were sending around 3.6 million tonnes of waste to landfills each year. While each household was producing more than a tonne of 'rubbish', the government estimated that 65 per cent of this material could actually be recycled or composted and used productively (NZ Ministry for the Environment (MFE), 2002).

In Auckland, the largest city in New Zealand, data showed that since 1983, the amount of waste disposed of by each person had increased by 73 per cent (MFE, 2002). But while the country's waste problem appeared to growing, one of the main difficulties was that much of the national waste data was either unclear or non-existent, making it difficult to identify specific behavioural solutions.

In 2002, the MFE launched the first New Zealand Waste Strategy (MFE, 2002). The strategy clearly identified the need to inform and educate local communities about the need to reduce the production of household waste and increase the recovery of useful resources such as green waste. It called for the implementation of a long-term public education and information programme, and included a number of voluntary targets, such as the delivery of national recycling facilities and the diversion of organic waste from landfills. One component of the strategy was a campaign, titled 'Reduce Your Rubbish'. The campaign was conceived and implemented by the MFE, in partnership with regional councils, territorial local authorities and business partners. It was the first time the MFE had worked in such an integrated way on a national programme to promote environmental awareness and action in the community.

PROJECT RATIONALE

In 2002, many of New Zealand's most important industries, such as farming, tourism and film production, had come to rely heavily on its 'clean and green' image. The New Zealand government wanted to help ensure that the reality continued to meet this image by finding a more effective way to help individuals take greater action to address pressing environmental issues, such as increasing waste, and reducing water and air pollution.

Against this backdrop, 'Reduce Your Rubbish' provided an opportunity to pilot a public information and education campaign and identify lessons for the development of other programmes to address important environmental issues.

Initially, the MFE wanted to produce a short media campaign to promote greater public awareness and support for the country's first ever national waste strategy. However, the Ministry's Waste Team realised that the launch of the strategy provided them with an ideal opportunity to directly encourage householders to take action to reduce the amount of rubbish they were producing.

The design of the campaign was based heavily on a successful community-engagement and a behaviour-change programme that had been developed by the Auckland Regional Council. 'The Big Clean Up' (Menzies, 2003) used an effective PR and advertising campaign to encourage more than 40,000 householders to join the membership programme and take simple steps to help reduce pollution and protect the natural environment. The 'Reduce Your Rubbish' campaign was adapted to focus specifically on the problem of household waste, while also meeting the needs of multiple stakeholders and a national audience. The Project Team included representatives from the Ministry for Environment, Local Government New Zealand, regional councils and territorial authorities.

 ## AIMS AND OBJECTIVES

The aim of the project was to raise awareness of New Zealand's growing waste problem and promote specific actions to help householders reduce their rubbish. But it was also specifically designed to test whether the central and local government could collaborate on future programmes to raise awareness and promote action on other major environmental issues.

Three objectives were set for the project:

○ Overall aim: Reduce the amount of household waste going to landfill.
○ Behavioural objectives: Increase rates of recycling and the composting of kitchen and garden waste, and encourage householders to buy recyclable or reusable products.
○ Strategic objective: Encourage improvements to the recycling/composting infrastructure and encourage industry to take greater responsibility for the total life cycle of its products.

 ## IDENTIFYING THE TARGET AUDIENCES

The campaign was to be initially aimed at the general public. However, in order to improve impact, segmentation was undertaken to identify those most likely to recycle/compost. Segmentation was attitudinally based and explored people's thoughts, feelings and behaviours towards environmental issues. Pre-campaign surveying classified respondents into three broad lifestyle segments:

1   Those with a totally environmentally considerate lifestyle where the environment is considered in almost everything they do.
2   A pragmatic lifestyle in which the environment is considered only when it is reasonable or practical to do so.
3   An unconcerned lifestyle which doesn't consider the environment at all.

These three segments were further broken down into seven sub-segments (detailed in Table 15.1).

The 'Slipping Greens', 'Available to Green' and 'Ambivalent to Green' groups were targeted as the groups where the greatest potential for behaviour change was most likely to occur. These segments then became the campaign's primary audiences.

Table 15.1 Attitudinal segmentation in targeted regions

Segment Name	% of target audience*	Characteristics
Dark Green	11%	Consider the environment in everything they do
Greens	19%	Committed to considering the environment, but not as passionate as dark greens
Slipping Greens	6%	Think they are green, BUT not sure it's worth the effort
Available to Green	24%	Really WANT to do better
Ambivalent to Green	8%	THINK they are green some of the time
Easy Greens	27%	Only do what practical, not interested in doing more
Browns	4%	Not green and willing to admit it!
No Classification	1%	

*Percentage of respondents across the 10 targeted regions in which the campaign ran.

SCOPING RESEARCH

Every effort was made to start with the target audiences' current understanding of the waste problem, and to establish what key behaviours the campaign should look to promote in order to maximise its chances of success. The research was in part a refinement process to see what people would most likely engage with.

Pre- and post-national phone surveys were conducted to:

1 Establish the segments.
2 Measure changes to attitudes and claimed behaviours as a result of the campaign.

A survey was sent to 2,000 members of the Auckland Regional Council's 'Big Clean Up' programme, asking them to consider the ease with which they could incorporate a range of rubbish reduction actions in their daily lives. The results of these surveys and follow-up focus groups were used to develop an eight-point plan, which was eventually refined down to three specific and achievable behaviours and calls to action for the campaign:

- Recycle as much as you can
- Compost kitchen and garden waste
- Reduce rubbish by buying reusable or recyclable products.

ACTIONABLE INSIGHTS

In September 2002, a national workshop on waste, environmental education and communication was held with representatives from the New Zealand Ministry of the Environment, local government and the business sector. The workshop was used to help develop the creative brief for the campaign and to help strengthen collaboration between these different stakeholder groups.

In addition to this, a research agency was commissioned to conduct focus groups in five different towns and cities to help develop a better understanding of the target segments and the key barriers to change. A key finding was that government had seemingly taken the 'problem' away from householders. For many people the rubbish problem was simply a case of 'out of sight, out of mind'.

The primary perceived costs of taking the actions recommended were the additional time required to separate recyclables or compost kitchen and garden waste; and reduced convenience of not using plastic bags or actively looking for recyclable or reusable products.

Another price barrier identified was that householders without compost bins would need to purchase one in order to compost their kitchen and garden waste. To address this issue, one of the project partners (the Warehouse[1]) provided discounted compost bins during the campaign period.

Research confirmed that the campaign needed to raise awareness of the problem and focus on some simple and positive things that everyone could do to make a difference. Key insights were that:

○ Many people thought they were already doing all they could with their own rubbish.
○ Some felt that technology was already being used to solve the problem, and several respondents believed that their recyclables were already being separated by the council at waste-treatment facilities.
○ Many people did not understand the problems associated with putting waste to landfills, such as generating methane or leachate.
○ Most people were motivated to recycle because it was seen as a useful way to conserve raw materials. Few people seemed to think that reducing the amount of waste to landfill was a key benefit of recycling.

Recycling was chosen as the key behavioural goal because that was where the audience could most easily connect with the wider waste-reduction message. The research was used to formulate three key messages:

1   'Rubbish – it doesn't go away'
2   'Rubbish doesn't break down in a landfill – recycle'
3   '65 per cent of your rubbish can be recycled or composted'.

The focus group findings and key insights were also used to determine the key actions that the project team wanted people to take. Actions were promoted that would:

○ Meet with the target audience's understanding of the issue.
○ Be simple and easy to introduce into their daily lives.
○ Match the availability of existing services (not all places had access to recycling).
○ Match the relevant targets set out in the waste strategy.

In addition, the research suggested that the entire waste-management system was not as joined up as it needed to be. There was potential for advertising to be used to encourage certain target groups to recycle and compost more of their 'rubbish'. But how could any positive gains be sustained and expanded over time unless the country's waste policy,

---

[1] The Warehouse is a national discount supermarket chain in New Zealand.

infrastructure and markets made it irresistible for people to recycle and compost the 65 per cent of their rubbish that was literally going to waste?

 STAKEHOLDER ENGAGEMENT

Prior to project start-up, the central campaign team lobbied New Zealand's 11 regional councils to participate in the programme and contribute to the central fund. At the time, 'waste' was not a core objective for many, but they saw benefits of working together to cost-effectively promote awareness and action. Local Government New Zealand[2] worked as a broker between the Ministry and the regional councils, to clearly outline the key benefits that would result if participating organisations were able to find new ways of combing their resources. Ten of the 11 regional councils signed up.

A large number of businesses were also involved in the project, including a national advertising company who provided pro-bono support, lobbying organisations and large retailers.

A dedicated project-management website was used to coordinate the design of the campaign plan, media materials and community-engagement activities among the large number of campaign participants at national, regional and local levels. The website included all the main project-management, creative and evaluation documents relating to the campaign.

BARRIERS

A competition analysis was conducted to identify competing barriers. The main competition identified included:

○ Busy lives: Most householders believed they were time poor. Therefore the campaign needed to focus on providing householders with quick and simple actions they could integrate into their everyday lives.
○ Low perceived need: Many householders did not believe that there was a problem in sending waste to landfills and many felt they were already recycling as much as they could.
○ A fear of 'trivial solutions': One of the most pressing needs was to find effective ways to reduce the high level of organic material that was being sent to landfill. However, many of the campaign partners felt that a focus on composting would be viewed as trivial.
○ More pressing environmental issues: At the time of the campaign, New Zealand was suffering a severe drought. The two key impacts of this were that (1) a great deal of the available free media space was used to cover the drought, and (2) people were more concerned about water restrictions (will I get a shower tomorrow?) than they were about the less immediate issue of waste reduction. The 'Target 10' power-saving campaign, with a budget of NZ$1.5M, was also a competitor.

Throughout the scoping, development and implementation phases, further barriers arose. The three key barriers were as follows:

1 Funding/budget: The core budget of NZ$400,000 was a considerable barrier, particularly given the cost associated with developing and implementing a national media campaign. Additional funding was secured from 10 of the 11 regional councils and in-kind/pro-bono support totalling approximately NZ$800,000 was generated through local stakeholders and businesses.

---

[2] A national body to improve coordination between central and local government.

2   Time-frame: The planning and execution of the project was undertaken over a 12-month period. This proved to be extremely challenging, particularly given the need for the project to be fully collaborative and involve the full participation and support of local government and private sector partners. The campaign itself ran for just three months which also limited its direct impact.

3   Pre-existing knowledge/understanding/prioritisation amongst key stakeholders: The issue of waste reduction was not a high priority for regional councils, and this acted as an initial barrier to engagement. A robust stakeholder engagement strategy, including the running of a national workshop on waste, communication and the environment helped address knowledge gaps amongst key stakeholders (including the Minster for the Environment) and facilitated buy-in. Positioning the project as a pilot to help trial methods of future collaborative working also helped to overcome initial concerns amongst stakeholders.

METHODS MIX

'Reduce Your Rubbish' was a national campaign which provided a central platform to support local initiatives to meet local audience needs. The national campaign provided consistent messaging and branding, while a wide range of local-level activities was geared towards facilitating the desired behaviours; for example, at the start of the campaign, kerbside recycling was not available to all households, and at some landfills there was no facility for green waste to be separated.

INFORMATION

A free web and phone service was developed to help householders learn how they could increase recycling and composting behaviour, for example, detailing where their local services were and who to call for assistance, etc. In addition to the website, householders were encouraged to make a public pledge to try and reduce the amount of waste they sent to landfill. Householders were then provided with a self-assessment checklist to help them identify some of the simple things their families could do to reduce their rubbish.

SUPPORT

During the campaign, the Warehouse sold subsidised compost bins made from recycled plastic under the banner of 'Reduce Your Rubbish'. The warehouse sent out direct mailings to 1.3 million households advertising the special offer.

PROMOTION – NATIONAL

A national TV advertising campaign ran for five weeks and was primarily targeted at 'Slipping Greens', 'Available to Greens' and 'Ambivalent to Greens', as these were the segments identified as being most likely to adopt the desired behaviours.

A phased approach to the advertising campaign was employed, and the first two advertisements screened were developed to get householders to acknowledge the problem. For example, one of the advertisements addressed the issue of rubbish going to landfill and informed viewers that much of it did not break down. These were followed by advertisements that were aimed at helping householders understand simple things they could do to address the issues raised in the earlier ads. More than 130 positive articles on the 'Reduce

EIGHT EASY WAYS FOR YOU TO REDUCE YOUR RUBBISH.

1. RECYCLE YOUR CARDBOARD, PAPER, GLASS, CANS AND TYPES 1 AND 2 PLASTICS
Call your local council to find out about your local services.

2. BUY ECONOMY SIZE PRODUCTS, CONCENTRATES AND REFILLS

3. IF YOU DON'T NEED A PLASTIC BAG, DON'T TAKE IT
Take your own bag to the shops.

4. BUY PRODUCTS WITH RECYCLABLE PACKAGING
Cardboard, paper, glass, cans, type 1 and 2 plastics.

5. COMPOST YOUR GARDEN RUBBISH AND KITCHEN SCRAPS AT HOME

6. MULCH YOUR LAWN CLIPPINGS

7. IF YOU CAN'T COMPOST OR MULCH AT HOME, KEEP YOUR GARDEN RUBBISH SEPARATE
Arrange a garden rubbish collection or take it to a transfer station for composting.

8. DONE ALL YOU CAN AT HOME? WHY NOT LOOK AT WHAT YOU CAN DO AT WORK?

Ministry for the Environment   Auckland Regional Council TE RAUHITANGA TAIAO   AUCKLAND CITY   0800 REDUCE   www.reducerubbish.govt.nz

Replace with your regional council black & white logo

Replace with your black & white T.A. logo

Figure 15.1   8 Point Plan advert

Source: Ministry for the Environment, New Zealand

Your Rubbish' campaign appeared in newspapers throughout the country. Notably, more than 50 per cent of the free publicity generated was about local politicians and householders entering the Household Challenge. (See Figure 15.2.)

This online competition was also developed to show householders how they could improve their rubbish-reduction activities. This complemented the national advertising and provided incentives for householders to reduce their rubbish. Over $10,000 worth of prizes, and a great deal of free promotion, was provided by some of New Zealand's leading businesses. As part of the challenge, many councils provided direct support to households on how they could reduce their rubbish. This entailed an advisor going to their homes to discuss with them directly how they could reduce their waste.

PROMOTION – LOCAL

Territorial authorities and local stakeholders also generated media coverage on TV, print and radio using individual media plans. Local promotions also included advertising on bus shelters and in-store promotions. Posters and stickers were distributed though councils. Local advertising and promotion was reinforced with community-based events and competitions. All local promotions were adapted around the national model, and included:

1   'Reduce Your Rubbish' website: This award-winning website allowed people to provide input and provided a portal to local initiatives. Visitors to the website could access information on waste and its impact on the environment, hints and tips, and directions to local services.
2   0800-RUBBISH: An 0800 phone service was established and promoted during the campaign. Householders calling the national hotline were automatically redirected to local councils for hints and tips and more information about local services and support. (See Figure 15.1.)

MONITORING AND EVALUATION

The Ministry commissioned an independent company to determine the effectiveness of the campaign in terms of (1) increasing people's awareness of issues surrounding waste/rubbish and (2) measuring changes in behaviour with respect to recycling, composting and responsible shopping.

A survey was conducted to measure impact. The survey incorporated the 10 participating regional council areas and analysed the data gathered in conjunction with the data gathered in the Auckland region under a separate contract. A total of 400 telephone interviews (40 per region) were conducted for the benchmark and follow-up. A random sample of all adults aged 15 and over was taken and quotas were set to balance gender split and ensure that single person/retired households were not over-represented.

In addition to the phone survey, the local councils measured recycling and waste disposal in their area, qualitative interviews were conducted with 40 householders who were aware of the campaign and media monitoring was used to track the number of positive articles printed.

FINDINGS

Nation-wide awareness of advertising about the rubbish issue was 42 per cent (a potential audience of more than 500,000 households). 28 per cent of New Zealanders said that

Replace with your regional council black & white logo

Replace with your black & white T.A. logo

Figure 15.2   Household Challenge advert
Source: Ministry for the Environment, New Zealand

they had seen or heard something specifically about the 'Reduce Your Rubbish' campaign. 20 per cent said that the campaign had a positive effect on their awareness, attitudes or behaviour.

Most thought the main message was recycling at 59 per cent, with 27 per cent saying the main message was about reducing packaging. Unfortunately the composting message barely registered, with just 6 per cent recognition.

The critical thing about the campaign impact is that 'claimed green behaviour' actually decreased significantly during the campaign, as many people began to reassess if their recycling and other rubbish-reduction behaviours were really as good as they'd originally claimed in the baseline.

Working with businesses such as the Warehouse national discount-store chain and the Living Earth compost company provided excellent opportunities to communicate the main campaign messages through existing communications channels. For example, the Warehouse provided significant messaging and branding in one of its weekly mailers sent to 1.3 million householders. In this mailer it provided a special reduced price of $24.95 on Vertex compost bins (made from recycled plastic). As a result of this promotion they sold more than 1,500 compost bins in just two weeks, putting over $40,000 worth of recycled plastic back into the marketplace.

The 'Reduce Your Rubbish Challenge' generated a lot of positive media: more than 130 positive articles on the 'Reduce Your Rubbish' campaign appeared in newspapers throughout the country and more than 50 per cent of these articles were about local politicians and householders entering the Household Challenge.

 LESSONS LEARNT

The key lessons included:

- The research indicated that, despite the relatively low cost of the campaign, the collaborative approach across the public sector delivered real benefits to participating organisations and the wider community. For example, the local councils were able to increase their recycling rates in their areas, without having to pay into the campaign directly. The campaign had a significant impact on public awareness and behaviour, particularly given the low budget and short time period involved.
- A range of communication tools were developed that could be used again at regional or national levels and the website provided a useful resource for householders across New Zealand for a further five years, finally being retired in 2009.
- The project team felt that the campaign tried to address too many behaviours and that there should have been a greater focus on one specific and measurable behaviour.
- There is a need to ensure that any simple calls to action are integrated with the provision of supporting services, incentives and policies.

The 'Reduce Your Rubbish' campaign achieved its objectives and demonstrated that national government, local government and the business sector can collaborate effectively to promote community action to protect the environment.

CHAPTER RECAP

This chapter has shown how working with commercial companies and the public sector to ensure that products and services are available for the target audience to follow through with their call for action needs to be in place for positive impacts on behaviour to be achieved.

In the next chapter we will learn how taking a social marketing approach can create a social as well as economic good.

 SELF-REVIEW QUESTIONS

1 Behaviour is dynamic. What people do one day might change the next day. In social marketing it is important to focus some efforts on those already doing the positive behaviour, to keep them in that classification. In this project the Dark Greens and Greens were already recycling and considering the environment in their actions. What interventions would you develop for them, and why?
2 The project discovered there was an assumption that positive environmental attitudes are needed to support behaviour change, but in many cases it appeared that people were prepared to act differently if it was easy to do so. What methods mix would you develop to make things easy for people to do the desired behaviour?

3 It was felt that the campaign tried to address too many different behaviours and there should have been a greater focus on one specific and measurable behaviour. If you were looking to address the problem outlined in this chapter, what specific behaviour would you have focused on and why?

REFERENCES

Colenso BBDO. (2002, Oct.) Creative brief for the 'Reduce Your Rubbish' Campaign. More online at: www.mfe.govt.nz/issues/waste/waste-pilot/creative-brief.html. Accessed Feb. 2011.

Feldhaeuser, Horst. (2003, June). Measuring the National 'Reduce Your Rubbish' Campaign. Prepared for the Ministry for the Environment by Research Solutions. New Zealand: Ministry for the Environment. Available online at: www.docstoc.com/docs/33774596/Measuring-the-national-Reduce-Your-Rubbish-campaign. Accessed Feb. 2011.

Menzies, Steve. (2003). Can social marketing provide a model to address New Zealand's major environmental problems? 'Reduce Your Rubbish' (April–June 2003). Conference Paper at Social Marketing for Social Profit (16–17 Oct. 2003), New Zealand: Ministry for the Environment. Available online at: www.mfe.govt.nz/issues/waste/waste-pilot/conference-paper.html. Available online at: www.mfe.govt.nz/issues/waste/waste-pilot/conference-paper.html. Accessed Feb. 2011.

NZ Ministry for the Environment. (2002, Nov.). Qualitative consumer feedback on waste and the waste reduction executions. Prepared by Colenso BBDO. New Zealand: Ministry for the Environment.

NZ Ministry for the Environment. (2010, March). The New Zealand Waste Strategy: Towards zero waste and a sustainable New Zealand. Available online at www.mfe.govt.nz. Accessed July 2010.

16 CO-PRODUCTION WITH THE PRIVATE SECTOR

VIGNETTE: 'THE HEART TRUTH', US DEPARTMENT OF HEALTH AND HUMAN SERVICES

This programme was launched to raise awareness of the high risk that heart disease has for women. The centrepiece of the programme is the 'Red Dress', which was launched as the national symbol for women and heart-disease awareness. Rather than delivering a traditional media campaign, the strategy has been to invest a much smaller amount of money than would have been needed for a national media campaign into a partnership and PR-driven strategy. This strategy involved the development of delivery partnerships with organisations from the retail, publishing, fashion and media sectors, as well as the NGO and public sectors.

One such partnership was with *Glamour* magazine, which helped the initial launch with a 15-page health story featuring Shania Twain, in a red dress, on the October 2003 magazine cover, and featured an interview with First Lady Laura Bush. Following this debut, *Glamour* now issues an annual 'Red Dress' feature.

Through its partnership strategy the campaign has generated awareness levels, and an ongoing delivery system, that could not have been purchased by the Federal Government.

This vignette shows how limited funds can be invested by government agencies to create sustained delivery coalitions with the for profit sector, to reach more people in a way that they would respond to.

For further information, please visit http://www.nhlbi.nih.gov/educational/hearttruth/.

ABOUT THIS CHAPTER

As we have seen already, a deep understanding of the target audience, together with an understanding of social norms and the particular enabling factors and barriers associated with adopting any new behaviour, is key when developing a successful social marketing programme. In this chapter we will build on this understanding by exploring how social marketing principles can be applied in the commercial sector, which has the added challenge of economic reality and specific social norms. The chapter demonstrates that by taking a social marketing approach new and innovative business processes can be introduced to create a social as well as an economic good.

CASE STUDY: PROJECT 50 PER CENT: REDUCING FISH DISCARDING THROUGH THE APPLICATION OF SOCIAL MARKETING

Sue Nelson, Kindred Social Marketing; Andy Revill, UK Centre for Environment, Fisheries & Aquaculture Sciences

PROJECT OVERVIEW

The Centre for Environment, Fisheries & Aquaculture Sciences (Cefas) is an internationally renowned scientific research and advisory establishment and the UK's largest and most diverse applied marine science organisation. This case study demonstrates that it is critically important to invest effort in engaging with stakeholders and potential partners when seeking to bring about a change in behaviour amongst a community. This case study is also interesting in that it is not only targeting its behaviour change at a group of independent professionals but also professionals who work in the commercial sector, where the very real issue of staying in business and making a return on your own and your shareholders' investments is a key motivation that needs to be considered.

PROJECT RATIONALE

Operating as an executive agency of the UK Department for Environment, Food and Rural Affairs (Defra), Cefas provides evidence-based scientific advice, conducts world-class scientific research, and facilitates marine projects with a range of partners both in the UK and internationally. The scientific research and practical trials conducted by Cefas have aimed to protect and better understand the marine environment. Cefas had worked for some time with trawlermen to attempt to measure and reduce the number of 'discards' they throw over the side of their boats, and some progress had been made. However, there was a great deal of room for improvement.

Discards are fish that are caught at sea and thrown overboard for a number of reasons (typically because these fish have no market value, or legislative constraints forbid their landing and sale because they are too small). Discarding in commercial fisheries is widely regarded as a waste of natural resources, disruptive to marine ecosystems and ethically undesirable. Globally, 7.3 million tonnes of fish are discarded every year.[1]

The Devon beam trawl fleet in the south-west of the UK had one of the highest discard rates of English and Welsh fisheries. Fishing has been a way of life in Brixham and its larger neighbour of Plymouth for almost 1,000 years, with the surrounding seas famous for their catches of sole, turbot and plaice, together with cuttlefish and scallop. But, as the fishing industry expanded, the UK Government and European Commission became concerned about the over-fishing of European waters. As well as prime fish destined for market, smaller juvenile fish – the future of fish shoals and the fishing industry – were also being caught up in large trawler nets.

---

[1] The UN's Food and Agriculture Organization estimate.

Beam trawler nets typically have a mesh size of at least 80 mm, which catches a high degree of benthos (typically larger starfish, decaying matter, shells, plants and debris). The benthos is ecologically important, but has no commercial value and is an unwelcome component of catches. There are also substantial catches of juvenile and non-commercial fish, for which there is no market or their landing and sale is forbidden by legislation. There is much debate as to whether these smaller fish live, after being thrown back into the water.

It has been clear for many years that conservation measures needed to be taken. However, early attempts to get fishermen together and discuss the use of new fishing nets that allowed juvenile fish to escape had only met with limited success. As Kenny Kemp, who has helped promote the success of this intervention. observed, 'the UK's fishermen weren't too keen on what they saw as government officials telling them how to catch fish. Increasingly, those who went out to sea felt pilloried for overfishing – and viewed as villains by ecological interest groups' (Kemp, 2010).

Cefas clearly knew that the behaviour of fishermen and boat owners has an impact on the sustainable success of reducing discards. Without their full cooperation and understanding of trial and research results, the take-up of potential improvements remained low. The behaviours that Cefas wanted to promote included adjusting the nets, so that they have bigger mesh sizes to allow smaller fish to escape. However, figuring out how to best configure the nets and the optimum shape and design is a difficult task, and requires the Cefas scientists to live and work on the boat alongside fishermen, recording the total number of fish caught and kept, or thrown overboard. The two large 'beams' on the boats of trawlers are ideal for trials as one side can be used as a control, against the other with the new net designs. If they have cooperation and can run sea trials working with fishermen in this way Cefas scientists can directly compare catches, including the amount of benthos on deck and the number of juvenile fish discarded. In so doing, they can demonstrate impact to the crew and the wider fishing industry. The new nets also had the added advantage of being lighter, causing less drag from the boat so less horsepower is used, resulting in fuel savings. These benefits were expected but field trials were essential and for this the active cooperation of fishing crews was needed.

Dr Andy Revill from Cefas was frustrated by the lack of progress and put this down to too many 'expert'-driven solutions being applied without fully understanding why fishermen were resistant to adopting what looked like effective practice. For example, Cefas launched a competition among Devon fishermen to develop their own net designs to reduce unwanted catch. The competition was moderately successful, but only the winner actually used the new net. Realising that a different approach was needed, and inspired by work promoted by the National Social Marketing Centre about change in other policy areas, Revill decided to commission a social marketing pilot programme to address the issue of changing behaviour amongst fishermen in the uptake and use of the new nets.

 ## AIMS AND OBJECTIVES

Cefas decided to use a social marketing approach to reducing discards, and pilot a project in the Devon beam trawl fleet to see what lessons could be learned. Cefas wanted the Devon beam trawl fleet to be the first commercial fishing fleet in Europe to reduce its discard levels to the most practical minimum level. It was thought that this could be up to 50 per cent of the current rate, so this became the aspirational target, even though there was a great deal of scepticism that such a turnaround could be achieved. The project became known by those working on it from Cefas, and amongst local fishermen, as 'Project 50 Per Cent'. The behaviours that were targeted were to enlist a sufficient number of crews from the two ports to work with Cefas to undertake trials that would involve the installation and correctly use fishing nets with larger mesh sizes to demonstrate that it was possible, by this relatively straightforward switch, to dramatically reduce the amount of discard without adversely affecting the target catch. The project began in the spring of 2009 and finished in March 2010.

The project was led by Dr Andy Revill, Team Leader, Applied Fisheries Science and Technology at Cefas, with funding from Defra. A social marketing consultancy, Corporate Culture, was contracted to assist with the project. The project was structured using the National Social Marketing Centre's Eight-point Benchmark Criteria (French and Blair-Stevens, 2008).

 IDENTIFYING THE TARGET AUDIENCES

The challenge, a reduction in discards by Devon's beam trawler fleet, required a focus on three target groups: fishermen, skippers and boat owners. Two target locations were selected: Brixham and Plymouth tow fishing ports in the south-west of the UK. These ports were selected because they were typical of ports around the country, so that if lessons were learnt they should be applicable in other areas across the UK.

 STAKEHOLDER ENGAGEMENT

Project officers understood that it would be essential to engage all of the target groups in the project if it was going to be a success. A plan was agreed by Cefas and its marketing agency to ensure that all three target groups were briefed about the project and were included in the scoping phase, to discover their views and thoughts about potential solutions. Cefas officers and inspectors were also briefed and encouraged to offer potential solutions. Stakeholder engagement also included personal visits and phone calls to European officials, Defra policy officials, local newspapers, radio stations, trade press, local councillors, MPs and industry figures to explain the project and its aims.

To develop a deep understanding of why fishermen were reluctant to use the new nets, Corporate Culture undertook a series of interviews with fishing skippers, boat owners, trawler agents and producer organisations. What they identified, according to Kemp, was a 'pent-up frustration within the fishing community'. Often fishermen felt that, even if they did take positive action it was rarely recognised by the public, environmental groups or the government. After the consultations, Dave Langdon, the owner of the beam trawler MFV Barentszee, who had taken part in the exercise, was pleasantly surprised: 'It was the first time that I've known a government organisation to work with the local fisherman and ask us how we could help. It opened up a different kind of discussion because we felt that our opinions were being valued.'

SCOPING RESEARCH

The initial social marketing brief was to:

- Gain a deeper understanding and insight into the behaviours of fishermen, including the barriers, incentives, disincentives, rewards and opportunities for changing discarding behaviour.
- Identify effective mechanisms to facilitate behaviour change.

The initial scoping stage with fishermen, skippers and owners therefore focused entirely on two-beam trawler fleets in Brixham and Plymouth, interviewing them individually or in pairs to gain an in-depth understanding of behaviours, barriers, incentives and attitudes. Individual interviews were also carried out with a range of stakeholders including Cefas researchers, industry leaders, fishery officers and Defra policy officials.

Existing research had already shown that:

- Fishermen believed when nets were modified it resulted in reduced profitability as it allowed fish to escape that could be sold. They also thought that modified nets were prone to 'chafe' (affecting the visual appearance of the caught fish, thereby reducing its saleability and price), and require too much maintenance.
- Large catches are appealing to fishermen even if subsequently many fish have to be discarded (the visual appeal of a trawl full of fish).
- There are few incentives or rewards for fishermen who reduce discards.

BARRIERS AND THE COMPETITION

The social marketing research responses were consistent between crew, skippers and owners, and opinions were strongly held. Below are some of the key insights gathered from fishermen about their own perceptions of their profession, discarding and EU quotas:

- Fishing is not an exact science: Despite the fact that many of the target group had been fishing all their adult life and knew specific fishing grounds intimately, the activity involves hunting around, trying areas and moving on if not successful. It is not a science where fish can easily be located. 'The old hunter-gatherer instinct', that's what a fisherman does – he hunts around.' A typical trip, with a crew of five or six men, will involve going far out to sea for at least five days at a time. It is physically hard and demanding work, sometimes in appalling weather conditions.
- Quotas: Quotas are debated at European level on the basis of figures compiled by scientists, such as those employed by Cefas. The fishermen understand why Cefas return to the same spot each year in order to gauge fish stocks but, as they see it, 'the fact that scientists don't find fish doesn't mean there aren't any – they swim around!' They believe there is a need for a strategy to track fish movements more extensively. They generally favour audit over sampling, and would prefer an observer on one boat for a full year, so they can really get to understand fish movements and levels, as the fishermen do.
- An innocent and ancient tradition: Fishermen believe that few industries are more 'innocent' (a word used often). It is the continuation of an ancient and honest tradition, which benefits local people and fishing grounds. They describe it as a worthy profession, rooted in history, providing food for the table and jobs in their community. They genuinely believe that fishing this way keeps the seabed in good condition. 'I believe it's got to be fished. It's like ploughing a field. It's got to be turned over.'
- Financially precarious: Fishing has become more financially difficult for crews, skippers and owners, especially those with small fleets or single vessels. They believe they are 'gambling with our families' incomes' and are frustrated that the public and the media do not understand quotas and how they are attached to boats. There are press reports that some trawlers can cost a million pounds, and this implies that fishing is a well-paid occupation with luxurious vessels, when in fact owners are buying old boats, and investing in quota for many years in advance with no surety of income. Crew get paid on the basis of the catch they return with, so incomes vary wildly across the year. Some crew claimed to have earned less than £20,000

in the previous year. All say they are working more days, shorter-handed and for relatively less money than 20 years ago.

- A dangerous occupation: Fishing is still a dangerous occupation, with all interviewees having lost a close friend or relative at sea. The UK fishing industry experienced 180 fatal accidents between 1992 and 2006.[2] UK fishermen are subject to a fatal accident rate 24 times higher than construction workers. 'We're steaming off in a boat not really designed to operate out there. It's pretty deep and it's a long way from home sometimes.'

- Policing: The fishermen are consistently monitored to see if they contravene any quota regulations or other aspects of EU legislation. Fishery officers inspect boats and catches, and have offices on the dockside where the catches come in. If catches are not recorded properly or trawlers have taken fish above their quota, they can be taken to court and fined heavily. Devon fishermen feel a huge sense of injustice at this. 'Something as innocent as fishing can become the victim of the Proceeds of Crime Act. It's abhorrent. Fishermen are not drug dealers, gun runners, or serious and organised criminals.'

- Fish stocks are abundant: All fishermen say there is a natural ebb and flow in levels of fish stocks year on year. Whilst they may become depleted at some point, in their own experience they always come back. It cannot be overstated that there is a universally and strongly held view that fish stocks are abundant, and that officials and scientists use flawed methods of assessment or are unduly influenced by environmental NGOs. 'I don't know where they get their figures from, I really don't … you could put your underpants in the water and catch a sole in them. They're sitting in their office and telling me it's a sole recovery zone. I'm laughing my socks off … the sole will start dying of old age soon.'

- Sustainable fishing: Many Devon fishermen expect their sons to continue the family tradition, describing their role as 'custodial'. They believe that good husbandry is in part responsible for the 'pristine' nature of the fishing grounds, and this is down to the way they fish (not the quota system or policing).

- The environment lobby: Fishermen feel they are repeatedly dealt an unfair blow in the press. 'To talk about raping and pillaging is disgraceful.' They find this wholly offensive and believe the environmental lobby and the media concentrate efforts disproportionately on discrediting trawling, and that they are not in a position to defend themselves. Many environmental NGOs have sophisticated press offices which portray fishermen as the 'bad guys', and they feel this is undeserved and would like a fair debate and understanding of the nature of their job.

There was clearly a need to reposition the relationship between Cefas and the fishing community, from one of suspicion, mistrust and misunderstanding to a new relationship of mutual respect, clear understanding and partnership.

ACTIONABLE INSIGHTS
As a result of the scoping phase, a number of recommendations were put forward to Cefas, along with a social marketing strategy and project plan for implementation.

 Recommendations included:

- Trust building through positive recognition: Devon fishermen needed professional help to put forward their views to the media and raise the profile of beam trawl fishermen (in general) and the reality of their trade. Helping fishermen to explain their profession and debate some of the key issues from a completely neutral stance, would positively place them at the

---

[2] According to the UK Maritime and Coastguard Agency, Marine Accident Investigation Branch.

centre of local and regional media attention. Stories and profiles of their work and where they live, would ultimately lead to better take-up of net trials and modifications, and engender more trust in Cefas, so that Cefas could work constructively and openly in partnership with fishermen going forward.

○ Defra communications and engagement: Defra, the sponsoring government department for Cefas, needed to better communicate their position, the dilemmas they faced, and the reasons for their eventual decisions to a range of audiences in the industry. The distribution of quotas amongst an incredibly diverse fishing industry, with enormous local differences, is complex, and decision-making is difficult. In the vacuum that is created by a lack of proactive and clear communications, the industry generates misinformation and rumour, which leaves Defra open to untrue accusations of not caring about fishermen and their communities when considering quota allocations. 'I just think the government doesn't want to help you, they would rather bankrupt you.'

○ Cefas reporting: It was accepted by all stakeholders that it was entirely appropriate that Cefas technical information and other scientific trials should be written up as 'academic' reports for scientists and experts. However, they also needed to be produced in formats that were digestible by fishermen and the general population. This meant 'translating' results and making them available to local fishermen using channels that they were comfortable with.

○ Ownership of new approaches: It was recognised by everyone that it was important to implement a programme of trials to test the use of different mesh net sizes to optimise the escape of juvenile fish. It was also agreed that the success of trials should not only be publicised but also publicly celebrated widely, with positive coverage in the media and locally with residents, to encourage positive recognition of fishermen's attempts to be more sustainable and to provide feedback and positive reinforcement to the fishermen themselves.

○ Policing: It was agreed that fishery officers should not relax policing standards. However, they needed to develop more positive relationships in the Devon communities in which they operate. The current relationship was sometimes seen as a barrier to recruiting fishermen for technical modifications, as the situation tended to perpetuate 'distrust' in anyone 'official', including Defra and Cefas.

As a result of this extensive effort to engage fishermen, skippers and boat owners in the process of undertaking new trials with reconfigured nets, ten crews volunteered to take part in the new experiments with larger mesh sizes.

INTERVENTION MIX

Following the in-depth scoping research, the researchers returned to Devon to present their findings face-to-face to the fishermen, skippers and owners before it was publicised or reported externally. Fishermen in the two ports were asked to participate in new net trials and their agreement was sought to be in media stories positively promoting the project. It was agreed that feedback on progress for each individual crew was important in keeping them involved for the long term. A marketing programme was planned to achieve four aims:

○ Explode myths and build trust between the stakeholders.
○ Give positive reinforcement to those taking part in the trials.
○ Provide feedback and show evidence of effectiveness of new approaches.
○ Build a partnership approach to change by making Defra's and Cefas's decision-making processes more transparent, and build more trust between Cefas and the fishing communities.

The key intervention to bring about behaviour change among the target groups in this project was the engagement work undertaken in the scoping phase, as this demonstrated a true commitment to developing a more collegiate and respectful relationship between Cefas and the fishing community. This was achieved by a great deal of stakeholder outreach, listening and feedback. In addition to this work, it was agreed that, as well as being reported back to Cefas in 'scientific' reports, trial results would also be reported back to fishermen, skippers and owners in the form of 'fact sheets', made available to all fleets and industry figures. These fact sheets would be clear, easy to interpret and accompanied by photos of the crew taking part in the trial on-board ship. They would also contain graphs and charts of all the relevant information about catches and discards using the new net configuration. Press and PR activity was also undertaken to highlight stories and photographs of local fishermen and how they were attempting to reduce discards to promote their contribution to environmental sustainability. Local and regional press began reporting on the trials and their progress, featuring the names and photographs of the crews involved. For the general public and the fishing community, a colourful newsletter was produced with fish recipes and tips for buying fish to cook. Other publicity materials were distributed to residents and visitors in local cafes, pubs, shops, restaurants and newsagents in the two ports, to raise awareness of the project.

MONITORING AND EVALUATION

Cefas officers working with each of the ten volunteer crews from Plymouth and Brixham recorded details of each fishing trip during the trial period. There records included not only the areas and times fished, but also the configuration of the nets and crucially the numbers and species of fish caught and the discards that resulted. What was also interesting in terms of process evaluation was that the fishermen who took part in the trials assisted the Cefas officers, not only by following their instructions, but also by making a number of suggestions for modifications to the fishing gear. In this way, the trials were influenced by actual fisherman with practical and commercial experience. The expertise of the fishermen was recognised and helped to improve the trials and their impact. In addition each of the new nets under trial had a slightly different design to help discover the best shape. Each skipper of each trial boat was involved in designing the net they would use and in this way their expertise was utilised, while their ownership of the project increased.

FINDINGS

In keeping with the process of partnership and trust building, in December 2009, at the end of the trials, an event was held to thank participating fishermen and present the final results to a local audience and the media. It was announced that the fishermen had successfully reduced the amount of juvenile fish discarded overboard. The unprecedented success that had been achieved by using modified nets was also widely reported in the local media, which helped to create excitement around the project and give positive reinforcement to all those who had taken part. The trials aimed to reduce the number of juvenile fish thrown overboard by 50 per cent. Many industry experts believed this to be an unrealistically high target. However, the results published at the event showed an unprecedented average reduction of 52 per cent, with one Devon beam trawler, MFV Geeske, reducing discards by 66 per cent. Dave Langdon, whose own trawler managed a 63 per cent reduction, said: 'It's the best thing for the industry in a long time and we've shown that we're trying to work in a sustainable fishing industry. Overall, we've achieved over 50 per cent reduction in the discarding of dead fish across the boats taking part in the pilot. It has been fantastic.'

Cefas demonstrated that, by putting effort into understanding the lives, attitudes and concerns of fishermen in detail, a constructive and successful partnership could be built, to achieve significant positive results. As quoted by the press, Dr Revill commented:

> Because we now have a much better understanding of what it's like to be a fisherman, and have built the project from the bottom up, the fishermen have achieved amazing results. They have been inspired by this approach and taken pride in what they have achieved.

The fishermen in the trial areas have now decided to apply for Marine Stewardship Council accreditation. The demand for certified sustainable seafood is very strong and the decision to pursue this certification is a positive move, which will enhance the status of those taking part, and be viewed by the wider public as the fishing industry's longer-term commitment to conserving the marine environment off the coast of southern England. The trials are now being rolled out to other areas of the UK.

LESSONS LEARNT

The key learning regarding the success from this case study is the need for project designers and implementation agencies to:

- Understand the attitudes and beliefs of the target audience.
- Understand the real and actual barriers to change – including commercial.
- Engage target groups in the design, development, implementation and evaluation of projects.
- Agree challenging and aspirational goals.
- Agree goals that are complementary to the commercial goals of the target audience if profit is a motive, i.e. reducing discards should not affect the commercial catch and, as shown in this case study, actually help with reducing fuel bills by using lighter nets.

CHAPTER RECAP

This chapter has shown that by understanding a target audience's deep-rooted beliefs, social norms and the economic constraints, interventions can be developed to trigger positive behaviour change. Without a deep level of insight from the programme team, this target audience's fatalism and scepticism could have been a significant barrier to change. This chapter has also shown that it is possible to work with the for-profit sector to create social solutions that are also economically sound and work for business. In the next chapter we will see how, when you have developed an effective project, the next challenge that you often face is how to industrialise it or scale it up so that it can have a population-level effect.

SELF-REVIEW QUESTIONS

1 What was the 'exchange' being offered to the fishermen in this case study?
2 What are some of the potential complexities or issues that might arise from trying to work with private sector? How might these be addressed?
3 If you were taking on the wider dissemination of this project to other fishing ports, list five things you would do to engage relevant stakeholders in other ports to adopt new nets. Remember to think about emotional, practical and economic issues that will need to be addressed.

REFERENCES

French, J. and Blair-Stevens, C. (2008). The National Eight Point Bench Mark Criteria for Social Marketing. London: National Social Marketing Centre.

Kemp, K. (2010, June). In for the long trawl: Special report. London: Corporate Culture.. www. corporateculture.co.uk.

17 'FRANCHISING' SOCIAL MARKETING

VIGNETTE: 'ECOTEAMS', GLOBAL ACTION PLAN

KEY WORD: FRANCHISING

The 'EcoTeams' programme is run by the award-winning charity Global Action Plan. The core 'EcoTeams' process was developed in the Netherlands in 1990, and run very successfully with a large proportion of the Dutch population through the 1990s. It was first introduced to the UK in Nottingham in 2000, and has subsequently been rolled out to households across the UK.

'EcoTeams' consists of a standardised package of support (e.g. planning tools), collateral (e.g. DVD and website) and facilitation ('EcoTeams' trained staff). Each team comprises a group of six people, who each represents their household. Teams meet once a month for five months, mapping out practical actions they can take to reduce environmental impact; and weighing and measuring waste to monitor progress.

To develop the most cost-effective model for widespread roll-out, three different delivery models were tested in the UK: 'fully-facilitated', 'semi-facilitated' and 'standalone'. The semi-facilitated model has proven to be most consistently cost-effective, and continues to be rolled out across England. Since 2000, more than 4,000 UK households have taken part in EcoTeams. In that time they have:

- Used 21 per cent less energy
- Lowered their carbon emissions by 17 per cent
- Cut waste by 20 per cent
- Spent £170 less on yearly household bills.

This case study appears in full on ShowCase, at www.thensmc.com. The EcoTeams website is at: www.ecoteams.org.uk.

This vignette makes the point that effective social marketing programmes can be 'standardised' and rolled out as a set package across multiple sites.

ABOUT THIS CHAPTER

Social marketing is typically commissioned by the public sector, and works to achieve a social good. However, as we have seen, this does not mean that it cannot learn lessons from the private sector, and take a business-orientated approach to developing and spreading strong practice. In many cases, rather than 'reinventing the wheel' and designing new programmes from scratch, social marketers might be better placed to implement or 'franchise' a proven model of practice, which has a high probability of delivering return on investment.

In this chapter you will learn how a successful programme to increase children's consumption of fruit and vegetables has been 'commercialised' and franchised, so that it is now delivered in multiple sites across the world, with the hope that it will one day be funded and rolled out nationally by governments worldwide.

CASE STUDY: FOOD DUDES HEALTHY EATING PROGRAMME: LEARNING TO LIKE FRUIT AND VEGETABLES

Fergus Lowe, Pauline Horne, Simon Viktor, Pauline Kelly, Sally Pears and Tracey Anthony: School of Psychology, Bangor University, UK.

This case study appears in full on the National Social Marketing Centre's ShowCase resource (www.thensmc.com), and further information is available on the 'Food Dudes' website at www.fooddudes.co.uk.

PROJECT OVERVIEW

'Food Dudes' is a school-based programme to increase children's liking and consumption of fruit and vegetables. It has evolved from 18 years of research by psychologists at Bangor University, Wales, and has been shown to consistently change children's eating habits in 16 days (Horne, 1995, 1998, 2008, 2010; Lowe, 2002, 2004, 2007). The programme was initially piloted in schools in England, Wales, and Scotland, but has now been launched across a number of sites internationally: from 2007, the Irish government rolled out 'Food Dudes' to all primary schools in Ireland (1,350 schools to date); in England, 137 schools have taken part in the programme across three sites; in Sicily, a pilot of six schools has been completed; and Phase 1 of the programme has also run successfully in schools in Utah and California. The success with which 'Food Dudes' has been rolled out in the UK and internationally demonstrates that social marketing programmes can be transferred effectively, regardless of location or culture, if the right intervention 'package' is developed and consistently applied.

PROJECT RATIONALE

It is widely accepted that, at 250 g, the average British daily intake of fruit and vegetables falls far below the recommended intake of 400 g (WHO, 1990). A diet lacking in the essential nutrients derived from eating fruit and vegetables can lead to a variety of serious illnesses, such as cancer and coronary heart disease (Renehan, 2008). 'Food Dudes' was specifically developed to encourage children and families to change their eating habits by including more fruit and vegetables in their diet, thereby promoting a healthier lifestyle.

'Food Dudes' not only increases fruit and vegetable consumption, but also reduces the intake of unhealthy snack foods, providing an effective means of tackling the global rise in childhood obesity and its related illnesses, both in childhood and later life.

'Food Dudes' uses three core principles of behaviour change – Role Modelling, Rewards and Repeated Tastings – in an innovative way by employing them in a school setting, whilst incorporating a home element that enables the whole family to participate and benefit from the programme.

 ## AIMS AND OBJECTIVES

'Food Dudes' is a programme designed to impact on childhood obesity. Its aims are to reduce consumption of unhealthy snacks and increase fruit and vegetable consumption. It measures performance by reported and observed consumption.

IDENTIFYING TARGET AUDIENCES

There are three main target audiences for 'Food Dudes':

- Primary-aged school children[1]
- The parents and families of these children
- The teachers of these children.

'Food Dudes' in its current format adopts a whole-school approach, aimed at primary-aged school children. Although Phase 1 of the intervention takes place at school snack time or lunchtime, the family as a whole is also targeted, as parental involvement is a key aspect of the programme's success. During Phase 2, teaching staff implement the programme in the classroom and act as role models and motivators for the children and each other.

The programme is also effective in special needs schools where children who previously were reluctant to even handle fruit and vegetables are now tasting and eating them (Wolverhampton Evaluation, 2009). There is also evidence that some children, who previously were fed a liquid diet, now readily eat fruit and vegetables. This population can also be prone to weight and dietary problems and 'Food Dudes' removes the barriers to change in this population by encouraging them to try novel foods in a fun and rewarding way.

A study using the same core principles has demonstrated that pre-school children at nursery can also learn to consume eight new fruit and eight new vegetable types,

---

[1] Primary-aged school children in the UK are aged between 5 and 11 and in years 1 to 6.

with effects maintained fully six months after the end of the intervention (Horne, 2010; Tapper, 1993).

 SCOPING RESEARCH

The scoping stage of the programme comprised extensive academic research and primary research with the target audience. Almost 20 years of behavioural psychological research by the Bangor Food and Activity Research Unit (BFARU) identified the key psychological factors influencing children's food choices, including theories about how children learn; how they emulate role models; how they respond to incentives; and how they acquire early taste patterns.

In addition, almost 450 children aged 2–7 took part in studies conducted in homes, schools and nursery settings to direct the development of the programme and pre-test educational materials with the target audience.

ORIGINAL RESEARCH

The BFARU pursued extensive research to identify the key psychological factors influencing children's food choices. The fact that children do not eat fruit and vegetables is clearly an issue that relates to learning and cultural phenomena. By examining psychological principles associated with learning and development, 'Food Dudes' researchers were able to create a pilot scheme that incorporated the key principles of social learning and applied them to the issue of taste acquisition (Lowe, 1998).

Based on this academic research, a pilot intervention was designed, for trial on a small scale. This trial was funded by the Economic and Social Research Council and Unilever, and involved more than 450 children, aged 2–7, taking part in studies conducted in homes, schools and nurseries. The programme template included two key elements: video adventures featuring the 'Food Dudes' superheroes, and small rewards to encourage children to taste the new foods.

All studies showed that the programme brought about significant long-term increases in children's consumption of fruit and vegetables. For instance, in one of the home-based studies with 'fussy eaters' (aged 5–6 years), children's consumption of targeted fruit rose from 4 per cent to 100 per cent, and of targeted vegetables from 1 per cent to 83 per cent. Targeted fruit consumption was still at 100 per cent, and vegetable consumption at 58 per cent, when the children were observed again six months later (Lowe, 2007).

PRE-TESTING AND DEVELOPMENT

Following these initial successes, the BFARU developed a stand-alone package to enable primary schools to implement the programme across all age groups.

In all schools, children were presented with fruit and vegetables at lunchtime, and fruit and/or vegetables at 'snack time' (immediately prior to morning break). The learning programme was then introduced in those schools selected for the intervention. In all of them this resulted in significant increases in pupils' fruit and vegetable consumption (Horne, 1995, 1998, 2004, 2008).

All new procedures and materials, including videos and educational materials, were pre-tested with children in primary schools in five areas across England and Wales.

THEORY-BASED INSIGHTS

'Food Dudes' is based on the 'Three Rs' of behaviour change (Lowe, 1998) that have been developed through an understanding of learning theory (Bandura, 1977; Keller, 1969; Mayer 2003), and taste acquisition theory (Birch, 1982; Pliner, 1982; Skinner, 1969; Zajonc, 1968):

- Role-Modelling
- Rewards
- Repeated Tastings.

ROLE MODELLING

Children learn to imitate new behaviours by watching those who they respect and like (Bandura, 1977; Birch, 1980; Clarke, 2009; Hardman, 2010). This is an essential element of the 'Food Dudes' Programme. For 15–20 minutes daily, for 16 days, the children watch a series of DVD adventures featuring 'The Food Dudes', a group of children who act as positive peer models. By eating fruit and vegetables, the 'Food Dudes' are shown to gain the superpowers they need to vanquish 'General Junk' and his 'Junk Punks' who are taking away the energy of the world by depriving it of healthy food.

REWARDS

Reinforcement theory suggests that rewarding positive behaviours leads to sustained behaviour change (Cameron, 2001; Skinner, 1953; Wardle, 2003). After watching the 'Food Dudes' DVD, children are encouraged to taste fruit and vegetables themselves. If they succeed, they earn 'Food Dudes Rewards' (such as small stickers or branded pens). A home pack helps to extend the programme's effects to the home environment and to recruit the support of parents in continuing to reward new behaviours at home.

REPEATED TASTINGS

Taste Acquisition Theory suggests that repeated tasting of new foods allows children to discover the intrinsically rewarding properties of fruits and vegetables, i.e. they actually come to like the taste (Birch 1982, 1987; Pliner, 1982; Skinner, 1969; Zajonc, 1968). With increased liking of fruit and vegetables, children then become more likely to eat these foods simply for their flavour, rather than for any external reward. In the process of starting to like these foods, children also develop a pride in being individuals who contribute to a school culture that is strongly supportive of fruit and vegetable consumption. This combination of biological and psychological factors is what maintains the children's change of eating behaviour over the long term.

 MARKETING MIX

The 'Food Dudes' programme has been developed as a stand-alone package that can be easily administered by primary-school staff across the full age range of pupils (i.e. from 4 to 11 years old). It is suitable for pre-school, Key Stage 1, Key Stage 2,[2] and special-needs children.

The programme is appropriate for lunchbox and school-meal children, and can be implemented and evaluated independently in a school or home setting or a combination of both.

The programme consists of the following separate phases:

PREPARATION

Baseline measurement (one to four days). During this phase, children's consumption of fruit and vegetables is measured before the 'Food Dudes' programme is introduced.

PHASE 1 (16 DAYS)

Phase 1 is the initial 16-day intervention phase, during which children are introduced to the 'Food Dudes' who, via DVD adventures, letters and rewards, encourage them to eat fruit and vegetables. This introduction provides opportunities for children to sample fruit and vegetables, and, in the process, develop a liking for them. Phase one procedures can either take place at snack time or lunchtime at school.

Each day, children are read a letter and/or watch a specially designed DVD episode, lasting six minutes, starring the 'Food Dudes'. (See Figure 17.1.)

DVDs: The 'Food Dudes' are young superheroes who are involved in saving the 'Life Force' from the 'Junk Punks', who plot to take away the energy of the world by depriving it of fruit and vegetables. The children watch the Dudes getting the better of the Punks in a series of video adventures. They see the Dudes eating and enjoying a range of fruit and vegetables while extolling their health-giving properties and taste, and see that these eating choices are integral to the Dude's winning strategy.

Letters: There are a series of short 'Food Dude' letters which teachers read out to their class. The letters are a key means of communication between the 'Food Dudes' and the children, providing important information about prizes and the benefits of eating a healthy diet, as well as giving encouragement and praise for the children's eating efforts.

The purpose of the 'Food Dudes' is to provide influential role models for children to imitate

Children are also given small rewards (e.g. juggling balls, pencils and pedometers) if they succeed in eating the piece of fruit or vegetable they are given. This gives them an incentive to follow the 'Food Dudes' healthy eating advice and ensure that children get enough repeated tastes of the foods to begin liking them for their own intrinsic qualities.

Home pack: Children are also provided with a 'Food Dudes Home Pack', to encourage them to eat more fruit and vegetables at home through the involvement of parents and a system of self-monitoring.

---

[2] Key Stage 1 children are aged between 5 and 7 and in years 1 and 2, whereas Key Stage 2 children are aged between 7 and 11 and in years 3 to 6.

Figure 17.1 'Food Dudes' super heroes

Developed by and used under licence by Bangor University. © Bangor University. All Rights Reserved

PHASE 2

Phase 2 is the 'maintenance' phase of the programme, in which the school supports the children's increased consumption of fruit and vegetables, for example through the use of class wall charts and certificates. This phase lasts for up to a year and the aim is for the school to move towards a self-sustaining system of rewarding fruit and vegetable consumption, to ensure that a culture of healthy eating is maintained over time.

In this phase, the programme continues to support fruit and vegetable eating, but with less intensity than during Phase 1. Classroom wall charts are used to record consumption levels of these foods, and as the children achieve more advanced goals they earn further rewards and 'Food Dudes' certificates.

PHASE 3

Phase 3 is ongoing, by which time schools will have developed their own systems of supporting healthy eating. It is also very important to involve the new intake of children each year, to introduce them to the 'Food Dudes' and the healthy eating culture of the school.

EDUCATION SUPPORT MATERIALS

The enthusiasm generated by the 'Food Dudes' programme provides an excellent vehicle for achieving educational goals across the curriculum. Education support materials have been designed around the 'Food Dudes' theme. Each pack contains suggestions and worksheets covering English, Mathematics, Science and Technology. These materials are not essential to the programme, but may be helpful to teachers.

Figure 17.2 'Food Dudes' branding

'FRANCHISING' THE PROGRAMME

'Food Dudes' was initially run in schools as a research programme. However, based on its consistently strong results, the programme has been commercialised and rolled out across funded sites as follows:

IRELAND (2007–ONGOING)

'Food Dudes' is being rolled out nationally to all primary schools in Ireland (1,350 schools to date), under the management of Bord Bia (the Irish Food Board). The programme is now fully funded by the Irish government's Department of Agriculture, Fisheries and Food, and the fruit and vegetables used for the programme are co-funded by the EU's School Fruit Scheme. Before the government agreed full funding for the programme, 'Food Dudes' was run as a pilot (from 2002–7). During this phase, the cost of the fruit and vegetables, and responsibility for distribution to some 10,000 children was borne by the fruit and vegetable industry. The industry's contribution was co-ordinated by Fresh Produce Ireland (the representative body for the fruit and vegetable industry in Ireland), an alliance of growers, distributors and progressive retailers, all dedicated to increasing the consumption of fresh produce among Irish children.

ENGLAND (2009–10)

The success of 'Food Dudes' in Ireland generated significant interest in England. Current projects include: Wolverhampton, running in 93 schools over three years, funded by Wolverhampton PCT; Bedfordshire, running in 14 schools over two years, funded by Unilever and Bedfordshire PCT; and Coventry, running in 30 schools over two years funded by Coventry Council's 'Cook and Eat Well' programme.

ITALY (2009)

A pilot based in six Sicilian schools has shown that social marketing programmes can be successfully transferred internationally. The pilot study in Sicily was supported by the Regional Agriculture and Forestry Agency, and a regional agricultural supplier provided the fruit and vegetables for the intervention.

USA (2009)

Utah and California have recently run pilots of Phase 1 of 'Food Dudes', showing that its materials and programme protocols are cross-transferable and effective in American elementary schools.

'Food Dudes' works as a commercial model because of its standardised approach to the behaviour-change process. In each site, the commissioning body buys a set programme package, consisting of a 16-day standardised intervention, all required materials and supplies (coordinated by the 'Food Dudes' team), as well as ongoing support for a full academic year. This 'package' compares favourably with competitors, who typically charge a daily fee for teaching children food preparation and cooking skills; or provide unsupported teaching resources for teachers to incorporate into standard lesson plans. By contrast, 'Food Dudes' charges a one-off fee per child, plus a licence fee, which is renewable annually.

Not only does this approach mean that the school has everything it needs to run and monitor the programme successfully, at a fixed price, it also appeals to prospective funding bodies, as the one-off, paid programme package is then sustainable by the schools independently beyond the initial support period.

Any income generated by this commercialised approach is reinvested in research to generate new approaches to behaviour change (e.g. using 'Food Dudes' to promote physical activity). The best-case scenario for the programme would be for governments worldwide to recognise the strong results 'Food Dudes' generates, and fund the programme at a national scale, as in Ireland.

MONITORING AND EVALUATION

'Food Dudes' is always evidence-based, and uses its own research findings to support and develop its theoretical constructs.

'Food Dudes' employs four standardised techniques to assess changes in eating behaviours:

- Evaluation questionnaires
- 24 hour Food-Recall Diaries (DIET-24)
- Weighed measures
- Direct observations with high levels of inter-rater reliability.

These assessment techniques help to maintain the accuracy of research data and outcomes.

The procedures and principles employed by 'Food Dudes' are in accordance with ISO 9000[3] standards and Prince2,[4] and are approved by the Project Management Institute (2008),[5] which ensure that work is delivered to time and cost. 'Food Dudes' employs a number of project managers and management procedures. For example: risk assessment and management, project planning and scope management, service-delivery monitoring, stakeholder and customer-care satisfaction, resources allocation and progress reports. These procedures allow the programme to be systematically managed and monitored throughout its life cycle. This allows the programme to meet its targets and function at the highest level when implemented.

RESULTS

'Food Dudes' has been shown to be effective at changing children's eating behaviours (Lowe, 2007) and has also been shown to increase fruit and vegetable consumption and

---

[3] ISO 9000 is a quality-management system, designed to help organisations ensure they meet the needs of customers and other stakeholders. The standards are published by ISO, the International Organization for Standardisation, and available through national standards bodies.

[4] PRINCE2 (PRojects IN Controlled Environments) is a process-based method for effective project management. It is a *de facto* standard used extensively by the UK government and is widely recognised and used in the private sector, both in the UK and internationally.

[5] The Project Management Institute serves practitioners and organisations with standards that describe good practices; globally recognised credentials that certify project management expertise; and resources for professional development, networking and community.

decrease consumption of other more calorically-dense and nutrient-poor snack foods (Wolverhampton Evaluation, 2009). The programme increases children's fruit and vegetable consumption within 16 days of the start of the programme (Horne, 1995, 1998, 2004, 2008; Lowe 2002, 2004, 2007).The programme's extensive history of published and unpublished research has shown that it always achieves its primary goal of improving the target audience's dietary intake (Lowe papers; Horne papers; Ireland, 2010; Wolverhampton, 2009; and Bedford 2009).

For instance, during pilot research, children in the intervention schools showed statistically significant increases in lunchtime fruit and vegetable consumption, irrespective of the school lunch setting (classroom or dining hall) or lunch type (packed lunch or school meal). In contrast, those children in the control schools either showed no statistical change in eating behaviour or significantly reduced their consumption of lunchtime fruit and vegetables.

In these early studies, the adaptive changes in eating behaviour were maintained in the four-month follow-ups. The long-term effectiveness of 'Food Dudes' was established in some of these early studies with a one-year follow-up. The effects of the programme were maintained over this time-frame.

Later studies have replicated earlier findings and extended them to show that: (1) increases in fruit and vegetable consumption can have a positive impact on unhealthy snack food consumption by displacing its consumption, especially at school lunchtime (Wolverhampton, 2009) and (2) the programme maintains its effectiveness over one year (Wolverhampton, 2009) and 2.5 years (Ireland, 2010).

Overall, 61 per cent of the children who received the programme in Wolverhampton showed an increase in fruit and vegetable consumption from baseline to follow-up. On average, children were consuming 4.95 portions of fruit and vegetables a day following the 'Food Dudes' programme. The programme's effects were maintained over a year – the Cohen's d effect size value was > 2 for the follow-up observations (Wolverhampton, 2009).

The programme is also proven to be most effective in those children who are classified as being the 'poorest eaters' at baseline because of their low consumption of fruit and vegetables. For example, the poorest eaters in the Wolverhampton Phase 1 rollout evaluation increased their fruit and vegetable consumption from baseline to follow-up by 2.65 portions.

The programme has also achieved some noteworthy secondary outcomes:

- Improvements in children's general health
- Improvements in children's levels of physical activity
- Improvements in children's school-based behaviour
- Improvements in familial and peer interactions. (Wolverhampton Evaluation, 2009)

In recognition of these strong results, the Wolverhampton project won the prestigious 'Chief Medical Officer's Gold Award' in May 2010, beating over 100 contenders.

 LESSONS LEARNT

Although 'Food Dudes' was initially implemented in schools as a research programme, by commercialising the programme, an income has been secured for investment in ongoing research and programme development. Positive elements include standardising the programme for multi-site application; using local supply and distribution networks for fruit and vegetables; and providing training for all coordinators and staff involved in implementation.

However, despite consistently strong results, future projects will be monitored at a central level, rather than giving control to individual regions/sponsors. By evaluating in this way the effectiveness of the programme can be maintained and implementation will be further standardised across regions, avoiding dilution or overlap with other initiatives.

CHAPTER RECAP

In this chapter we have seen how a successful approach to behaviour change can be rolled out as a 'standardised' package across multiple sites. We have also seen how this 'commercialised' approach can be taken without jeopardising the local effectiveness of each project. As a final point, this chapter has suggested that, by taking a proven intervention that offers an agreed set of collateral and support at a 'fixed price', social marketing commissioners can achieve a greater sense of the likely impact of their investment, while local implementation teams gain the security of having a fully established programme that arrives fully designed and 'ready to roll'.

In the following chapter you will learn how to take a holistic approach to social marketing, and address more than one behavioural 'issue' under one programme, to reflect the complexity and inter-relatedness of behaviours.

SELF-REVIEW QUESTIONS

1 'Food Dudes' is unusual in that it offers social marketing commissioners a 'standardised' intervention and support package. Consider the relative strengths and weaknesses of this approach, and list five benefits and five potential risks.
2 Commercialisation of the programme enables ongoing investment in research and continual development of the 'Food Dudes' offer. In what ways might the scope of the 'Food Dudes' programme be expanded, to influence other behaviours in children?
3 Select a behaviour-change issue of your choosing, that has been addressed successfully by a previous social marketing programme. How might you approach the task of commercialising this offer, and what challenges might arise along the way?

REFERENCES

Bandura, A. (1977). *Social Learning Theory*. New Jersey: Prentice-Hall.

Bedford Evaluation, 2009: Final Report, Bangor University, Bangor Food and Activity Research Unit, Bangor, UK.

Birch, L. L. (1980). Effects of peer models' food choices and eating behaviours on pre-schoolers' food preferences. *Child Development*, 51: 489–96.

Birch, L. L. and Marlin, D. W. (1982). I don't like it, I never tried it: effects of exposure on two-year-old children's food preferences. *Appetite*, 3: 353–60.

Birch, L. L., McPhee, L., Shoba, B. C., Pirok, E. and Steinberg, L. (1987). What kind of exposure reduces children's food neophobia? Looking vs tasting. *Appetite*, 9: 171–8.

Cameron, J., Banko, K. M. and Pierce, W. D. (2001). Pervasive negative effects of rewards on intrinsic motivation: the myth continues. *The Behavior Analyst*, 24: 1–44.

Clarke, A. M., Ruxton, C. H. S., Hetherington, L., O'Neil, S. and McMillan, B. (2009). School intervention to improve preferences for fruit and vegetables. *Nutrition and Food Science*, 39: 118–27.

Hardman, C. A., Horne, P. J. and Lowe, C. F. (2010). Effects of rewards, peer-modeling and pedometer targets on children's physical activity: A school-based intervention study. *Psychology and Health*, 1: 1–19.

Horne, P. J., Hardman, C. A., Lowe, C. F., Tapper, K., Noury, J., Madden, P., Patel, P. and Doody, M., (2008). Increasing parental provision and children's consumption of lunchbox fruit and vegetables in Ireland: The Food Dudes intervention. *European Journal of Clinical Nutrition*, 1–6.

Horne, P. J., Lowe, C. F., Fleming, P. F. J. and Dowey, A. J. (1995). An effective procedure for changing food preferences in 5–7 year old children. *Proceedings of the Nutrition Society*, 54: 441–52.

Horne, P. J., Lowe, C. F., Bowdery, M., Egerton, C. and Tapper, K. (1998). The way to healthy eating for children. *British Food Journal*, 100: 133–40.

Horne, P. J., Tapper, K., Lowe, C. F., Hardman, C. A., Jackson, M. C. and Woolner, J. (2004). Increasing children's fruit and vegetable consumption: a peer-modelling and rewards-based intervention. *European Journal of Clinical Nutrition*, 58: 1649–60.

Horne, P. J., Greenhalgh, J., Erjavec, M., Lowe, C. F., Viktor, S. and Whitaker, C. (2011). Increasing pre-school children's consumption of fruit and vegetables: A modelling and rewards intervention – paper in press (*Appetite*).

Ireland Phase 3, 2010: Final Report, Bangor University, Bangor Food and Activity Research Unit, Bangor, UK.

Keller, F. S. (1969). *Learning: Reinforcement Theory*. New York: Random House.

Lowe, C. F., Horne, P. J. and Hardman, C. A. (2007). Changing the nations diet: a programme to increase children's consumption of fruit & vegetables (working paper 5). Bangor University, Bangor Food Research Unit, Bangor, UK.

Lowe, C. F., Horne, P. J., Tapper, K., Bowdery, M. and Egerton, C. (2004). Effects of a peer modelling and rewards-based intervention to increase fruit and vegetable consumption in children. *European Journal of Clinical Nutrition*, 58: 510–22.

Lowe, C. F., Horne, P. J., Tapper, K., Jackson, M., Hardman, C., Woolner, J., et al. (2002). Changing the nation's diet: A programme to increase children's consumption of fruit and vegetables (technical report). Bangor University, Bangor Food Research Unit, Bangor, UK.

Lowe, C. F., Dowey, A. and Horne, P. J. (1998) Changing what children eat. In A. Murcott (ed.), *The Nation's Diet: The Social Science of Food Choice* (pp. 57–80), London: Addison-Wesley Longman.

Mayer, Richard E. (2003). *Learning and Instruction*. Upper Saddle River, NJ: Merrill Prentice-Hall.

Pliner, P. (1982). The effects of mere exposure on liking for edible substances. *Appetite*, 3: 283–90.

Project Management Institute. (2008). *A Guide to the Project Management Body of Knowledge (PMBOK Guide)*, 4th edn. Pennsylvania: Project Management Institute, Inc.

Renehan, A. G., Tyson, M., Egger, M. Heller, R. F. and Zwahlen, M. (2008). Body-mass index and incidence of cancer: A systematic review and meta-analysis of prospective observational studies. *Lancet*, 371: 569–78.

Schagen, S., Blekinkinsop, S., Schagen, I., Scott, E., Teeman, D., White, G., Ransley, J., Cade, J. and Greenwood, D. (2005). Evaluation of the school fruit and vegetable pilot scheme: Final report. London: Big Lottery Fund. Available oneline at: www.nfer.ac.uk/nfer/publications/NFS03/NFS03_home.cfm?publicationID=196&title=Evaluation%20of%20the%20School%20Fruit%20and%20Vegetable%20Pilot%20Scheme:%20final%20report.

Skinner, B. F. (1953). *Science and Human Behavior*. New York: Macmillan.

Tapper, K., Horne, P. J. and Lowe, C. F. (1993). The Food Dudes to the rescue! *The Psychologist*, 16: 18–21.

Wardle, J., Herrera, M. L., Cooke, L. and Gibson, E. L. (2003). Modifying children's food preferences: The effects of exposure and reward on acceptance of an unfamiliar vegetable. *European Journal of Clinical Nutrition*, 57: 341–8.

Wolverhampton Evaluation, 2009: Final Report, Bangor University, Bangor Food and Activity Research Unit, Bangor, UK.

World Health Organization. (1990). *Diet, Nutrition and the Prevention of Chronic Diseases*. WHO Technical Report Series No. 797. Geneva: World Health Organization. Cited in the National School Fruit Scheme Report. Available online at: www.okfoods.org.uk/School%20Fruit%20 Scheme.pdf.

Zajonc, R. B. (1968). Attitudinal effects of mere exposure. *Journal of Personality and Social Psychology*, 9: 1–27.

18 CHANGING BEHAVIOURS HOLISTICALLY

VIGNETTE: 'HULL PCT – STRATEGIC SOCIAL MARKETING FOR PUBLIC HEALTH COMMISSIONING'

KEY WORD: HOLISTIC SOCIAL MARKETING

Hull Primary Care Trust (PCT) oversees public-health services and healthcare provision for Hull, UK. The PCT has taken a large-scale, strategic approach to social marketing, applying its principles to the development of all public-health programmes for the area, and developing a commissioning organisational structure that is built around social marketing principles.

Senior commissioning leads and public-health staff have undertaken social marketing training, and consumer insight findings have been used to inform strategic planning and commissioning of services such as smoking cessation, weight management and alcohol. In addition, senior policy leads have mapped key performance indicators, target audiences, and activity across inter-connected public health work streams, to streamline activity and reduce replication.

By taking this city-wide approach, duplication across work programmes has been minimised and consistency of social marketing and public-health delivery has increased.

For further information visit: www.hullpct.nhs.uk.

This vignette makes the point that social marketing can be undertaken at a macro scale, rather than on a project-by-project basis. It also shows that a cross-programme approach can yield benefits by reducing overlap and improving coordination of related services.

ABOUT THIS CHAPTER

As we discussed in Chapter 1, the process of capturing and spreading learning is crucial to social marketing, as it enables programmes to be adapted, evolved and rolled out, based on a sound understanding of impact.

In this chapter we will explore:

○ How what started as a brief to re-design a smoking cessation service, evolved into a more ambitious programme to develop a multi-service, holistic lifestyle support programme.

○ How this modified service has continued to grow and develop since its launch in 2008, as service impact has been achieved, and new service elements have been integrated under the brand.

○ How developing social marketing on a cross-cutting scale can enable programme planners to increase service alignment and build consistently around customer insight.

CASE STUDY: 'VITALITY' LIFESTYLE SERVICE: PROVIDING SUPPORT HOLISTICALLY

Henna Ali, NHS South West Essex/City University, London; Ian Wake, NHS South West Essex

This case study appears in full on the National Social Marketing Centre's ShowCase resource (www.thensmc.com), and further information is available on the 'Vitality' website at www.lovevitality.org.

 PROJECT OVERVIEW

'Vitality' is a holistic health and well-being service for south-west Essex, which supports individuals to improve their health by making simple lifestyle changes. The service was developed as a result of a research exercise to understand barriers to quitting smoking. However, this research identified that residents did not want a service directed only at smoking cessation. Instead they wanted a lifestyle programme which integrated healthy eating, smoking cessation, exercise, stress management and alcohol advice.

The 'Vitality' project was carried out by NHS South West Essex (a Primary Care Trust) for the area of South West Essex, UK. An NHS Primary Care Trust (PCT) is part of the National Health Service in the UK, that provides some primary and community services or commissions them from other providers, and is involved in commissioning secondary care for a local area. The programme started with focus groups being held in July 2007, with the recommendations being made in October 2007. First-phase development and implementation work continued until March 2008 and the programme is ongoing, as NHS South West Essex continues to implement new service-user recommendations, and to evaluate performance. As the programme continues to grow, it is beginning to incorporate more service offers. For example, programme leads are now working with community pharmacists to integrate services.

The budget for the initial programme of work was £250,000.

PROJECT RATIONALE

NHS South West Essex is responsible for improving the health and reducing health inequalities for a population of 420,000 people, across the areas of Thurrock, Basildon, Billericay, Wickford and Brentwood. Its area covers a mixed urban/rural geography, and includes both relatively affluent and relatively deprived towns. A recent Public Health Report has highlighted that a ten-year gap in life expectancy exists between the most and least deprived wards in South West Essex (Annual Report, 2008). This is unsurprising given the high levels of deprivation in many wards[1] within Basildon and Thurrock (two of the most deprived areas). According to the local 'Smokefree Basildon: Tobacco Control Strategy' (2006) and National Statistics Online, Basildon has six wards in the top 20 per cent most deprived in England and Wales; four out of ten of its wards are the most deprived in South Essex; six out of nine wards rank in the top ten most deprived against the income deprivation indices; and four out of nine wards are ranked in the top ten most deprived against the health deprivation and disability indices (Smokefree Basildon, 2006). Thurrock has a very similar demographic make-up and similar levels of deprivation to Basildon.

Within the UK, socio-economic inequalities in ill health take the form of a social gradient where people who are from a higher socio-economic status (SES) have better health and limited disabling illnesses, whereas people from low SES display poorer health (Graham, 2004).

Behavioural risk factors, such as smoking, cause significant health inequality between people from different social classes (Siahpush, 2005). Not only do a higher percentage of people from a low socio-economic status smoke, it was also highlighted that smokers who are from a low SES smoke for more years of their life than people in a higher SES. Helping people to quit smoking is thus a key activity in reducing health inequalities across south-west Essex.

The health and financial burden of smoking, in conjunction with social inequalities in smoking behaviour (e.g. people from low SES smoking for a longer duration), suggest that smoking can increase social class differences in the standard of living and health. Thus, facilitating and encouraging people from low SES to quit smoking will not only be beneficial to the public health policy of the UK but also to the social policy which will see a decrease in the inequality gap.

Research was therefore carried out in South West Essex to identify the most effective approach to supporting smoking cessation within local communities.

 AIMS AND OBJECTIVES

The aims of the programme were to:

○ Understand the barriers that local residents from deprived communities face in quitting cigarettes.
○ Explore how these barriers to quitting cigarettes might be overcome.

The overarching behavioural goal of 'Vitality' was to increase the number of four-week quitters[2] in Basildon and Thurrock, and to meet the government's required four week quit targets of 2,428 quitters during 2007–8.

---

[1] Electoral 'wards' are the key building block of UK administrative geography, being the spatial units used to elect local government councillors.

[2] A smoker is counted as a 'four-week quitter' if s/he is a 'treated smoker', is assessed (face to face, by postal questionnaire or by telephone) four weeks after the designated quit date (minus three days or plus 14 days) and declares that s/he has not smoked even a single puff on a cigarette in the past two weeks.

IDENTIFYING TARGET AUDIENCES

Targeting of the 'Vitality' service was based on two segmentation variables:

GEOGRAPHIC

The programme focused on areas of low socio-economic status within south-west Essex, as these are the areas that tend to have the highest smoking rates. For instance, in Basildon, one in every three adults is a smoker. Geography is thus a significant factor in identifying communities with significant health and support needs.

DEMOGRAPHIC

The research phase aimed to understand gender-related and generational differences, by conducting focus groups with men under 30 years and over 31 years; and women under 30 years and over 31 years.

SCOPING RESEARCH

Scoping research for the programme involved a qualitative study with potential service users. The reason for selecting this model was that this type of research is inductive, generates hypotheses and has a focus on how and why things happen, rather than that they happen.

Six focus groups were held with males and females to discuss what barriers they faced in quitting cigarettes, and how they felt these barriers might be overcome. The sample of this study consisted of 33 participants, split into the following categories:

- Pregnant women over 18 (two groups)
- Men between the ages of 18 and 29
- Men over 30 years of age
- Non pregnant females between the ages of 18 and 29
- Non pregnant females over the age of 30.

All focus-group sessions were voice-recorded and transcribed, before being analysed using abbreviated grounded theory. 'Grounded theory' (Corbin and Strauss, 1990) enables researchers to analyse individual and interpersonal processes and look at how they are developed, maintained or transformed (Charmaz, 2003), and from this understanding build up a theoretical understanding of why people think and act as they do.

 ACTIONABLE INSIGHTS

Focus groups generated a detailed understanding of the barriers to successful quit attempts; ways in which the target population felt these barriers might be overcome; and their reactions to different marketing and support propositions:

HOLISTIC SERVICE

The most fundamental insight identified during focus groups was that people did not want the stop-smoking service that was on offer, which only offered stop-smoking advice, and which was run in isolation from other healthy lifestyle services. Instead, they wanted an integrated service, which could look at their health in a holistic manner, rather than focusing on smoking in isolation.

Focus-group participants associated their smoking behaviour with a number of factors, including weight gain, stress management and alcohol. They also held a common view that, by quitting cigarettes, weight would be gained, stress would increase and drinking alcohol would become less enjoyable: 'I'd rather smoke than be fat.' Because of the inter-relatedness of health issues, support services would also have to be planned and delivered in an interconnected way, rather than in silos.

BRAND RECOGNITION

Scoping research also identified that the most significant source of competition for the programme was the issue of brand recognition. People were confusing existing NHS stop-smoking service promotions with other stop-smoking promotions that were running at the same time (e.g. commercial promotions on nicotine replacement therapy (NRT) products). They were also failing to connect all of the different advertisements that the PCT had placed to promote its services, as there was no unifying brand. Instead, each stop-smoking team was referring to itself by location (e.g. 'Thurrock Stop Smoking Service', or 'South Essex Stop Smoking Service'), alerting the programme team to the fact that a new, unifying brand would be required as part of the marketing mix.

SELF-EFFICACY

Research participants identified that they did not have confidence in their own ability to quit smoking. The participants claimed to lack 'willpower' in order to quit smoking and feared failure. The majority of the research population were from lower socioeconomic groups and it was found that these participants had a very restricted range of opportunities available for reward. As smoking is seen as a reliable source of reward, they did not have confidence in their ability to quit smoking and replace it with another rewarding activity. The programme team would thus need to build a strong exchange element into the marketing mix, in order to offer an appealing and achievable alternative to smoking.

RELATIONSHIP WITH HEALTHCARE PROFESSIONALS

A major barrier to quitting smoking was identified as the lack of empathy towards the smoker from healthcare professionals. Most often, research participants reported that they could not speak to their General Practitioner (GP, also known as Primary Physician) regarding smoking, due to the professional's negative body language and a feeling of being rushed during health appointments. Participants found healthcare professionals to be judgemental, sometimes patronising and dictatorial in their attitude to stopping smoking, which discouraged people from accessing services.

Research also identified issues around the type or accuracy of information being provided by healthcare professionals. For example, midwives had reportedly provided pregnant smokers with incorrect information, such as advising that it was okay to continue smoking during pregnancy, or suggesting that if the pregnant woman quit smoking during pregnancy, their unborn child would experience withdrawal symptoms and stress.

 MARKETING MIX

One size does not fit all. In response to research insights, NHS South West Essex concluded that it needed to evolve the services it was offering to the public, and evolve the way in which it marketed these services. Silo working was not delivering, and user research had demonstrated that the health-improvement team needed to adopt more integrated working practices and service delivery.

Based on the results obtained from the focus groups the changes to be made were divided into two categories: service reconfiguration and promotion.

SERVICE RECONFIGURATION (PRODUCT, PLACE AND PRICE)

It was agreed that, instead of a traditional stop-smoking service, a lifestyle programme which integrated factors such as healthy eating, smoking cessation, exercise, stress management and alcohol advice would be developed. If people were reporting that they would 'rather be a smoker than be fat', then the PCT needed to provide them with help and advice on healthy eating and exercise, alongside smoking-cessation advice.

Based on feedback, it was concluded that this integrated programme would work best if it was tailored to individuals' needs. It was also important to increase self-control and self-efficacy within the population. It was proposed that this could be done by providing them with a lifestyle programme which would make them feel healthy and emphasise all-round well-being.

SERVICE PATHWAY

The treatment pathway for the new service was therefore designed as shown in Figure 18.1. This treatment pathway maps the intended customer pathway into and through the new service, outlining the following steps in the process:

1   Referral and needs assessment: Having been referred into the service by a frontline health professional, individuals complete a 'Health Needs Assessment Questionnaire' (HNQ). The HNQ is conducted by a 'Vitality' staff member with all clients who have been referred into stop-smoking services (and now other services too, such as the obesity service). It was also intended that this questionnaire would be made available online when the fully integrated service was launched, allowing individuals to self-refer to services. A pilot of this online assessment programme is currently under development.
2   Service selection: Based on the results of their HNQ, individuals are able to access a complementary suite of 'Vitality' services, including smoking cessation; nutrition; exercise; alcohol; stress; and cardiovascular disease management.
3   Lifestyle modification: All 'Vitality' services encourage and empower clients to use the 'Lifestyle Goal Setting Tool', which helps individual to plan and implement long-term lifestyle modifications, so that any changes they make whilst engaged with services can become part of a longer-term solution.

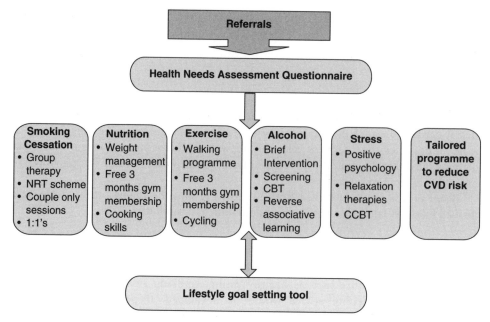

Figure 18.1 'Vitality' flow chart

Artwork created by Perception Advertising Limited, 101 Park Road, Brentwood, Essex, CM14 4TT, UK

HOLISTIC SUPPORT

In addition to core smoking-cessation services, 'Vitality' now also provides:

- 8 walking programmes running per week
- 12 weight-management groups running per week
- 8 cooking-skills programmes running per week
- Two-week waiting list for in-house weight management
- 16 stop-smoking drop-in sessions running per week.

The number of programmes running under the 'Vitality' brand has significantly increased since the launch of 'Vitality', reflecting the extent to which the programme has snowballed beyond its original scope, to redesign the stop-smoking service. As the programme continues to gain reputation, additional new services will be further integrated, so that clients can access an increasingly wide selection of support under a single umbrella brand.

CUSTOMER CHOICE

Programme planners were also aware that there needed to be an increase in service choice, via options such as one-to-one sessions, couple only sessions (as people wanted to quit with their partner and not in groups), trial sessions (to allow people to make up their minds and boost their confidence in available services) and telephone support. Services were developed in response to these insights, and telephone and internet support services were also made available.

HEALTHCARE PROFESSIONALS

To respond to issues around interaction with health professionals, 'Vitality' also provides training for GPs and midwives, to raise their own self-awareness about their body language, the tone in which they offer information. Both GPs and midwives are important sales-people for 'Vitality', and the training draws heavily on undertaking role play, as evidence suggests that this an effective training approach (Lowry, 2004).

PROMOTION

Research revealed the need for a strong, unified brand for the new holistic lifestyle service. Therefore, in addition to these substantial service modifications, a strong promotional element also underpins 'Vitality'. (See Figure 18.2.)

To ensure that the new brand was widely recognised and understood, promotional activity commenced in March 2008 and continued throughout the year. Promotional activities included:

○ Media relations: Press releases, coverage in local newspapers, online news website coverage.
○ Advertising: On bus shelters, billboards in central locations, half billboards in supermarkets and bus advertisements.
○ Telemarketing: Direct mail to all households within the area, targeting all businesses with more than 20 employees and all schools. Schools were targeted because female focus-group participants said that they read all the materials their children bring home from school. In total, businesses and schools have so far requested 40,000 'Vitality' booklets.

Figure 18.2 'Vitality' branding

Artwork created by Perception Advertising Limited, 101 Park Road, Brentwood, Essex, CM14 4TT, UK

- Newspapers: Advertising across all local newspapers, as well as an advertorial in the women's section of the highest circulation local newspaper every month (as women said they always read this section of the newspaper).
- 'Vitality' website: Providing information about all current services and allowing people to refer themselves online. The website will soon be extended to contain a chat forum and once the health needs questionnaire is complete NHS South West Essex will be putting that online so people can start building their own stop-smoking programmes. (See Figure 18.3.)

 ## STAKEHOLDER ENGAGEMENT

The key stakeholders for this project were as follows:

- NHS Stop Smoking Service
- Primary Care Trust Board of Directors (responsible for commissioning services)
- PCT Provider Services Board (responsible for delivering services)
- Local pharmacies
- Local doctors/primary-care physicians
- Acute sector (local hospitals)
- Local councils

Figure 18.3 'Vitality' marketing collateral

Artwork created by Perception Advertising Limited, 101 Park Road, Brentwood, Essex, CM14 4TT, UK

- Local schools
- Local businesses
- Local leisure providers.

Research findings were disseminated to as many senior people within the PCT as possible, to obtain buy-in for implementation of recommendations. Once buy-in was secured from the board and the local stop-smoking service, research was disseminated to the regional Smokefree Alliance (an organisation based locally with representation from key stakeholders working in the field of tobacco).

Once implementation began, local pharmacies, GPs and the local hospital were also made aware of the changes being made to the stop-smoking service. This has ensured that the service continues to grow, evolve and spread. (See Figure 18.4.)

MONITORING AND EVALUATION

The impact of 'Vitality' has been evaluated using a range of outcome measures, including:

- Number of people joining the service, completing programmes and successfully quitting smoking. This data has been compared to data collected prior to the launch of the new service.
- Number of calls to the freephone number and hits to the website, allowing evaluation of impact of marketing work.
- Awareness questionnaires to ascertain brand recognition.

Figure 18.4   'Vitality' marketing collateral

Artwork created by Perception Advertising Limited, 101 Park Road, Brentwood, Essex, CM14 4TT, UK

RESULTS

QUIT TARGETS

- Prior to service redesign the stop-smoking service was hitting the government's national four-week quit target, but often by only a small margin.
- 2007/8: exceeded the four-week quit target by 32 per cent.
- 2008/9: NHS South West Essex exceeded its four-week quit target despite a significantly increased target being set.
- 2009/10: NHS South West Essex achieved an additional 400 quits from target.

CALLS AND WEBSITE HITS

- 412 per cent increase in call volume to smoking-cessation services, from an average of 25 calls per month to an average of 132 calls within three months.
- 6,000 telephone enquiries in 2008/9 and 9,000 telephone enquiries in 2009/10.
- 7,303 hits to the website from launch in March 2008 to March 2009.

There is a 50 per cent brand awareness of 'Vitality' amongst general public in South West Essex (Ali, 2009), which shows that, in a short period of time, the programme team have been successful in significantly raising the profile of the new service.

The number of new services offered under the 'Vitality' umbrella continues to grow, and discussions are currently under way to explore the opportunity of including community pharmacists in the programme. This snowball effect demonstrates the success of using a holistic approach to service delivery that transcends the usual public-health silos against which services are traditionally divided.

 LESSONS LEARNT

The 'Vitality' programme team have successfully created a strong, unified brand; a multi-component healthy lifestyle service; and a unifying 'vision' that coheres all services under this umbrella.

However, one of the biggest challenges 'Vitality' faced in its development was to overcome entrenched public-health team and service structures, whereby people from different teams (e.g. smoking, weight management, alcohol support, stress management) worked as completely separate entities. Across these individual teams, a large number of services were being run, but without much coordination, and often with significant cross-over and duplication. By bringing these disparate services together under one brand, not only did 'Vitality' offer an improved customer experience, it also improved the effectiveness and efficiency of public-health delivery and commissioning. Making changes to any developed service is a hard task, however, and even more so when you are trying to change the entire culture and sub-structures of an organisation in order to achieve your ambitions.

Executive sponsorship and management buy-in were crucial in driving the organisational changes that 'Vitality' needed in order to succeed. In addition, a concerted effort was made to engage and support key frontline staff to work in a more integrated fashion. Staff were trained in health areas where they lacked confidence, or had no previous training, to ensure that they were comfortable discussing and delivering a wide range of services to their clients (e.g. obesity, stress management and nutrition, rather than just smoking cessation). Without this investment in developing the skills sets of frontline staff, the 'Vitality' service could not have grown beyond its original scope as a simple smoking-cessation service.

CHAPTER RECAP

This chapter has shown how a clear focus on customer requirements has enabled a strong, holistic lifestyle support service to be developed, which exceeds and has evolved beyond the original programme design brief. In this chapter we have also seen how this integrated approach to service delivery has generated a momentum that means additional service elements continue to be incorporated into the 'Vitality' offer.

In the next chapter we will see how a national programme to tackle childhood obesity built detailed evaluation mechanisms into its structure, to demonstrate impact across a range of indicators.

SELF-REVIEW QUESTIONS

1 The original brief for this social marketing programme was to develop a better smoking-cessation service. However, as we have seen, the revised service offer drew in a wide range of additional programmes, such as weight and stress management. What challenges might arise from growing the scope of a programme like this, and how might you manage them?

2 One of the key insights from this case study was that staff needed support and training to enable them to work across a range of health specialities (i.e. not just smoking cessation). What other approaches, beyond staff training, would help you to embed a programme and ensure its sustainability wasn't threatened by local resistance to organisational change?

3 'Vitality' is still growing and developing three years after its launch. As opposed to more time-bound, short interval interventions, this illustrates how social marketing can be about a long-term, sustained process of change. How might your approach to developing and managing a long-term social marketing programme differ from a shorter-term campaign, and what steps would you need to take to ensure longevity of your programme?

REFERENCES

Ali, H., Kanapathy, J. and Marway, P. (2009). 'Vitality' Brand Awareness Report. NHS South West Essex Annual Report of the Director of Public Health, South West Essex PCT. (2008). Available online at: www.swessex.nhs.uk/about-us/dms/.

Charmaz, M. (2003). Grounded theory. In J. Smith (ed.), *Qualitative Psychology: A Practical Guide to Research Methods* (pp. 81–109). London: SAGE.

Corbin, J. and Strauss, A. (1990). Grounded theory method: Procedures, canons, and evaluative criteria. *Qualitative Sociology*, 13: 3–21.

Graham, H. (2004). Tackling inequalities in health in England: Remedying health disadvantages, narrowing health gaps or reducing health gradients? *Journal of Social Policy*, 33: 115–31.

Lowry, R. J., Hardy, S., Jordan, C. and Wayman, G. (2004). Using social marketing to increase recruitment of pregnant smokers to smoking cessation service: A success story. *Public Health*, 118(4): 239–43.

Siahpush, M., Heller, G. and Singh, G. (2005). Lower levels of occupation, income and education are strongly associated with a longer smoking duration: Multivariate results from the 2001 Australian National Drug Strategy Survey. *Journal of the Royal Institute of Public Health*, 119: 1105–10.

Smokefree Basildon: Tobacco Control Strategy. (2006). Basildon Primary Care Trust, Basildon, UK.

19 THE IMPORTANCE OF EVALUATION

VIGNETTE: ROAD CREW

Based in Wisconsin, USA, Road Crew is one of five US projects funded by the National Highway Traffic Safety Administration, seeking a 5 per cent reduction in alcohol-related crashes in the pilot communities. Pioneered in several rural Wisconsin counties, it represents an innovative approach to drink-driving.

Before drinkers go out for the evening, they arrange a ride with Road Crew. Vehicles pick up customers at their home, drive them around from bar to bar, then deliver them home safely at the end of the night. Rather than asking people not to drink, or not to drive, Road Crew provides a service solution, which keeps communities safe from drink-drivers whilst adding to the fun of a night out by providing a way for people to socialise. Evaluation has been a key component of the Road Crews success, to demonstrate that it works but also to convince funders, stakeholders and users that it is an effective programme that saves lives and money.

As of February 2008, Road Crew had:

- Grown to provide service in six Wisconsin counties, serving 36 communities
- Given over 97,000 rides
- Prevented an estimated 140 alcohol-related crashes
- Saved an estimated six lives.

Comparing the estimated cost of avoiding a crash by implementing Road Crew at US$6,400, and the cost to a community to recover from a crash at $231,000, Road Crew has shown savings estimated at over $31 million.

This case study is available in full on ShowCase at www.thensmc.com.

This vignette shows how clear evaluation enable programme impact to be monitored and celebrated.

ABOUT THIS CHAPTER

Well-constructed and well-executed evaluation should be a feature of all social change programmes and is not a unique feature of social marketing. However, as we saw in Chapter 2 the learning and change that flows from evaluation is also key part of the social marketing planning process. In this chapter we will review a case study that not only represents a well-planned programme but also one that set out from the very beginning to evaluate its work in terms of both efficiency and effectiveness.

This chapter explores a large-scale case study, that provides a good example of a comprehensive approach to developing a social marketing programme. In particular it illustrates three key learning points:

- When developing a large-scale intervention, aimed at creating a population level-change across complex behavioural agendas (food consumption and exercise), it is necessary to set out very clear and measurable programme objectives.
- Robust evaluation is essential for sustainability of large-scale programmes.
- Building a coalition of support from across civic society will be key in developing programme viability.

CASE STUDY: 'CHANGE4LIFE': TACKLING OBESITY AT A POPULATION LEVEL

David Shaw, Social Marketing Consultant; Alison Hardy, UK Department of Health's 'Change4Life' team.

PROJECT OVERVIEW

As part of the last government's public-health strategy, there was a commitment to develop a three-year social marketing programme, to tackle the growing problem of obesity in the UK. The Department of Health (DH) developed the programme in conjunction with the Department for Children, Schools and Families (DCSF) and other government departments, non-government organisations (NGOs), academics and a number of commercial-sector partners.

This was a substantive national programme that adopted a planned social marketing research and insight-driven approach. The research that shaped the project was undertaken in 2007 and 2008. This culminated in the development of the 'Healthy Weight Healthy Lives: Consumer Insight Summary', published in November 2008. The research findings informed the development of the cross-government national marketing programme, called 'Change4Life'. £75 million was allocated to the programme over three years, with a launch to stakeholders in December 2008 followed by a public launch in January 2009. An adult programme was launched in February 2010, to accompany the child-focused first stage.

'The remit of Change4Life's is preventative not remedial. The programme was not set up to recruit overweight or obese children into weight-loss programmes, but to change the way all of us raise and nourish our children, with the aim of creating a cohort of 5- to 11-year-olds who have a healthy relationship with food and activity. (See Figure 19.1.)

Figure 19.1   The 'Change4Life' logo

PROJECT RATIONALE

The prevalence of obesity in the UK has trebled since the 1980s. By 2005, nearly a quarter of adults in England will be obese (Health Survey for England, 2002). It was estimated that about a third of adults and a fifth of children aged 2–10 years would be obese by 2010, and nearly 60 per cent of the UK population could be obese by 2050 (see Figure 19.2). This could mean a doubling in the direct healthcare costs of overweight and obesity, with the wider costs to society reaching £49.9 billion by 2050 (Government Office for Science, Foresight Report, 2007). In response to the Foresight Report, and several other national reviews, the UK government published *Healthy Weight, Healthy Lives: A Cross Government Strategy for England* in January 2008. This set out the ambition to be the first major nation to reverse the rising tide of obesity. (See Figure 19.2.)

AIMS AND OBJECTIVES

The 'Change4Life' programme aimed to bring about a societal shift in attitudes and behaviour, resulting in fewer people becoming overweight and obese. To achieve this it aimed to:

- Create a societal movement under the 'Change4Life' banner that would speak to and for the public on issues relating to diet and activity, and underpin all public-facing marketing and communications activity.
- Create a segmentation model that would allow resources to be targeted to those individuals who are most in need of help (i.e. whose attitudes and behaviours place their children most at risk of excess weight gain).
- Provide insight into why those individuals hold the attitudes and behave they do.
- Create a communications campaign to change those attitudes.
- Provide 'products' (such as handbooks, questionnaires, wall charts, web content) that people could use to help them change their behaviours.
- Signpost people to services (such as breastfeeding cafés, accompanied walks, free swimming and cookery classes).
- Bring together a coalition of local, non-governmental and commercial-sector organisations to use their influence to change behaviours.

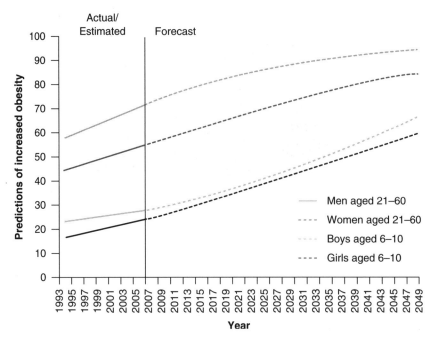

Figure 19.2 Predictions of increased obesity in England

Source: Foresight Report.

'Change4Life' aimed to 'reframe' obesity, away from a cosmetic issue of personal appearance, towards an issue of poor health outcomes and to personalise behaviours such as poor diet and low physical activity levels as critical risk factors.

Targets for the first year of the campaign were:

- To reach 99 per cent of families living in England (defined as an opportunity to see the campaign).
- For 82 per cent of all mothers with children under 11 to recall the advertising campaign (as measured by the tracking study).
- For 44 per cent of mothers with children under 11 to recognise the 'Change4Life' logo (as measured by the tracking study).
- For 100,000 families to complete 'How are the Kids?' questionnaires.
- For 200,000 families to join 'Change4Life' (defined as registering their details with us).
- For 33,333 families to still be involved with 'Change4Life' after six months.
- To generate 1.5 million responses (calls, web visits or paper responses).

These stretch targets were developed in conjunction with the UK Central Office of Information (COI), by examining what had been achieved by other government campaigns of a comparable size and by using COI's Artemis[1] forecasting tool.

---

[1] The UK Government's Central Office of Information is a government agency that provides guidance, support and coordination of government communications and marketing activity.

IDENTIFYING TARGET AUDIENCES AND CONDUCTING SCOPING RESEARCH

The initial target audiences for 'Change4Life' were the 1.4 million families who have children aged under 2; the 3 million families with children aged 2–10 whose children are most at risk of weight gain; pregnant women; and those ethnic minority communities (particularly black African, Bangladeshi and Pakistani) where levels of childhood obesity are particularly high.

Market research conducted for the programme, conducted with households with children aged 2–10 years, identified that families could be grouped into six distinct clusters according to their attitudes and behaviours. Data were gathered from a sample of 883 children and their families via three questionnaires, and one additional survey, which focused on attitudes and behaviours in relation to physical activity. A cluster analysis was carried out and participating families grouped into six clusters.

Qualitative insight research conducted for the programme set out to explore the attitudes and behaviours demonstrated by the clusters in more depth. The research was split into four stages:

- Stage 1: The research team interviewed members of the 'Change4Life' programme's expert review group to capture expertise and insights.
- Stage 2: Families were asked to carry out pre-tasks, including making a short film, 'A day in the life of my kids'; recording a week's worth of 'kitchen cam' footage; and keeping diaries recording what they ate and how much physical activity they undertook.
- Stage 3: Researchers spent two days with each family in the four priority clusters observing their behaviour, carrying out formal interviews with both parents and children, and accompanying them to the supermarket and out to dinner.
- Stage 4: Families in the four priority clusters took part in workshops looking at the intervention strategies and marketing concepts developed for 'Change4Life'.

ACTIONABLE INSIGHTS

Key insights from qualitative and quantitative research with families included:

- While people know obesity is an issue (93 per cent of UK parents agree that 'childhood obesity is an issue of national importance') they do not realise that it is their issue (only 5 per cent of parents believe that their child is overweight or obese).
- Parents routinely underestimate the amount of food that they and their children eat, and overestimate the amount of activity that they undertake.
- A host of behaviours the research suggests are unhealthy (such as spending a lot of time participating in sedentary activities) have no perceived risk for parents.
- Healthy living was perceived as a middle-class aspiration.
- Parents prioritise their children's immediate happiness over their long-term health, the link between poor diet and sedentary behaviour today and future health outcomes was not understood.

An overview of the research findings and the methodologies used was published in a *Healthy Weight, Healthy Lives Consumer Insight* summary. The conclusion was that, before behaviour change could be achieved on any significant scale, families would need to:

○ Be concerned that weight gain has health consequences
○ Recognise that their families are at risk and take responsibility for reducing that risk
○ Know what they need to do to change
○ Believe that change is possible.

It was also felt that propensity to change could increase when:

○ People are asked about their own behaviours
○ Information is personalised
○ People are encouraged to create their own goals
○ People can see how their behaviours are benchmarked against others
○ They are able to record their own progress
○ They are given feedback, reminders and rewards.

These assumptions had implications for the overall shape of the programme and how it would be delivered. The staging and shape of the year one activity was based on a hypothetical model of behaviour change. In developing this model, the programme team drew heavily on the academic literature around behaviour change, on previous behaviour change programmes (particularly tobacco control) and on other interventions (often smaller-scale, face-to-face programmes) that had successfully changed behaviours in the past.

This led to a working hypothesis for how behaviour change might be created, represented in Figure 19.3. It was recognised that this model was overly rational and simplistic, and the team did not expect individual families to travel neatly and sequentially through each stage. Rather the assumption was that individual families would move at their own pace, sometimes fast, sometimes slow, sometimes stalling, lapsing or even going backwards for a time through the process of change. However, it was considered to be a reasonable overview of what might be expected to happen at a population level.

 STAKEHOLDER ENGAGEMENT

To create a societal movement, there was a need to mobilise a wide network of organisations, both public and private, that could influence and support families. This included healthcare professionals, teachers, child-minders, local authority staff, charities, NGOs and commercial organisations. 'Mobilising the Network' started in 2008, before any direct communication to the public. The aim of this phase was to ensure that, when the public did attempt to change behaviours, it met an informed and supportive local environment. An enormous amount of work was undertaken in this stage by local authorities, Primary Care Trusts, Strategic Health Authorities, the Regional Government Offices and commercial and NGO partners to prepare for the public launch. The scope and scale of partnership working that was achieved was unprecedented. The

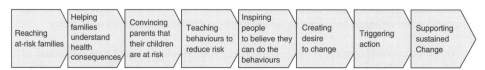

Figure 19.3   Working hypothesis for creating change in relation to the 'Change4Life' objectives

Source: HM Government (2010).

programme team worked with representatives to develop a governance framework and campaign guidance to ensure best practice. In addition to a wide range of NGO and public-sector organisations at local, regional and national level, the programme also set out to create a long-term alliance with a large number of commercial-sector organisations. Full details of all commercial partner activity can be found at www.nhs/'Change4Life'/pages/partners.

The programme also set out to recruit what was termed 'local supporters'. These supporters could be someone from the community, whose job it is to promote healthy lifestyles, or an individual who has influence with the target audience (such as a member of a community-minded voluntary group, club or registered charity). What distinguished them was that they would be willing to do more than help their own families. At the launch, there were about 8,000 individuals signed up as local 'Change4Life' supporters.

COMPETITION

Competition analysis demonstrated that key issues included lack of awareness, lack of knowledge and time pressures. All of these competing forces influenced the delivery approach that was developed. The potential competition from food retailers was also anticipated, and a network of commercial-sector organisations was developed to ensure that many of the biggest companies in the UK pledged to support the programme.

 MARKETING AND INTERVENTION MIX

With regard to product development, 'Change4Life' developed a wide range of products for different target groups, such as the 'How are the Kids?' self-assessment questionnaire and feedback system. Each product was developed for a specific behaviour and for a specific target audience.

With regard to promotions, the programme involved:

- Paid-for advertising (including television commercials, newspaper advertising and posters).
- Sponsorship of Channel 4's *The Simpsons*.
- Direct and relationship marketing (including a customer relationship programme, delivered both online and offline).
- Digital communications (including a website, email marketing and online display advertising).
- Public relations.
- Partnership marketing (the creation and dissemination of messages and offers by 'Change4Life' partners); and communications aimed at stakeholders (such as the health and teaching workforces).

'Change4Life' also communicated with the public by means of materials distributed to healthcare professionals, via benefits mailings and through schools. At-risk families were invited to join 'Change4Life' and were sent a questionnaire called 'How are the Kids?' to assess their current behaviours.

 PRE-STAGE: MOBILISING THE NETWORK

Unlike traditional public-health information campaigns, which begin with top-down and centrally delivered messages, this programme began with over six months of engagement with partners and with workforces, local service providers, potential local supporters and NGOs, so that, when national marketing started, the public would encounter an informed and supportive local environment. It also enabled those organisations that provide services and commission marketing of their own to join up their activities with the national effort.

This phase included social marketing training (including briefing on the research findings), face-to-face presentations and direct marketing. For example, the Secretary of State for Health wrote to 220,000 individuals who are active in grassroots organisations and the Chief Medical Officer and the Chief Nursing Officer wrote to every general practitioner, practice nurse, midwife, health visitor and health trainer in England. This phase is ongoing and has grown as the campaign has developed. There are currently 50,000 people who have signed up to be 'Change4Life' supporters and are helping families to change their behaviour.

PHASE ONE: REFRAMING THE ISSUE

In January 2009, 'Change4Life' was launched officially to the public with television and print advertising, an information line and a campaign website. People who responded to the campaign were sent a welcome pack of materials, including a handbook for Healthy Happy Kids, a wall chart detailing target behaviours and stickers for their children. The brand identity was 'Change4Life'. This identity was selected because:

- The words contain both an imperative (change) and an aspiration that the change will be long term ('4life'). The double meaning of '4life' also stresses longevity (i.e. in order to live longer) and quality of life.
- It is accessible and fun.
- The logo contains little 'people' whose presence gives the identity humanity.

The launch advertising explained the link between weight gain and illness (particularly Type 2 diabetes, cancer and heart disease) and reduced life expectancy ('lives cut short'), and positioned this as an issue that could affect the majority (9 out of 10) of families in the future. It also told people where to go for more help and advice.

PHASE TWO: PERSONALISING THE ISSUE

The next phase helped people recognise that their own families may be at risk of developing obesity because of their current behaviours. The main marketing mechanic for this phase was 'How are the Kids?', a questionnaire on children's health and activity which was distributed to over five million at-risk households. 'How are the Kids?' was positioned as an opportunity to see how modern life is affecting the individual's family and provides a route in to a long-term CRM programme.

PHASE THREE: ROOTING THE BEHAVIOURS

To change behaviour people need to know what to do and be convinced that they can carry out the desired behaviour. This means making what is being proposed understandable and actionable, and if possible easy to do. The 'Change4Life' research phase had defined the behaviours that parents should encourage their children to adopt if they are to achieve and maintain a healthy weight as:

- Reduce fat intake, particularly saturated fat
- Reduce added sugar intake
- Control portion size

- Eat at least five portions of fruit and vegetables per day
- Establish three regular meal times each day
- Reduce the number of snacks eaten
- Do at least 60 minutes of moderate-intensity activity per day
- Reduce time spent in sedentary activity.

Prior to the launch of 'Change4Life', only one of these (eat at least five portions of fruit and vegetables per day) had any real traction with the public (via the national '5 A Day' initiative).

To make the required behaviours real and achievable, 'Change4Life' and its partner agencies created a user-friendly, memorable language for describing them and supplied tips that translated each behaviour into real situations to which our target audiences could relate. In summary the desired behaviours were promoted as follows (see also Figure 19.4):

1 Reducing sugar intake ('Sugar Swaps')
2 Increasing consumption of fruit and vegetables ('5 A Day')
3 Having structured meals, especially breakfast ('Meal Time')
4 Reducing unhealthy snacking ('Snack Check')
5 Reducing portion size ('Me Size Meals')
6 Reducing fat consumption ('Cut Back Fat')
7 60 minutes of moderate-intensity activity ('60 Active Minutes')
8 Reducing sedentary behaviour ('Up & About').

Figure 19.4 The eight 'Change4Life' key behaviours
Source: HM Government (2010).

PHASE FOUR: INSPIRING PEOPLE TO CHANGE

For people to move from an intention to change to a real change, they needed to be convinced that change is possible (i.e. believe in their own ability to change) and normal (i.e. that people like them are already making changes). This stage of the programme sought to inspire people to believe that change is possible ('I'm in') and convince them that change is already happening ('We're in'). This includes editorial in local press and local radio advertising, detailing local services and events, as well as local people telling stories of how they managed to change their families' behaviours.

PHASE FIVE: SUPPORTING PEOPLE AS THEY CHANGE

All campaign materials gave at-risk families the opportunity to sign up to an ongoing CRM programme that supports behaviour change. The CRM programme provides encouragement, information and support for families to get their children eating better and moving more. Some families will want more support than marketing can provide and 'Change4Life' will signpost these families to face-to-face interventions at a local level. This programme is delivered both online and by post.

 MONITORING AND EVALUATION

There were three high-level themes to the evaluation programme:

- Monitoring campaign exposure and visibility to target audience.
- Investigating the impact on families.
- Tracking the development of a social movement.

Such a large and complex intervention required a mixed-method approach to evaluation, to provide a rounded view of the campaign. A 'Change4Life' Tracker Survey was developed and used to evaluate awareness of, and response to, the campaign and its impact on attitudes and behaviours. The tracking study is carried out by the British Market Research Bureau (BMRB). The survey commenced in November 2008, when a baseline of key measures was established, and the full study has been running since January 2009. The questionnaire is updated on a monthly basis in order to ensure that the latest campaign activity is monitored. However, the majority of core questions have remained consistent throughout in order to provide trend data.

An academic study using a randomised design and control group to gauge the impact of 'Change4Life' marketing materials upon family behaviour was also developed. The study was led by University College London and contains a combination of quantitative and qualitative approaches.

The COI Artemis database[2] was also built into the evaluation design. Artemis holds response data for all government campaigns, and enabled the team to assess the cost-effectiveness of the marketing activity in terms of the volume and nature of responses generated.

---

[2] COI Artemis currently contains data for 54 campaigns across a variety of government departments, enabling comparisons to be made in terms of efficiency and effectiveness.

Longer-term use of proxy data was also developed at a population and sub-population level. Additionally over time, routine survey data will support tracking of behaviour change, body-mass index (BMI) change and other longer-term health outcomes. These surveys and weight measurement programmes include the Health Survey for England, the National Travel Survey and the National Diet and Nutrition Survey.

Ultimately, 'Change4Life' aims to establish whether there is a link between changes in behaviours and changes in weight, and between changes in weight and improved health in the longer term, thus allowing us to calculate the return on marketing investment in terms of savings to the state and quality adjusted life years (QALYs) to the individual. It is planned that economic evaluation of the programme will also be carried out.

In February 2010, as part of its commitment to a more open and reflective approach to social marketing evaluation, the government published a full evaluation report of the 'Change4Life' programme (HM Government, 2010). Some of the key results are reported below.

FINDINGS

The campaign reached 99 per cent of targeted families by the end of January 2009. Awareness of the advertising campaign peaked at 87 per cent in March 2009 and remained high throughout the year.

Logo recognition exceeded its target, reaching 88 per cent in September–November 2009 and closing the year at 87 per cent. In the first 12 months, 413,466 families 'joined' 'Change4Life', by registering their details by telephone, post or on the website. This figure had grown to 477,632 by August 2010. In England, 346,609 families sent in 'How are the Kids?' questionnaires, of whom 288,487 (85 per cent) provided enough information for the 'Change4Life' team to provide them with a personalised response. Even though 'How are the Kids?' is no longer being promoted, responses continue to come in at average of over 200 per day.

Some 200,000 at-risk families were included in the postal (more expensive) version of the Customer Relationship Management (CRM) programme, which comprised four separate packs of additional information and resources. A further 90,000 people received a lower-cost electronic version of the CRM programme.

The programme had a target of 33,333 families entering the CRM programme to still be interacting with 'Change4Life' after at least six months. In order to measure continued interaction, the team put coupons into the CRM packs to incentivise a response (e.g. 'send this back to receive a free ring binder'). While response does not in any way signal behaviour change, it does prove that the packs were opened, read and that the recipients were sufficiently interested to interact further with 'Change4Life'. The second CRM pack (sent out at least six months after people joined 'Change4Life') received over 44,833 responses.

Counting all postal, online, face-to-face and telephone responses, 'Change4Life' generated 1,992,456 responses, exceeding the target of 1.5 million.

Independent audits by COI concluded that 'Change4Life' had the fastest awareness build of any government campaign that they had ever monitored; and had in the 'How are the Kids?' Questionnaire the most efficient engagement tool ever recorded in the government's Central Office of Information's Artemis database.

In addition, over 200 partner organisations from the private, public and third sector have signed the terms of engagement to support the campaign.

With regard to the local supporters programme, at the start of the campaign there were 8000 signed up; by the July 2010 there were over 32,000. Asked whether they intended to sustain their involvement with 'Change4Life' in the next year, only 5 per cent of local supporters said that their involvement would decrease; 44 per cent said they expected their involvement to increase; and 51 per cent said it would stay the same. (See Table 19.1.)

Additionally 44 per cent of primary schools, hospitals, general practices, town and village halls, children's centres, pharmacies, nurseries, libraries and leisure centres displayed 'Change4Life' materials. Over 25,000 local supporters used 'Change4Life' materials to help them start conversations regarding lifestyles, with over one million people. NHS staff ordered over six million items of 'Change4Life' material to distribute to the public. Primary schools generated over 50,000 sign-ups to 'Change4Life'. Local authorities and primary-care trusts joined up their own activities and created new ones, such as street parties and road shows. With regard to the actual targeted behaviours, there have been encouraging increases in awareness of the eight behaviours (see Table 19.2).

The tracker survey has shown a high degree of claimed behaviour change, with three in ten of mothers who were aware of 'Change4Life' claiming to have made a change to their children's behaviours as a direct result of the campaign. This equates to over one million mothers claiming to have made changes in response to the campaign. Almost all mothers (99 per cent) claimed that their children did at least one of the 'Change4Life' behaviours at the pre-stage, and this remained constant throughout the year.

Encouragingly, the number of mothers claiming that their children do all eight behaviours increased from 16 per cent at the baseline to 20 per cent by quarter four. This also showed

Table 19.1 Summary of year one targets and achievements

	Year one Target	Year one Achievement
Reach (% of all mothers of children under 11 who had an opportunity to see the advertising campaign)	99%	99%
Awareness (% of all mothers with children under 11 who recalled seeing the Change4Life advertising)	82%	87%
Logo recognition (% of all mothers with children under 11 who recognised the Change4Life logo)	44%	88%
Response to *How are the Kids?* (total number of questionnaires returned electronically, by post or from face-to-face marketing)	100,000	346,609
Total responses (including website visits, telephone calls, returned questionnaires)	1,500,000	1,992,456
Sign-up (total number of families who joined Change4Life)	200,000	413,466
Sustained interest (total number of families who were proven to still be interacting with Change4Life six months after joining)	33,333	44,833

Source: HM Government (2010).

Table 19.2   Reported behaviour change at end of year one

Behaviour	January 2009 (327) %	October–December 2009 (823) %
5 A Day	80	73
Sugar Swaps	6	26
Me Size Meals	4	36
Snack Check	5	15
Cut Back Fat	14	21
Meal Time	5	14
60 Active Minutes	8	26
Up And About	9	13

Source: HM Government (2010).

seasonality, climbing steadily throughout the year (18 per cent in the spring, 20 per cent in the summer and 24 per cent in the autumn, dropping slightly in the winter).

The proportion of families having adopted at least four of the behaviours has also increased. The programme has not only encouraged families who already had relatively healthy lifestyles to become even more healthy; it has also persuaded people with much less healthy lifestyles to make an effort to improve their health.

If the claimed data equate to actual change, an extra 4 per cent of families (about 180,000) are now practising all eight behaviours. However, we know that reported behaviour is often not accurate. In order to address this issue, the programme also used 'Basket Analysis' data provided by retailers to track actual shopping behaviour. This approach employs a variety of methods, including geo-demographic profiling of store loyalty-card data (to see what sort of people bought what sort of products), and the use of in-home scanners (so that panellists, who have already provided demographic information, can automatically upload data on all of their purchases). Individuals give their consent for their information to be used in this way, and the data is presented once it has been anonymised and aggregated.

In a pilot study, objective measures were used to monitor the actual purchasing behaviour of 10,000 of the families who were most engaged with 'Change4Life'. The analysis compared purchases made at Tesco supermarket during September, October and November 2009 with the same period in 2008 (i.e. pre-'Change4Life'). To factor out the impact of pricing and sales promotion, a control group of 10,000 non 'Change4Life' families who were demographically comparable, and whose purchasing in 2008 matched the intervention group, was also reviewed. Profiling confirmed that the highly engaged 'Change4Life' households did contain a large proportion of lower-income families, confirming that the people who are engaging with 'Change4Life' are from the right target audience segments. However, more significantly, the analysis also found differences in the purchasing behaviour of the intervention group relative to the control.

In particular, there were changes in the purchases of beverages among 'Change4Life' families, who favoured low-fat milks and low-sugar drinks.

In addition to questions of programme impact, the 'Change 4Life' programme also incorporated measures to assess the value for money of the programme. An independent review[3] of the media buying for the 'Change4Life' campaign highlighted considerable savings across all media channels:

- Securing sponsorship of *The Simpsons* for less than 50 per cent of the market price.
- Over-delivering launch TV by 20 per cent (achieving 20 per cent higher ratings than paid for).
- Added value of over £700,000 across press partnerships and display advertising.
- In all, over £6 million worth of media savings were made across the year, the equivalent of 40 per cent of the actual spend.

The COI's Artemis tool also gave the 'Change4Life' team more information about the cost effectiveness of the programme. The original COI Artemis forecast (based on the media plan) was for 100,000 returns at an average cost per response of £5; cost per active response of £22; and cost per intermediate conversion of £27. These forecasts were themselves bullish: the average cost per response across government campaigns is £13, the average cost per active response is £115 and the average cost per intermediate conversion is £303. How are the Kids? delivered a cost per active response of £10 and cost per intermediate conversion of £15, making it the most cost-effective response mechanism in government.

The government investment in 'Change for Life' also attracted other marketing spend. The original investment in the DH campaign attracted:

- £1.5 million in spend from other government departments.
- A further £7.5 million of national partner activity.
- £12,457,572 in free media space for the launch.
- £532,393 in free media around the sponsorship of Channel 4's *The Simpsons*.
- £200 million in commitments by the Advertising Association consortium.

 ## LESSONS LEARNT

WHAT WORKED WELL

In the first annual evaluation the report, the 'Change4Life' team set out the following lessons about what had helped to make the programme so successful:

- Embedding 'Change4Life' within the broader policy context. The programme is not an add-on, it is an integral part of Healthy Weight, Healthy Lives. It has helped to bind the policy together and explain it to the public.
- Basing the programme on the latest evidence, including evidence generated through ongoing campaign research and monitoring, sharing that evidence base widely and seeking expert opinion to guide decisions where the evidence base was limited.
- Engaging specialist suppliers, all of whom, while outstanding in their own field, are also capable of working together in a spirit of cooperation.
- 'Open source' marketing: the creation of sub-brands and allowing partners to create their own sub-brands, content and programmes, encouraging them to feel that they are part of a bigger initiative.
- Building a coalition of partners, including the commercial sector, non-governmental organisations and other government departments.

---

[3] The source is Manning Gottleib OMD, a communications agency

○ Working to engage the local NHS and the schools. Pre-existing networks, such as regional obesity leads, regional physical activity leads and healthy schools coordinators have all worked hard to promote the movement in their areas.

○ The 'Change4Life' brand identity, created by the ad agency M&C Saatchi (and the claymation television advertising developed by Aardman Animation) captured the imagination of the public and made it possible to land some hard-hitting messages in an engaging and charming way. It has also provided a rallying call for those already working in the area.

○ The 'How are the Kids?' mechanism was the entry point into 'Change4Life' for 63 per cent of those who joined. Without it, we would have ended the year with a database of only 149,458 families, about 50,000 short of our target. In addition, we know that families who joined 'Change4Life' through 'How are the Kids?' engaged more frequently with other aspects of the programme.

WHAT WORKED LESS WELL

The campaign was developed (and is being delivered) at great speed. The team report that they would advise others contemplating such a programme to:

○ Spend more time on the 'Mobilising the network' phase: on reflection, there was an underestimation of the amount of time it would take to engage properly.

○ Start the CRM programme sooner: many families waited months for their first CRM pack. The CRM programme should have been ready to go out to families as soon as they joined 'Change4Life'.

○ Develop more products for professionals, such as teachers and doctors, who have a professional interest in combating obesity.

○ The evaluation from the first year's activity made it clear that more targeted approaches would be needed for specific subsections of the community. It also revealed that it was significantly more cost effective to recruit people into the programme via peers and by using public sector institutions such as schools, than via mass-media advertising or on-street promotions. During the second phase of the programme, more effort will be put into providing materials for schools to encourage children to make pledges to change their diet and/or activity levels, and developing a clearer role for the 'Change4Life' sub-brands and 'Change4Life' ambassadors. The programme will also be producing targeted interventions and materials for pregnant women, and parents of children under the age of two, as well as targeted interventions and materials for ethnic minority communities and for middle-aged adults.

CHAPTER RECAP

The 'Change4Life' programme shows how evaluation should and can be built into social marketing programmes and also how it can be used to help modify the programme as it develops. By applying evaluation that looks at both the impact on behavior and the cost benefit of interventions this case study shows that evaluation can also help make best use of the funds available. Evaluation is also a key feedback mechanism for funders and in the case of state-sponsored programmes politicians. The evaluation of the 'Change4Life' programme has helped it continue in the UK despite a change of government. In this way evaluation has helped sustain the programme and thereby increase its chance of having a bigger effect.

SELF-REVIEW QUESTIONS

1 If you were asked to pick out five key strengths of the 'Change4Life' programme what would they be?
2 From the description of the 'Chage4Life' programme, what would you say were the strengths and weaknesses of its evaluation strategy?
3 Choose a behaviour-change issue you would like to tackle. How would you evaluate whether your selected interventions had worked effectively? What difficulties might arise during the evaluation process?

REFERENCES

Cross Government Obesity Unit, UK Department of Health and Department of Children, Schools and Families. (2008). Healthy Weight, Healthy Lives: A cross government strategy for England. London.

Government Office for Science. (2007, Oct.). Tackling obesities: The Foresight report. Future choices – lifestyle change – evidence review. London.

UK Department of Health. (2002). Health Survey for England. London: Department of Health.

UK Department of Health. (2008). Healthy Weight, Healthy Lives, insight summary. Produced by the Central Office of Information for the Department of Health and the Department for Children, School and Families. London.

UK Department of Health. (2010, Feb.). Change 4 Life, one year on. London: Department for Health. Available online at: www.dh.gov.uk/en/Publicationsandstatistics/Publications/Publications PolicyAndGuidance/DH_112529.

OVERVIEW AND TOP TIPS

In this book we have set out five key themes that capture what we think to be the main features of the social marketing mindset. These are:

- Citizen Orientation
- Clarity of Purpose
- Coalition Building
- Combination of Approach
- Continuation, Learning and Evaluation.

In Chapter 1, we set out to develop a greater understanding of the nature of social marketing and some of the key principles that underpin its practice. In Chapter 2 we covered the social marketing planning process and in subsequent chapters illustrated how both the key social marketing principles and planning steps can lead to the development of powerful social change programmes.

Social marketing is more a science than an art. It should be driven by data and research, testing and refinement. Social marketers don't like guessing – it is too difficult, and often results in an expensive waste of precious public funds. Like all complex activity, social marketing takes both in-depth study and practical experience to build up real expertise. This book has been designed with the aim of helping practitioners and students build their understanding of social marketing by reviewing real-life case studies, not all of which are prefect, and most of which did not achieve everything they set out to do.

We want to end this book with a final set of tips that have been developed from our own personal experience in helping people around the world develop social marketing programmes. We hope you find them helpful and, like the rest of this book, we hope they help you to avoid some of the pitfalls many have encountered before.

10 TIPS FOR DEVELOPING AND IMPLEMENTING A SOCIAL MARKETING PROGRAMME

1   Actively engage individuals and communities and partners and stakeholders: Engage communities in the development, delivery and evaluation of solutions.
2   Focus on behaviour: Set explicit objectives and tailor interventions to achieving measurable behavioural goals.

3 Segment and succeed: Use behavioural and psychological data as well as demographic and service data to segment target audiences and inform the intervention mix.

4 Combine approaches: Use a mix of interventions including information, service change, policy , education, enforcement and design to bring about change.

5 Sustain and fund appropriately: Deliver programs that can be sustained over time at a cost effective level to bring about measurable improvement.

6 Tackle the competition: Understand social, economic environmental and psychological forces that may be prevent or restrict change and develop strategies to reduce these.

7 Harness all possible assets: Develop interventions and co-delivery through coordinated effort on the part of the public, for profit, and NGO sectors.

8 Develop theory and science informed: Have a clear and consistent model of practice that is informed by research based theory and best practice.

9 Learning culture: Develop a learning culture that invests in capturing what is learnt from interventions, both positive and negative and permit experimentation.

10 Coordinate and integrate: Ensure synergy between intervention strategies and broader policy aims and policy drivers and coordinate action between international, national and local efforts and between sectors and departments.

4 THINGS TO AVOID

1 Don't let people think that Social Marketing is just about flashy promotional events, materials development, mass or new media promotions.

2 Don't develop interventions that are only driven by what 'experts' think people need.

3 Don't undertake actions that are not informed by market research or client insight.

4 Don't run programmes or projects that you don't evaluate.

FINAL TIP

Remember, the first duty of a Social Marketer is to market social marketing to non-marketers. We need to ensure that a marketing mindset is embedded within all our organisations so that they can become more effective and efficient.

INDEX

Research Methods Books from SAGE

DISCOVERING STATISTICS USING SPSS THIRD EDITION

ANDY FIELD

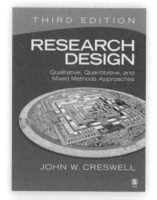

THIRD EDITION

RESEARCH DESIGN

Qualitative, Quantitative, and Mixed Methods Approaches

JOHN W. CRESWELL

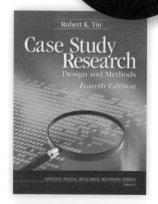

Robert K. Yin

Case Study Research

Design and Methods

Fourth Edition

APPLIED SOCIAL RESEARCH METHODS SERIES

Second Edition

QUALITATIVE INQUIRY & RESEARCH DESIGN

Choosing Among Five Approaches

John W. Creswell

Doing a Literature Review

Chris Hart

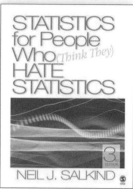

STATISTICS for People Who (Think They) HATE STATISTICS

NEIL J. SALKIND

SECOND EDITION

INTERVIEWS

Learning the Craft of Qualitative Research Interviewing

Steinar Kvale
Svend Brinkmann

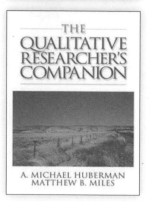

THE QUALITATIVE RESEARCHER'S COMPANION

A. MICHAEL HUBERMAN
MATTHEW B. MILES

Basics of QUALITATIVE RESEARCH 3e

Juliet Corbin
Anselm Strauss

www.sagepub.co.uk